Learning to Plan Modern Languages Lessons

Learning to Plan Modern Languages Lessons contains a wealth of guidance and ideas for those learning to teach in secondary schools. Drawing on extensive experience and research in the field, it offers detailed explanation of basic lesson planning methods and the principles that underpin them, illustrated by worked examples of well-planned lessons.

The book shows how to progress from planning smaller activities to full lessons to sequences of lessons, and how to ensure progression for your students. Specific aspects of language learning such as grammar and culture are explored, together with ideas for how to make your planning skills more effective in the long-term through collaborative and reflective practice. Starting from a presentation, practice, production (PPP) model of language teaching, the book aims to:

- provide structured, practical starting points in lesson planning for beginning teachers of modern languages (ML);
- deepen knowledge and understanding of ML as a subject and how it is learnt (pedagogical subject knowledge), in order to inform and support planning decisions;
- develop understanding of lesson planning as part of a planning cycle;
- enhance understanding of strategies and professional development opportunities to promote the further improvement of planning abilities.

Including reflective/discussion tasks and example lesson plans *Learning to Plan Modern Languages Lessons* is a must-read book for beginning and more experienced teachers of any modern language.

Cheryl Mackay is a freelance education consultant. She started her career as a teacher of ML (French and German), then Head of Department; and has worked in a range of different secondary schools in the UK. She was responsible for the initial training and education of ML teachers at St Martin's College in Lancaster (now the University of Cumbria) and Newcastle University, UK. She has written on the teaching of thinking skills in ML lessons and on the experiences of beginning ML teachers.

Learning to Plan Modern Languages Lessons

Understanding the Basic Ingredients

Cheryl Mackay

LONDON AND NEW YORK

First published 2019
by Routledge
2 Park Square, Milton Park, Abingdon, Oxon OX14 4RN

and by Routledge
52 Vanderbilt Avenue, New York, NY 10017

Routledge is an imprint of the Taylor & Francis Group, an informa business

© 2019 Cheryl Mackay

The right of Cheryl Mackay to be identified as author of this work has been asserted by her in accordance with sections 77 and 78 of the Copyright, Designs and Patents Act 1988.

All rights reserved. The purchase of this copyright material confers the right on the purchasing institution to photocopy pages which bear the photocopy icon and copyright line at the bottom of the page. No other parts of this book may be reprinted or reproduced or utilised in any form or by any electronic, mechanical, or other means, now known or hereafter invented, including photocopying and recording, or in any information storage or retrieval system, without permission in writing from the publishers.

Trademark notice: Product or corporate names may be trademarks or registered trademarks, and are used only for identification and explanation without intent to infringe.

British Library Cataloguing-in-Publication Data
A catalogue record for this book is available from the British Library

Library of Congress Cataloging-in-Publication Data
Names: Mackay, Cheryl, author.
Title: Learning to plan modern languages lessons : understanding the basic ingredients / Cheryl Mackay.
Description: London ; New York, NY : Routledge, 2019. | Includes bibliographical references.
Identifiers: LCCN 2019002120 (print) | LCCN 2019008916 (ebook) | ISBN 9780203729731 (eBook) | ISBN 9781138304833 (hardback) | ISBN 9781138304840 (pbk.)
Subjects: LCSH: Languages, Modern—Study and teaching (Secondary).
Classification: LCC PB35 (ebook) | LCC PB35 .M23 2019 (print) | DDC 418.0071/2—dc23
LC record available at https://lccn.loc.gov/2019002120

ISBN: 978-1-138-30483-3 (hbk)
ISBN: 978-1-138-30484-0 (pbk)
ISBN: 978-0-203-72973-1 (ebk)

Typeset in Bembo
by Swales & Willis Ltd, Exeter, Devon, UK

Contents

List of figures *viii*
List of tables *ix*
List of boxes *xi*
Acknowledgements *xii*
List of Abbreviations *xiii*
Preface *xiv*

Introduction   1

Distinctiveness of modern languages as a school subject 1
View of language learning that underpins the book 2
Putting it into practice 4
View of learning to plan that underpins the book 5
Purpose and aims of the book 6
How to use the book 7
Overview of the book 7

List of references for Introduction   9

Part I
Getting started   11

Introduction to Part I 11

1   Basics done well   13

Drilling 13
Teacher TL use and output modification 18
Summing up Chapter 1 22

2   Planning for individual activities   23

Introduction to the activities 23
Planning boxes 24
Overview of the activities that follow and how they are organised 25
PPP model: early stages 27
PPP model: practice stages 33
PPP model: starting to use the language 53
PPP model: using the language for real and letting go 61
Reflecting on the activities in Chapter 2 63
A final word about learning to plan 63
Conclusion to Part I 64

List of references for Part I   65

Part II
Well-planned lessons — 67

Aims of Part II 67

3 Planning whole lessons — 69

Introduction 69
Lesson structure 70
A word about lesson objectives 72
The lesson plans which follow 72
Overview of the lessons that follow and accompanying narrative 73
Two French lessons: Year 11 and Year 7 73
Two contrasting Year 8 Spanish lessons 79
Year 7 German lesson with a top set class 86
Year 7 German lesson with a bottom set class 89
Year 8 Spanish lesson 95
Summing up Chapter 3 99

4 Lesson planning process — 102

Introduction 102
Lesson planning 102
Lesson evaluation 103
Learning intentions 103
Writing lesson plans 106
Summing up Part II 109

List of references for Part II — 112

Part III
Planning for a balanced language learning experience — 113

Introduction to Part III 113

5 Different sorts of ML lessons — 115

Introduction 115
The value of culture 116
The importance of grammar 122
Cultivating creativity 136
Exploiting literature 141
Independent learning 147
Summing up Chapter 5 152

6 Longer-term planning — 153

Introduction 153
What is longer-term planning and why does it matter? 153
Units of work 154
Planning a unit of work 154
End of unit tasks 160
Planning a sequence of lessons: planning checklist 163
Evaluating longer-term plans and planning 163
Summing up Chapter 6 165
And finally . . . two recommendations 165

List of references for Part III — 166

Part IV
Getting better at planning — **169**

7   Developing your planning abilities during the ITE period — 171

Feedback on planning 171
Joint planning with your mentor 172
Extended lesson review 174
Learning together with your mentor 176
Summing up so far 176
Planning related dilemmas 176
A look ahead . . . 181

8   Next steps — 182

Introduction 182
Pen portraits of five RQTs 182
Interviews with five RQTs 187
Summing up Chapter 8 198

List of references for Part IV — 199

Final reflections — 200
Annotated list of further reading and sources — 202
Index — 205

Figures

0.1	The PPP model as a cycle	5
0.2	Learning to plan cycle	6
1.1	Example of a drilling sequence	14
1.2	Drilling the pronunciation of '*le bureau de renseignements*'	16
1.3	Teacher's TL output in the drilling sequence	18
1.4	Starter list of TL modification strategies	20
2.1	PPP model as a continuum	23
2.2	Screen for '*En un café bar*'	26
2.3	Example of a 'repeat if true' transcript	34
2.4	Screen for '*Freizeit*' (German hobbies)	35
2.5	Listening grid	48
2.6	Screen for guessing game with jobs (*les métiers*)	49
2.7	Sample guessing game script in French (*les métiers*)	50
3.1	Text used in English conversation group lesson	70
3.2	German substitution dialogue for bottom set Year 7 lesson	94
3.3	Spanish substitution dialogue for Year 10 lesson	94
3.4	French substitution table for Year 9 lesson	95
3.5	Planning for a balance of stirrers and settlers	99
3.6	Thinking through your discipline plan	100
4.1	The planning cycle	103
4.2	Why is it important for beginning teachers to write lesson plans?	106
5.1	Intended learning outcomes: some examples	115
5.2	Resource needed for Year 10 German lesson (*Vorsätze für das neue Jahr*)	128
6.1	Sample staircase of progression for '*les dernières vacances*'	156
6.2	Example of a sequence of lessons	157
6.3	Planning checklist for end of unit tasks	161
6.4	Task sheet for fashion show	162
7.1	Learning to plan cycle	176
8.1	Example of a treasure hunt pupil response sheet	183
8.2	Example of a learning objectives slide	186
8.3	Linguist of the lesson poster	187

Tables

1.1	Target language observation sheet	21
2.1	Overview of Chapter 2	25
2.2	Mini-plan of Activity 1, What number is …? What is number …?	27
2.3	Mini-plan of Activity 2, What's missing?	30
2.4	Mini-plan of Activity 3, Mouthing	32
2.5	Mini-plan of Activity 4, Repeat if true	36
2.6	Mini-plan of Activity 5, Noughts and crosses	38
2.7	Mini-plan of Activity 6, Listen and respond	41
2.8	Mini-plan of Activity 7, Listening comprehension	45
2.9	Mini-plan of Activity 8, Guessing game	51
2.10	Mini-plan of Activity 9, Spot the fib	54
2.11	Mini-plan of Activity 10, Mini-survey	57
2.12	PPP model and the role of the teacher	63
3.1a	Example of a clearly structured lesson	71
3.1b	Commentary on the example of a clearly structured lesson	71
3.2	Overview of Chapter 3	73
3.3a	Year 11 French lesson plan: '*Comment est-il/elle?*'	74
3.3b	Commentary on Year 11 French lesson: '*Comment est-il/elle?*'	75
3.4a	Year 7 French lesson plan: '*Tu as des frères ou des sœurs?*'	76
3.4b	Commentary on Year 7 French lesson: '*Tu as des frères ou des sœurs?*'	77
3.5a	Year 8 Spanish lesson plan 1: 'Spanish drinks'	80
3.5b	Commentary on Year 8 Spanish lesson: 'Spanish drinks'	81
3.6a	Year 8 Spanish lesson plan 2: '*En un café bar*'	82
3.6b	Commentary on Year 8 Spanish lesson: '*En un café bar*'	83
3.7a	Year 7 German top set lesson plan: '*Mein Stundenplan*'	87
3.7b	Commentary on Year 7 German top set lesson: '*Mein Stundenplan*'	88
3.8a	Year 7 German bottom set lesson plan: '*Mein Stundenplan 2*'	90
3.8b	Commentary on Year 7 German bottom set lesson: '*Mein Stundenplan 2*'	91
3.9a	Year 8 Spanish lesson plan: 'Spanish presents'	96
3.9b	Commentary on Year 8 Spanish lesson: 'Spanish presents'	97
3.10	Learning to teach: lesson planning prompts	101
4.1	Two examples of generic lesson evaluation templates	104
4.2	Lesson plan template 1	107
4.3	Lesson plan template 2	108
4.4	Outline lesson planning template 1	109
4.5a	Outline lesson planning template 2	110
4.5b	Completed outline lesson plan for Year 8 Spanish	111
5.1	Overview of Chapter 5	116
5.2a	Year 9 French lesson plan: '*Tu préférerais visiter le Maroc ou la Suisse?*'	118
5.2b	Commentary on Year 9 French lesson: '*Tu préférerais visiter le Maroc ou la Suisse?*'	119
5.3a	Year 6 French CLIL lesson plan: 'French speaking painters'	120
5.3b	Commentary on Year 6 French CLIL lesson	121
5.4a	Year 9 German lesson plan: introducing word order with '*weil*'	125

List of Tables

5.4b	Commentary on Year 9 German lesson: introducing word order with '*weil*'	126
5.5a	Year 10 German lesson plan: introducing the future tense	130
5.5b	Commentary on Year 10 German lesson: introducing the future tense	131
5.6a	Example of a story in French: '*L'Histoire d'Henri*'	132
5.6b	Commentary and planning task relating to the story: '*L'Histoire d'Henri*'	133
5.7a	Example of a planning grid for teaching the perfect tense	134
5.7b	Commentary and planning task relating to the planning grid	135
5.8a	Year 8 French lesson plan: '*Déjeuner du Matin*'	143
5.8b	Commentary on Year 8 French lesson: '*Déjeuner du Matin*'	144
5.9	Example of an authentic resource to discuss: '*Notizen auf dem Küchentisch*'	146
5.10a	Year 10 French lesson plan: independent reading skills in French	148
5.10b	Commentary on Year 10 French lesson: independent reading skills	149
6.1	Unit of work template	158
6.2	Unit of work for '*les dernières vacances*'	159
6.3	Checklist for planning sequences of lessons	164
7.1	Lesson evaluation prompts	175

Boxes

2.1	Planning box for What number is …? What is number …?	28
2.2	Planning box for What's missing?	30
2.3	Planning box for mouthing	32
2.4	Planning box for repeat if true	36
2.5	Planning box for noughts and crosses	40
2.6	Planning box for listen and respond	43
2.7	Planning box for listening comprehension	46
2.8	Planning box for guessing game	52
2.9	Planning box for spot the fib (with class of beginners)	55
2.10	Planning box for mini-class survey	60
2.11	Planning box template	62
8.1	Will explains how he plans his ML lessons	189
8.2	Catherine plans her lessons for the week ahead	189
8.3	Exploiting the game of Battleships	191
8.4	Marilu's formula for starts of lessons	193
8.5	Josh explains about his teaching context	193
8.6	An example of critical reflection	194

Acknowledgements

A huge debt of gratitude is due to each of the following teachers who helped me write the book:

Will Good

Catherine Wallace

Josh Guerbaai

Marilu Gonzales Berrospi

James Rivett

I would like to thank each of them for their willingness to be interviewed and for the substantial contributions they each made to Chapter 8; also for their feedback on earlier versions of the planning dilemmas in Chapter 7. Part Four could not have been written without them.

I would also like to thank Wendy Ward and Bev Hewer for sharing their ideas for lessons (Chapters 2 and 6 respectively); Vee Harris for sharing her planning grid (Chapter 5); Stephen Fawkes for his ideas relating to creativity (Chapter 5); Marianne Claussen-Lange for *Notizen auf dem Küchentisch* (Chapter 5). I would also like to acknowledge that the front cover design was created using WordClouds.com.

Much of this book is based on lesson plans and ideas of past PGCE students, both at St Martin's College in Lancaster and at Newcastle University. Unfortunately, I no longer remember all of their names. Rather than mention some and not others, I would like to acknowledge all of them here anonymously and thank them very much for sharing their planning with me. .

I also need to acknowledge all my former colleagues from whom I have learnt so much and whose thinking has helped shape this book. In particular, at St Martin's I would mention James Burch and Jenifer Alison; and at Newcastle University, David Westgate, Rachel Lofthouse and Vivienne Baumfield.

And I should acknowledge the two anonymous reviewers of an early draft, and thank them for their helpful comments.

Finally, heartfelt thanks to my dear husband, Colin, for his endless patience, cups of tea and eye for detail that have helped me throughout this process, but particularly when I needed it most.

Abbreviations

ALL	Association for Language Learning
CLIL	Content and Language Integrated Learning
CLT	Communicative Language Teaching
CPD	Continuing Professional Development
ITE	Initial Teacher Education
ITT	Initial Teacher Training
LO	Learning Objective(s)
ML	Modern Languages
NQT	Newly Qualified Teacher
PDC in MFL	Professional Development Consortium in Modern Foreign Languages
PGCE	Postgraduate Certificate of Education
PPP	Presentation, Practice, Production
RQT	Recently Qualified Teacher
SEN	Special Educational Needs
SLA	Second Language Acquisition
TES	Times Educational Supplement
TL	Target Language

Preface

There are two things I believe in very strongly. The first of these is the value of learning modern languages; the second is the importance of planning.

My own life has, without question, been enriched through my knowledge, sometimes quite limited, of different languages. Languages have helped me form lasting friendships and brought me into contact with a great many interesting people. Languages have fuelled my curiosity about other countries and cultures and enabled me to start to think like a local when visiting now familiar countries, especially Germany. Above all, languages have enabled me to see that what we have in common is much greater than what divides us. As a teacher of French and German I taught in different secondary schools. I came across pupils who loved learning languages, but also some who hated the subject. But in all that time I didn't come across a single pupil who was not capable of learning another language nor anyone who didn't benefit in some way from language learning. As a result, I passionately believe that every child, regardless of home or academic background, should have the opportunity to benefit from learning another language.

Over many years as a PGCE tutor, it has been my privilege to observe some exceptionally good language lessons taught by beginning teachers. Lessons where everyone is visibly engaged and making an effort to progress, where different pupils are demonstrating different strengths, where pupils are encouraged to speak French, German or Spanish and where pupils leave the lesson with a tangible sense of achievement. Without exception, the strongest teachers were not only very good in the classroom, they were also very good at planning. Over the years, there have also been a few beginning teachers who struggled to make progress and found ML teaching very difficult. In more cases than not, the root cause of their difficulties lay with lesson planning. Learning to teach languages is not easy; but – all other things being equal – it is planning that makes the difference between success and failure.

One of the difficulties facing beginning teachers is that teaching in schools tends to draw on tacit knowledge; so teachers' planning is not always visible to PGCE students or trainees. This book sets out to make planning more visible to beginning teachers of ML. My main purpose in writing the book therefore is to help beginning teachers to plan language lessons that will make a difference to the lives of the pupils they are teaching in schools.

Learning to Plan Modern Languages Lessons was originally conceived rather like a cookbook for beginners. In this way, this book aims to develop understanding of key elements to think through when starting to plan modern languages lessons and to provide insight into the rich diversity of learning that is possible within our subject. A good cookbook offers so much more than just recipes themselves, it helps aspiring cooks to learn and to understand the basics so they are able to adapt and develop their own recipes and dishes; it inspires aspiring cooks to want to cook and to know more about the ingredients, the background to the dishes and the countries they come from. I hope that this might be a fitting analogy for the book I have written.

Introduction

Learning to plan is central to learning to teach. Apart from the classroom management and performance skills needed in the classroom, it is difficult to think of anything more important for aspiring teachers to learn during the period of their initial teacher education (ITE). But what is lesson planning and why is it important?

Planning is for learning, that is the function of lesson planning. This involves thinking through how we intend pupils' learning to progress in the lessons we teach and how lesson time can best be exploited to maximise progression in pupils' learning. This is not just a matter of ensuring that learning opportunities are in place. Planning also involves thinking through how learning might develop for all pupils, regardless of their apparent ability, aptitude or motivation for language learning. In short, planning is needed so that learning potential can be fully exploited. There can be no doubt that if all pupils are to learn and to make progress, this will not happen by chance. Decisions need to be made about the content of the lesson, how that content will be organised and about the resources required. The extent to which planning decisions ought to be written down and in what detail is a moot point, one which will be discussed later in the book. For now, the key point is that it is the quality of thinking that has informed the written plan that makes the difference to learning.

Learning to plan makes a critical contribution to the development of teaching expertise: 'it is through planning that teachers are able to learn about teaching and through teaching that they are able to learn about planning' (Mutton et al., 2011, p 399). But planning does not happen in a vacuum, it draws on different knowledge bases that are essential for teaching and, by implication, planning. Of particular relevance here is a teacher's pedagogical content knowledge (Shulman, 1987). This refers to an amalgam of knowledge of your subject, or the subject content that you are teaching, with subject pedagogy. Research into great teaching highlights the importance of such knowledge; the most effective teachers have deep knowledge of the subjects they teach, including understanding of how the subject is learnt. Indeed, pedagogical content knowledge and quality of instruction are the two biggest factors that contribute towards great teaching (Coe et al., 2014). The focus here on lesson planning in ML is therefore deliberate.

Distinctiveness of modern languages as a school subject

In essence, planning a ML lesson is different from planning a science or PE lesson, although there may be some similarities. This book gets to the heart of what distinguishes ML and ML learning from other school subjects and discusses implications for planning and teaching.

Over the years, many wise and learned scholars have written much that is still true about the distinctiveness of ML as a school subject. Two of my favourites are Wilga Rivers and Eric Hawkins.

Rivers once said 'as language teachers we are the most fortunate of teachers – all subjects are ours. Whatever the children want to communicate about, whatever they want to read about, is our subject matter' (1972, p68). As regards the subject content of ML, she makes a very valid point and one which celebrates the uniqueness of our subject. In a sense our subject is 'content-free' and as linguists, therefore, we do have much scope for creative thinking in our planning. In his address to the ALL Language World Conference (York, 1999), Hawkins referred to language as 'the defining attribute of humanity', reminding us of the unique, civilising effect of learning a foreign language. Hawkins was a passionate advocate of the benefits for young people of learning other languages, of being aware of and curious about language (Hawkins, 1999). To sum up, it is good for children and young people to learn languages: language learning develops the intellect, provides a basis of practical skill and is good for the soul. It is this rich combination of possibilities that makes us unique amongst school subjects, and this is something we can capitalise on in the lessons that we create.

Like other subjects we have our fair share of declarative knowledge, or emphasis on learning 'about' or learning 'that'. As language teachers, we draw on a range of different, subject-specific bodies of knowledge. These include knowledge and understanding of how the language works; of cultural aspects; and of works of literature. Like some other subjects, we also have a significant extent of procedural knowledge, or emphasis on learning 'how to'. Unlike other subjects, however, skills of listening, speaking, reading and writing are learnt and developed in and through another language. The crucial point here is that in ML we are expecting progress in relation to pupils' knowledge of and about the language we are teaching and also in relation to what they can use that language to do.

We also have subject-specific challenges. Principal amongst these is the challenge of getting pupils to speak in another language. There are numerous factors that make this a challenge; some of which are outwith the control of the individual teacher. Conceptualising the process of how classroom learners develop the ability to express themselves freely in another language is a challenge in itself. Another distinctive feature of our subject is that alongside generic theories of learning, we have another body of theory that helps our understanding of how we might best promote successful language learning in the ML classroom. By this I mean ideas relating to second language acquisition (SLA). We are fortunate in having a body of SLA theory and research to draw on. Mitchell and Myles argue 'SLA research offers a rich variety of concepts and descriptive accounts, which can help teachers interpret and make better sense of their own classroom experiences, and significantly broaden the range of pedagogic choices open to them' (1998, p195).

Having outlined some of the distinctiveness of ML as a school subject, I will turn now to the learning of our subject and signpost some of the key ideas that have informed the writing of this book.

View of language learning that underpins the book

As a beginning teacher you will hear different views or theories about the best way to teach languages. Amongst them is a view that there is no best way and that it is a matter of trying different things. Whilst I would agree that it is good to experiment and be open to new ideas, I do think however that there are dangers in assuming that 'anything goes'. There may not be one single theory that accounts for or explains all aspects of language learning, but that does not mean that there is no consensus about key principles that have stood the test of time. In fact, we have learnt a lot about what makes for successful language learning and I would like to draw attention here to some of the key principles that lie behind this book. But before doing that, it is necessary to clarify the term 'successful language learning'.

The current national curriculum for modern languages in England, published in 2013, states that 'The teaching should enable pupils to express their ideas and thoughts in another language and to understand and respond to its speakers, both in speech and in writing' (Department for Education, 2013). This is one of the stated purposes of the curriculum, which further aims to ensure that all pupils 'speak with increasing confidence, fluency and spontaneity, finding ways of communicating what they want to say, including through discussion and asking questions, and continually improving the accuracy of their pronunciation and intonation' (Department for Education, 2013).

Outside of England and the UK, it is assumed that the development of communicative language competence is the core aim of language teaching and learning. Most notably, *The Common European Framework of Reference for Languages* is based on the assumption that the aim of language teaching is to make learners competent and proficient in the language they are learning (Council of Europe, 2001).

I have taken it for granted, therefore, that communication is the goal of ML teaching and learning. Accordingly, the book is based on planning learning sequences that lead to communication; those sequences might take place in the course of one lesson, or over the course of several lessons. In essence, this falls under the umbrella term of communicative language teaching (CLT) or teaching 'approaches that aim to develop communicative competence through personally meaningful learning experiences' (Littlewood, 2013, p3).

Three documents, discussed shortly, have informed my thinking on some key principles of CLT.

The first is a chapter from the final report of the National Curriculum Modern Foreign Languages Working Party, published in 1990. This working party, chaired by Martin Harris (then vice chancellor of Essex University) and made up of other ML educators from different universities, schools and local authorities, was charged with advising the government on appropriate programmes of study for our subject. It was on the basis of this report that the then Secretaries of State for Education and Science and for Wales formally outlined their proposals for the inclusion of ML as a foundation subject in the National Curriculum for England and Wales. Unfortunately, this highly significant report is no longer in print. I have particularly drawn on the chapter entitled 'Sounds, words and structures' which elucidates the view of ML teaching and learning that underpinned the proposals. Of particular relevance here is the following distinction:

a) Practice (pre-communicative or reinforcing exercises);
b) Performance (realistic and independent communication);
c) Clarification (demonstration of how the model works).

The first is necessary, and the last may be very helpful, but the purpose of both is to promote better performance.

(NC Modern Foreign Languages Working Group, 1990, p54)

The second document is the *Languages Review*, published in 2007. This review was commissioned by the government to review existing languages policy; its remit was to examine what more could be done to improve the uptake for languages at age 14. The subsequent report was jointly written by Ron Dearing and Lid King, then Department of Education and Skills (DfES) National Director of Languages, and followed consultation and collaboration with key partners and stakeholders. Dearing and King address the question 'Is there a 'right way' of teaching?' Summing up a widely held consensus about language learning, they conclude that successful language learning takes place when the following conditions are in place:

- Learners are exposed to **rich** input of the target language;
- They have many opportunities to **interact** through the language;
- They are **motivated** to learn.

In addition, Dearing and King concur that 'learners need to **understand** both what and how they are learning if they are to have long-term success' (2007, Appendix 2, p29; the use of bold is the authors' own not mine). By this they mean that learners are able to understand and talk about how language works and to benefit from feedback on their performance. Citing Professor Rosamond Mitchell, they refer to this as the need to 'capitalise on language learners' relative cognitive maturity' (Dearing and King, 2007, p30).

The third and most recent document is a set of eight principles of language teaching. The principles are based on research evidence, particularly from the UK context. They were drawn up by the Professional Development Consortium in Modern Foreign Languages (PDC in MFL), a consortium of specialists in language learning from the Universities of Reading and Oxford together with leading classroom language teachers. The Consortium was established in 2012 in order to support the professional development of teachers of ML. The background to their work as well as links to the research are available on the PDC in MFL website. There are three points of particular significance. Firstly, four of the eight principles relate to 'oral interaction' in the target language (TL) and – by implication – exposure to the TL. Secondly, four of the principles refer to (learner) strategies, highlighting the importance of explicit instruction in those. Thirdly, and most importantly, one principle underpins all the others and that is principle eight which states that:

> The principal focus of pedagogy should be on developing language skills and therefore the teaching of linguistic knowledge (knowledge of grammar and vocabulary) should act in the service of skill development not as an end in itself.

(PDC in MFL, 2012)

Across these three documents, some important principles have been identified by leading authorities and widely respected experts within the field of ML education in the UK. In each case the aim of language learning is seen as learning to use the language, rather than learning about the language or learning words and phrases just for the sake of it. The authors of these documents highlight the central importance of speaking or using the TL to communicate as an end in itself and also as a vehicle for learning. The idea that we learn a language through using it to say things we want to say is indicative of a communicative approach to language teaching. Finally, the documents accord a secondary, but important, role to explicit learning about the language and to strategy instruction.

Informed by my reading of these documents, the book takes the view that successful language learning is likely to happen when classroom practices are made real and meaningful to learners and when the goal is to teach learners to be able to use the language effectively for their communicative needs. Hiep refers to this as the 'spirit of communicative language teaching' (2007, p196).

The version of CLT which best fits my purposes is summed up and endorsed as follows:

> A weaker version of CLT, including varying degrees of implicit-explicit focus on form, but with the underlying thrust being the communication of meaning, is still now the most enduring form of instruction supported by the research evidence.

(Macaro, 2003, p60)

In terms of pedagogy, I take the view that there is no one conceptually pure method, nor *can* there be one 'best method' (Mitchell and Myles, 1998, p195). Harris et al., referring to a discussion with Professor Rosamond

Mitchell, make the point that 'we need to accept that classroom learning is messy' (2001, p17). They highlight at least three types of learning going on in the languages classroom and argue that it is our responsibility to make sure that we offer pupils a diet of all three:

1. A behaviourist approach to learning. There is a need for pupils to memorise unanalysed chunks of language and to revisit and re-use that store of learning.
2. A cognitive approach to learning. Pupils should have knowledge of and be able to talk about the language. Sometimes pupils need to be pushed to greater accuracy or stretched to be more ambitious.
3. A more experiential, unconscious approach to learning, also known as language acquisition, as conceived by Krashen (Krashen and Terrell, 1983). Pupils need to have adequate exposure to the language, so they can acquire the language implicitly.

(Harris et al., 2001, p17)

I will draw on each these approaches in what follows, referring to different ideas and concepts from SLA, and sometimes more generic theories of learning from psychology. Thus I will be advocating an eclectic approach to pedagogy, but I hope to do so in a principled and reasoned way.

Putting it into practice

Planning lessons which result in successful language learning is a difficult task, particularly for beginning teachers who are also, at the same time, having to demonstrate various other competences, skills and expectations. It can be useful, especially at the outset, to have a framework or model to guide planning. I would like to introduce here the basic model of language teaching that particularly informs Parts I and II of this book. When starting to consider how learning might develop in the ML classroom, I will be drawing on a PPP (presentation, practice, production) model of language teaching.

For the purposes of this book, PPP acts as a basic model to explain CLT and a starting point for lesson planning. PPP has been recommended as particularly helpful for beginning teachers, not least because many of the basic decisions about how to sequence lessons and steps to follow in the classroom have already been made for them (Maftoon and Sarem, 2012).

It is worth noting, however, that PPP means different things to different people. The original PPP model pre-dates the advent of CLT. It was originally used as a lesson format for teaching grammatical structures, at a time when 'language' was equated with 'grammar' and the point of learning a language was to master the grammar of that language (Richards and Rodgers, 2014). Since then, and particularly with the advent of CLT, the PPP model has been modified and developed for use in a variety of contexts and for different pedagogic purposes (Maftoon and Sarem, 2012).

Given that several interpretations of PPP exist, I would like to outline here my take on the main ideas. The model I will be using in this book as a starting point for lesson planning is represented as a cycle (see Figure 0.1).

The cycle shows the traditional PPP sequence. The first phase of the sequence is the presentation of new language. This might, for example, involve the teacher speaking, using a video or a written text to introduce pupils to new language items or chunks of language that they are going to learn. This is followed by a practice phase with ample opportunities for pupils to practise and manipulate the new language in order to learn, for example, pronunciation, meaning, spelling, and grammatical features. Finally comes the production phase, where pupils are given the opportunity to use the language in a more creative or authentic way to express things that they want to say or write, combining it with previously learnt language or perhaps with new language that they have found out for themselves.

It should be noted that these phases do not remain watertight, they are defined more by what the teacher emphasises. For example, some items of language will be met and practised *in* use, some *before* use. It is also worth noting that each phase requires the teacher to create a context for what is being taught and to make meanings clear. This point is discussed further in Part I.

Just to be clear, I am *not* advocating this model as a complete representation of how languages are learnt. Critically, this model does not refer explicitly to grammar. Learning how the rules of how a language works is a hugely important part of language learning; how best to achieve this, however, is far from straightforward. Explicit grammar teaching will be dealt with separately in Part III. For now, it is assumed that patterns in the language or grammatical features will be picked up implicitly if the language is met and practised in context and meanings are clear.

For the purposes of this book, Parts I and II will draw on this simple model as a guide to inform the planning of learning sequences and lessons, during the early stages of learning to teach.

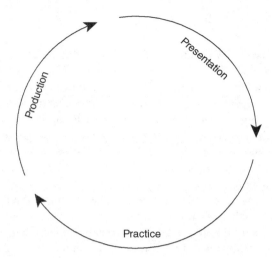

FIGURE 0.1 The PPP model as a cycle

Traditionally PPP is presented as a linear model. However, I think there are advantages in viewing it as an ongoing cycle and I am grateful to David Westgate for first introducing me to this way of conceptualising PPP. The cyclical nature of the model reminds us of the need for repeated practice and recycling of language in different contexts and for various purposes. Over time, pupils need plentiful opportunities not only to practise but also to use the language to say and write what matters to them. Pupils don't just pick up language in one topic and then remember it forever; nor is the language bound to any one topic, language can and should be transferred across topics to ensure progression. Rather like a spiral, the circumference of the cycle expands and learning deepens, as fluency, accuracy and complexity of language use develop over time.

I like this model because it reinforces the need for continual practice. Sometimes things can go awry if pupils are expected to produce the language before they have had adequate practice. By that I mean that pupils might complete the task in English rather than in the TL, or they might be distracted and give up on the task if they don't feel able to complete it in the TL. As a result, learning and progress suffer. Beginning teachers can easily underestimate just how much practice is needed in order to prepare pupils well for confident language production.

The model also highlights that practice in itself is not the end goal of language learning. It is vitally important that pupils are given regular opportunities to use the language to express themselves in speaking and writing. Otherwise, they are missing out on the whole point of language learning! Not to mention the huge sense of progress and achievement that can result from knowing that you can express yourself and be understood in another language. Without the production stage, we are denying pupils the opportunity to progress and realise their potential. So opportunities for production need to start as early as possible in a pupil's language learning experience and they need to be frequent features of lessons.

Finally, I think this is a model to which learners can relate. Some learners, for example, might relate the cycle to how they learn in PE. They might be familiar with their PE teacher starting the lesson by presenting or modelling a particular move or technique in tennis or rounders. The class then spends most of the lesson engaged in practising this before having the opportunity to incorporate their new learning into an actual game at the end of the lesson. Similar parallels might also be drawn with learning to dance, ride a bicycle or play a musical instrument. Of course, this is not to say that learning to ride a bike is the same as learning to speak a language! But if we can help learners to see links or parallels between how they are learning in ML and how they are learning outside of the ML classroom, then this is surely a good thing.

View of learning to plan that underpins the book

Learning to plan is integral to learning to teach. It is not the case that you learn to plan first, perhaps at university, and then go into school to learn how to teach. The process of lesson planning is the means by which beginning teachers gain an understanding about teaching and learning. In this sense, learning to plan is fundamental to your story as a beginning and developing teacher. It contributes to your developing expertise

Introduction

and is built into progressive expectations for your development during your period of ITE, for example your PGCE or training year.

In writing this book I have drawn on the work of Trevor Mutton, Hazel Hagger and Katherine Burn (Mutton et al., 2011). In particular, I have taken the view that planning is a complex process and one which involves a range of decision making. This book is concerned with the decision making of beginning teachers of ML. Mutton et al. distinguish between two different phases of teaching: pre-active teaching and interactive teaching. The former refers to pre-lesson planning, the latter to what goes on during the lesson in the classroom. Of particular relevance here are choices made during the pre-active phase of teaching. We cannot ignore, however, decisions made during the interactive teaching phase and those are also considered in the book. Mutton et al. argue that part of learning to plan is learning about the relationship between pre-active and interactive phases of teaching, and what pre-lesson planning can and cannot achieve.

A final point is that learning how to plan does not stop at the end of the ITE period. You will have learnt lots by the end of that phase and be able to demonstrate sufficient skill and expertise to be employed as a newly qualified teacher. But the development of teaching expertise takes much, much longer. Learning how to plan makes a critical contribution to that development and is a feature of beginning teachers' learning well beyond the ITE period (Mutton et al., 2011).

A useful way of conceptualising the relationship between planning, teaching and learning to plan is to think in terms of a 'plan, do, review' learning cycle, as outlined in Figure 0.2.

There are two key points to note here. The first is that experience, of planning and of teaching, does not on its own lead to improvement; it is learning from experience that makes the difference. The habit of reviewing their experience, reflecting on and evaluating the planning and teaching that has taken place, helps beginning teachers to develop understanding of their subject and how it is learnt and assists them to improve their practice. The second point is that learning from experience does not mean that there is no place for theory. Theory can help us to make sense of our experience, especially when things don't go as planned, and can be the creative spark for solving problems and dilemmas.

Purpose and aims of the book

The book is written primarily for beginning teachers and does not assume any particular prior knowledge or experience of planning; sections of the book may also be of relevance to school or university mentors.

The main purpose is to *help* teachers to plan language lessons that will make a difference to the lives of the pupils they are teaching in schools. Rather than telling you how to plan lessons, the emphasis is on unpacking some of the key decisions that go into planning for learning in ML, and the rationale behind those, so that you can start to plan your own lessons and sequences of lessons. The emphasis is also on encouraging beginning teachers to be proactive in taking responsibility for their own learning and development.

The aims of the book are as follows:

- To provide structured, practical starting points in lesson planning for beginning teachers of ML;
- To deepen knowledge and understanding of ML as a subject and how it is learnt (pedagogical subject knowledge), in order to inform and support planning decisions;

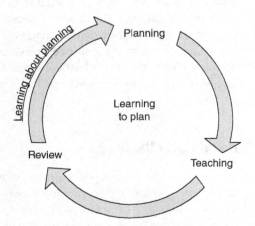

FIGURE 0.2 Learning to plan cycle

- To augment understanding of the range of different learning that is possible within ML;
- To develop understanding of lesson planning as part of a planning cycle;
- To start to develop an understanding of well-planned lessons and how this relates to ML;
- To begin to gain a longer term perspective on teaching and learning in ML;
- To enhance understanding of strategies and professional development opportunities to promote the further improvement of planning abilities;
- To start to attain an insight into how planning abilities might progress across the course of the ITE period and thereafter.

How to use the book

The book has been broadly structured to follow the typical trajectory of the ITE period. So, early chapters relate to planning experiences at the start of the school year, whilst later ones are more relevant for the second or final teaching placement and beyond. The book starts with relatively simple, limited examples and progressively moves to more complex and nuanced planning. Some parts of the book might be less relevant to you or less of a priority than others at any given time. It is absolutely fine to dip in and out of different parts. The book has been written so that each of the parts is largely self-contained, with its own list of references.

To support the narrative, you'll find lots of exemplary material in the book, particularly plans for lessons and for shorter learning sequences. Most of the lesson plans have been adapted from plans written by beginning teachers. The plans are there to be used; but please bear in mind that these are only examples of what is possible and should not be interpreted as foolproof recipes. So, please try out the mini-plans and lesson plans and evaluate them, referring back to the narrative or suggested wider reading in the light of your experience. That way you are likely to learn more.

Distributed through the book, you'll also find lots of reflective/ discussion tasks, both in the narrative and in commentaries that accompany lesson plans. These are designed to promote further learning. Rather than attempt them on your own, I would suggest that – if possible – you try and complete these tasks with others, perhaps with fellow beginning teachers or your school mentor. Interaction with others will help you to learn more from the tasks.

Overview of the book

Part I: Getting started

This part of the book introduces some practical ideas that you can plan for early on in the ITE period. There is an initial focus on the skill of drilling new language and strategies for modifying language input to make it comprehensible to pupils (Chapter 1), followed by a selection of activities and short games (Chapter 2). There is detailed information about the different elements to think through when planning for these. The accompanying narrative relates activities to different stages of the PPP model and explains a bit more about the pedagogic purpose of each.

Part II: Well-planned lessons

The theme of this part of the book is planning whole lessons. Chapter 3 introduces a selection of lesson plans for French, German and Spanish. There is a commentary with each to highlight some of the thinking behind each plan. The accompanying narrative explains about lesson structure and other features of well-planned lessons; and introduces further elements of planning such as assessment, differentiation and behaviour. Chapter 4 introduces the planning cycle, including lesson evaluation, and discusses the purpose of written lesson plans with some sample templates.

Part III: Planning for a balanced language learning experience

In this part of the book we move away from PPP and start to take a longer term perspective on ML teaching and learning. Chapter 5 introduces a variety of different elements of the ML curriculum that together help to provide a balanced language learning experience. There are examples of lesson plans, including grammar teaching, culture and creativity. These are accompanied by commentaries which look more closely at some of the planning decisions made. The accompanying narrative discusses the different elements and implications for planning and learning. Chapter 6 then turns to longer term planning with a particular focus on planning for progression across lessons. There are some worked examples from different stages in the planning process, including a suggested template to use for medium term planning.

Part IV: Getting better at planning

The focus of this last part of the book is *your* learning, specifically the development of your planning abilities, both during the ITE period (Chapter 7) and during the early stages of your teaching career (Chapter 8). Chapter 7 includes specific ways in which you can learn from working with a mentor; it also considers possible dilemmas or problems that beginning teachers might face with planning and provides some suggestions for how they might be addressed. Chapter 8 focuses on the different experiences of five recently qualified teachers in ML and how their planning and understanding of the point of planning have progressed since their ITE period.

Finally . . .

The book concludes with some final reflections and an annotated list of further reading and sources to further support, and deepen understanding of, planning for learning in ML.

References for Introduction

Coe, R., Aloisi, C., Higgins, S. and Major, L.E. (2014) *What makes great teaching? Review of the underpinning research*. Project Report. Sutton Trust: London. Available at https://www.suttontrust.com/research-paper/great-teaching/ (accessed November 2018).

Council of Europe (2001) *Common European framework of reference for languages: learning, teaching, assessment*. Cambridge University Press: Cambridge. Also available at https://www.coe.int/en/web/common-european-framework-reference-languages/ (accessed November 2018).

Dearing, R. and King, L. (2007) *Languages review*. Final report. Department for Education and Skills. Available at https://www.languagescompany.com/wp-content/uploads/the-languages-review.pdf (accessed November 2018).

Department for Education (2013) *The National Curriculum in England: languages programmes of study*. Available at: https://www.gov.uk/government/publications/national-curriculum-in-england-languages-progammes-of-study (accessed November 2018).

Harris, V., Burch, J., Jones, B. and Darcy, J. (2001) *Something to say? Promoting spontaneous classroom talk*. CILT: London.

Hawkins, E. (1999) *Listening to Lorca: a journey into language*. CILT: London.

Hiep, P.H. (2007) Communicative language teaching: unity within diversity. *ELT Journal*, 61(3), pp193–201.

Littlewood, W. (2013) Developing a context-sensitive pedagogy for communication-oriented language teaching. *English Teaching*, 68(3), pp3–25. Available at: http://journal.kate.or.kr/wp-content/uploads/2015/01/kate_68_3_1.pdf (accessed November 2018)

Macaro, E. (2003) *Teaching and learning a second language: a guide to recent research and its applications*. Continuum: London.

Maftoon, P. and Sarem, S.N. (2012) A critical look at the presentation, practice, production (PPP) approach: challenges and promises for ELT. *BRAIN*, 3(4), pp31–36. Available at: http://www.edusoft.ro/brain/index.php/brain/article/view/442/490 (accessed November 2018)

Mitchell, R. and Myles, F. (1998) *Second language learning theories*. Arnold: London.

Mutton, T., Hagger, H. and Burn, K. (2011) Learning to plan, planning to learn: the developing expertise of beginning teachers. *Teachers and Teaching*, 17(4), pp399–416.

NC Modern Foreign Languages Working Group (1990) *Modern foreign languages for ages 11–16*. Final Report. Department for Education and Science.

PDC in MFL (2012) *Research for Language Teaching*. Available at: http://pdcinmfl.com (accessed November 2018).

Richards, J.C. and Rodgers, T.S. (2014) *Approaches and methods in language teaching*. Third edition. Cambridge University Press: Cambridge.

Rivers, W. (1972) *Speaking in many tongues*. Newbury House: Rowley, Massachusetts.

Shulman, L.S. (1987) Knowledge and teaching. *Harvard Educational Review*, 57(1), pp1–22.

PART

Getting started

Introduction to Part I

The context for this part of the book is the early stages of the ITE period, when beginning teachers are getting their first teaching experiences in the classroom or working with pupils in small groups outside the classroom.

Beginning teachers are introduced to a bank of skills and activities that they can try out for themselves in the early stages. Based on the PPP model, the broad aim here is to develop understanding of how these basic ingredients might contribute to language learning and to consider implications for planning.

Chapter 1 focuses on the skills of drilling and TL modification. Chapter 2 then looks in detail at a sample of ten activities, some of which incorporate those skills, covering different phases of the PPP model.

CHAPTER

Basics done well

I have chosen to focus here on the skills of drilling and TL output modification. In my view, these skills are worth learning because they can both, in different ways, add to the quality of learning in any ML classroom. You can expect to use them in most, if not all, of your language lessons.

I have included them here because both of these skills depend in the first instance on careful planning. Especially during the early days of learning to teach, this can involve very deliberate and detailed planning of short episodes that might take just a few minutes or even seconds of classroom time to deliver. The planning involved might seem very time consuming but please don't be disheartened by this. With practice this planning will become easier and the delivery of these skills in the classroom will become more automatic.

Drilling

Within the context of the ML classroom drilling goes hand-in-hand with repetition of key language that we want pupils to learn; drilling usually comes in short intense bursts. The point of drilling is to provide learners with repeated exposure to the same, selected language and the opportunity to repeat that language for themselves. Repetition is a necessary part of language learning; it helps pupils to memorise and internalise language input: how to say it, what it means, plus any salient grammatical or formal features of the language, such as gender. Even the most capable and talented linguists benefit from hearing the same structures many times and repeating to themselves new language that they come across.

The mini-plan in Figure 1.1 shows what a typical drilling sequence might look like; I have based this on a model first introduced to me by James Burch. In terms of the PPP model, new language is presented and practised. Please bear in mind that this is just one possible way of drilling the new language.

It is worth noting that within this drilling sequence the teacher plans to pay attention to slightly different aspects of learning. Let's look a bit more closely at the different stages of the sequence.

(i) In the first part of the sequence (points 1–5), the teacher provides short bursts of repeated exposure to the language s/he wants pupils to learn. In so doing, s/he is presenting a model for pupils to imitate later on in the sequence. The learning focus here is comprehension.

(ii) The next part of the sequence (points 6–7) is about pupils repeating after the teacher exactly what they hear. The teacher uses different techniques to vary this, but essentially this is mechanical repetition practice. The new learning focus here is pronunciation.

(iii) The final part of the sequence (points 8–10) is less mechanical. Pupils start to repeat, or reproduce, the new language independently of the teacher. The new learning focus here is memorisation.

In short, drilling serves different learning purposes. These have been separated out here for the sake of clarity. In reality, these various layers of learning build on each other within the sequence. For example, learning to comprehend what the new language means continues throughout the sequence.

Planned repetition practice to support comprehension and pronunciation is not always paid the attention it deserves, especially at the planning stage. This may be because it is perceived as low level; it does not involve any higher order thinking or creativity. Yet, this sort of repetition is fundamental to language learning and the ability to lead the class in short bursts of choral repetition is a very useful teaching skill. It is true that drilling, or the need for repetition, cannot always be planned. It is a skill that ML teachers need to be able to draw on at any stage in a lesson, if it is judged that an individual or group of learners needs to hear and repeat the model again. For example,

Basics done well

Language Content of Drilling Sequence

C'est [contextualising phrase] … le collège
                                         le marché
                                         le stade
                                         le bureau de poste
                                         le bureau de renseignements
                                         la cathédrale
                                         la gare
                                         la plage
                                         la piscine

A possible drilling sequence might be:

P= pupils. T= teacher.

1. Using a visualiser, T reveals and points to pictures in order (1-9) and says the language.
2. If there is any doubt about meaning, T elicits English from P.
3. T says language in random order, P supply numbers.
4. T hides / covers up the pictures and plays memory game:
   "What number was …?"
5. T goes rapidly through pictures saying the language. P say "right / wrong" if language matches, does not match the picture.

   NB Up to this point, P have heard the language many times but have not yet had to produce it.

6. T says the language, P repeat after the teacher (various techniques- normal speed and volume, quickly, slowly, loudly, quietly, louder and louder, only boys, only girls)
   Really drill the difficult one *le bureau de renseignements*
7. P repeat with actions, preferably suggested by them. In case actions not forthcoming, have possible mimes worked out yourself as a backup.
8. T says number / performs mime and P produce language independently of T. If needed, continue with mouthing – P lip read what T is saying.
9. Various memory games:
   "What was number …?" (covering up all the pictures)
   "What's missing?" (having covered up one or more pictures)
10. Copy down new vocabulary + contextualising phrase. Preferably elicit the language first from P, so they tell T what to write. T says the language again when writing the language on the board for P to copy.

FIGURE 1.1 Example of a drilling sequence

most of the class may be mispronouncing a keyword or an individual pupil may repeatedly struggle with a particular structure. This applies to any stage of learning right up to A-level.

That said, probably the best place for beginning teachers to practise and hone their drilling skills is within the context of planned repetition practice. I will focus in the next five sections on key planning decisions associated with repetition practice when presenting new language to the class. These relate to the following:

- The language content;
- Making the meaning clear;
- Pronunciation;
- Drilling techniques;
- Monitoring and checking pupil progress.

Decisions about the language content

When planning to drill new language, the first decisions you need to make relate to the language content of the drill itself, or the 'content language'. In the first instance, this literally means: what language will you model for pupils to repeat? How much language and in what order?

As a general rule of thumb about seven new pieces of information are recommended for one drilling sequence. Please note this does not necessarily mean seven words! New vocabulary is going to be easier to learn if encountered within a context that helps pupils see how different items are connected. Context is very important for meaning. From a learning point of view, this applies specifically to the linguistic context within which new language is first encountered. For example, it may be quite impressive for pupils to learn how to say in French the names of nine places in the town, such as the town hall or the train station.. However, without a structure to provide linguistic context, what can they do with the words they have learnt? Consider what difference it makes if pupils encounter and learn those lexical items in conjunction with a contextualising phrase or question. The phrase might be as simple as '*c'est . . .*' or '*c'est . . .?*', '*je cherche . . .*' or '*où est . . .?*' etc. Essentially this is learning chunks of language that carry meaning rather than isolated or decontextualised words. This means that pupils are not just learning words (e.g. the French for names of places in a town); they are learning to do things with the language (e.g. to use French to identify or ask the whereabouts of places in a town). Even more significantly, research tells us that learning 'prefabricated chunks' (Mitchell and Myles, 1998, p12) is helpful to longer-term language learning progress and particularly in relation to grammatical patterns. The acquisition of grammar is considered further in Chapter 6.

When presenting and drilling new language, try to think in terms of chunks of meaning; make use of contextualising phrases or questions so that pupils are learning to use the language, rather than isolated words. Get this right, and you have the best possible basis for exploiting learning potential in the classroom. Your choice of contextualising phrase will depend on why you are teaching this language in the first place. What will pupils be using this language to do? What meanings could they communicate using this language?

Depending upon the topic or context, consider also if there is a best order in which to drill new language. An important point here is to be aware of possible patterns in the language that might help learning. For example, if introducing different hobbies in French, you might want to group together all the phrases with '*je joue au . . .*' and drill those separately from phrases with '*je joue du . . .*'. With some classes you might start with the simplest items first, probably the ones that sound most like English or are simplest to pronounce; with other classes you might start with the most difficult item and choose a drilling technique so that the class can hear it more often or repeat it in a more memorable way than the other items you are drilling.

The upper panel of Figure 1.1 shows what the outcomes of planning decisions about content language of the drill might look like.

Decisions on how to present the language and get the meaning over

A criticism levelled at repetition is that it is possible for pupils to repeat everything they hear, but without necessarily understanding what they are saying. In my opinion, repetition without meaning should be avoided. To make best use of learning time, you want pupils to know what they are saying when they are repeating the model. A priority when planning therefore is thinking through how you will make the meaning clear to your learners. Once you have identified the content that you want to drill, the next step is to think through how you will present that language so that pupils understand what it means. Learning starts with meaning. Pictures, photographs and film can be very useful, as can artefacts or objects to hold; mimes and actions are also helpful ways of conveying meaning, both of vocabulary items and whole phrases. It is best to be prepared to use a variety of different methods rather than relying on one all the time. In the drilling sequence in Figure 1.1, for example, pictures and actions are used to convey the meaning of the different places in town and pointing is used to demonstrate the connotation of '*c'est*' [this is ..].

Consideration of pronunciation

Then pronunciation needs to be considered. Start with yourself, be sure that you know how to pronounce the language you will be drilling; particularly if you are teaching your second or third language, you might want to check with a native speaker or, if none is available, at least check with the class teacher. Then consider pronunciation from the learners' point of view. Planning is an opportunity to consider any likely difficulties that learners may have: any words or sounds they might struggle to pronounce or get mixed up with. It is also a time to think through how best to help pupils acquire the correct pronunciation. For example, with longer words or groups of words (e.g. *le bureau de renseignements*), this might involve breaking down the utterance down into syllables before building it back up again.

To sum up so far, what you are aiming for is a manageable and meaningful chunk of accurate language, with a clear pattern if that is important, and messages that are comprehensible without unnecessary recourse to English translation. Then you can plan *how* you are going to drill it and decide on what drilling techniques you will use.

Drilling techniques

There are different ways of approaching this. Two common approaches are as follows. The first is to introduce all of the language in one go (for example, by pointing to pictures and saying the language), then check comprehension before starting any repetition practice. With this approach, you might use a variety of techniques to check comprehension, so that pupils hear the language many times before being asked to repeat. This is the approach modelled in Figure 1.1. An alternative approach is to introduce and drill the new language bit by bit, checking

A possible drilling sequence might be:

1. **Focus on the difficult word: *renseignements*. Build up from the end**
   T says the final syllable *ments,* P repeat after the teacher
   T says the final two syllables *nements*, P repeat after the teacher
   T says the final three syllables *seignements*, P repeat after the teacher
   Etc. until whole word is repeated

2. **Ping-pong – syllable for syllable**
   Start with *renseignements.* T and P alternate. T begins and says the first syllable, P the second syllable, T the third etc. until the end of the word. Then swap over, P begin and say the first syllable, T the second etc.
   Then do the same for the whole phrase and again swap parts.
   Then do the same again at speed.

3. **Sit down on key word / most difficult word**
   P stand up. One P begins and says the first word, go round the class each P says the next word of the phrase, when you run out of words start the phrase again. Sit down when you say *renseignements* and remain seated. Keep going until just one P is left standing.

4. **Re-construct the phrase**
   T randomly distributes each of the words that make up the phrase, one word to each P (*c'est/le/bureau/de/renseignements*). P stand up and move round the classroom each repeating the word they were given. P group up with other P who have the other words needed to reconstruct the phrase. Once completed, P in each group repeat the phrase again, rest of the class listen and comment on pronunciation.

5. **Cloze test in air – whole phrase**
   T says the phrase but misses out one of the words. P say the missing word.
   P do this in pairs

6. **Independent repetition of the phrase**
   P chant the phrase five times in their own time
   P chant the phrase five times getting louder and louder
   P chant the phrase again five times in one breathe

Alternatively, you might just do a few of these until you are happy that most of the class can confidently pronounce '*le bureau de renseignments*' from memory and know what it means.

FIGURE 1.2 Drilling the pronunciation of '*le bureau de renseignements*'

comprehension of each as it is introduced and drilled, and gradually building up a chain until all the new items have been introduced and drilled. With this incremental approach, pupils are progressively repeating more and more of the language as new items are added to the chain (e.g. *C'est le college, c'est le marché, c'est le stade* etc.). If you are introducing seven items, the first item will have been heard and repeated at least seven times until all of the items have been introduced and the chain completed.

An advantage of thinking this process through at the planning stage is that you can approach the drilling of difficult words in a methodical way, and ensure variety. It may take ten minutes just to drill one lexical item, as illustrated in Figure 1.2.

The trick is to break down the drilling sequence so that the ten minutes are spent in repeated but varied practice progressing to independent repetition. In my experience, this is time well spent and is certainly more effective than spending ten minutes mechanically repeating the same word or words in exactly the same way like robots. This is monotonous and robotic. Monotony means poor learning; we are not robots, we need variety!

It is important to recognise that the process of helping pupils overcome pronunciation difficulties, especially in the early stages of language learning, takes time and patience. The process is slow and repetitive and it helps to accept that not all of the issues can be overcome in one lesson. You may well need to pick up again on pronunciation of the same words in the next lesson.

Monitoring and checking pupil progress

Planning how you are going to drill new language is not just a matter of choosing what drilling techniques to use. It is equally important to think through how you will check what impact, if any, those techniques are having on pupils' learning and how you might address any difficulties that arise. For example, a useful way to check progress in learning pronunciation is to ask the whole class to repeat together without the teacher. This frees up the teacher to listen to the quality of the choral repetition and get a general indication of how well the class as a whole are progressing. As well as pronunciation, you will also need to check and recheck pupil comprehension.

Checking and rechecking comprehension is fundamental to language teaching and nowhere more so than during the presentation and drilling of new language. It is like a plate that is continually spinning, checking and rechecking until we are confident that learners are repeating, practising and using the language with meaning. Strategies for checking comprehension need to be planned as an integral part of your teaching. For example, a quick way to check comprehension is to point to pictures and say the language, with pupils saying 'right/wrong' (yes/no; true/false etc.) depending on whether the language does or does not match the picture.

Developing your practice

You will learn much from observing experienced ML colleagues and how they present and drill new language. Try and arrange for such an observation if you can; for example, your mentor may be able to model for you particular techniques and strategies that s/he finds helpful. A useful observation task, especially early on in your ITE period, is to focus on:

- Strategies that the teacher uses to check pupil comprehension. How does the teacher pick up on difficulties or misconceptions that some pupils may have?
- Strategies that the teacher uses to check pupil pronunciation. How does the teacher deal with mispronunciation?

Checklist of key questions to guide your planning of drilling sequences

To sum up, key subject-specific decisions need to be made when you are planning for repetition practice, or drilling. A checklist of key questions to guide your planning follows:

- **What language content will you be drilling?**
- **How will the language be contextualised?**
- **Are there any particular aspects of comprehension that might need special attention?**
- **How will you check comprehension?**
- **Are there any particular aspects of pronunciation that might need special attention?**
- **How will you drill for pronunciation?**
- **How will you check pronunciation?**

And finally... a word of caution about drilling

Teaching is not an exact science, it is practically impossible to predict precisely how many times a class or individuals within that class will need to repeat something before they can pronounce it with reasonable accuracy. Instead of trying to second guess this, accept that not all decisions can be made at the pre-lesson planning stage and that you will need to make some decisions in the classroom. Mechanically repeating after the teacher involves only limited intellectual engagement; unless managed in short, snappy, meaningful bursts, it can quickly lead to monotony and boredom. For this reason it is important not to overmilk this sort of drilling. Once it has fulfilled its pedagogic purpose for *most* pupils in the class, move on. Remember you can always return to further drilling and repetition practice later in the same lesson or in a subsequent lesson. So, even if you had planned to spend longer on it, move on to the next activity once you are satisfied that most of the class have a reasonable grasp of the key learning points, especially pronunciation and comprehension.

Teacher TL use and output modification

So far, I have concentrated on the language content that you will plan to teach pupils. Alongside this, planning also needs to consider other language to which pupils will be exposed in the classroom. To be clear, I am referring here to exposure to the TL (sometimes referred to as L2), rather than to English (or L1). TL exposure includes recorded material, reading material and the TL used by the teacher and other pupils. However, it is the teacher's own use of the TL that I want to focus on here.

There are many reasons why the teacher's use of the TL is important for learning (Pachler et al., 2014; Macaro, 2000). Perhaps the most important point is that the teacher can model for learners what it means to use a language to do things. For example, teachers typically use the TL to praise and encourage pupils, give instructions and explain activities, tell stories and engage in small talk or banter. The more we can do this, the more learners get the message that learning a ML is not just learning *about* the language, it is also learning *to use* the language to do things.

Through the language that s/he uses, which I'll refer to here as 'TL output', the teacher is also modelling for pupils different forms of the language and exposing them to language that they might use themselves. Over time, constant repeated exposure to frequently used words and structures really helps learning, implicitly. Research shows, for example, that there are high levels of pupil use of the TL when routines and instructions, reactions and simple requests are conducted in the TL and when the TL is the predominant language for setting up tasks (see Macaro, 2000).

Figure 1.3 shows what this might mean in practice. It lists the sort of language that pupils might be exposed to during the drilling sequence laid out in Figure 1.1. The numbers in Figure 1.3 refer to the numbered points in that sequence.

1. *Regardez ici. Regardez et écoutez-moi. Numéro X c'est ...*
2. *Qui peut traduire en anglais? En anglais?*
3. *... c'est quel numéro? Numéro un? Numéro deux? Numéro trois?*
4. *Plus difficile maintenant. Alors, un petit test de mémoire. ... c'était quel numéro?*
5. *Si c'est correcte, vous dites "oui" et vous faites comme ça* (thumbs up gesture), *si ce n'est pas correcte, vous dites "non" et vous faites comme ça* (thumbs down gesture)
6. *Répétez. Toute la class répétez. Les filles répétez. Les garcons répétez. Vite, vite, vite. Lentement. Doucement. Plus fort.*
7. *Levez-vous. Qui peut faire un mime pour ...? Un mime pour ... s'il vous plait. Bravo! Bonne idée! Excellente idée! Fantastique! Asseyez-vous.*
8. *A vous maintenant. Moi je fais un mime et vous la class vous dites le français.*
9. *Maintenant un petit test de mémoire. Numéro X c'est ...? Qui peut dire le français? Qui a une idée? Lève la main sit u as une idée. Qu'est-ce que tu penses? Plus difficile maintenant, qu'est-ce qui manque?*
10. *Ouvrez vos cahiers. Quelle est la date aujourd'hui? Quel est le titre aujourd'hui? Copiez la date. Copiez le titre. Alors on écrit les phrases en français. Phrase numéro un, qui peut dire le français? C'est ça! Excellent! C'est le collège. Copiez le français. C'est-le- col-lè-ge.*

FIGURE 1.3 Teacher's TL output in the drilling sequence

The first thing to note is that the teacher is constantly using the TL, but relying on a quite limited range of vocabulary and structure and using simple rather than complex constructions. Some words are used repeatedly, such as different adverbs to command others to do something in a particular way or the use of adjectives to give praise. Some structures are used again and again, such as the imperative form to give instructions and the interrogative with who + modal verb + infinitive to elicit volunteers. These are examples of verbal devices that teachers can employ to make the TL they are using comprehensible to the pupils they are teaching. In the same way that a physicist cannot simply walk into a science lesson and regurgitate her/his university notes, nor can French teachers simply walk into a French lesson and start speaking French as if they were speaking to native speakers. An important part of learning to teach, in any subject, is learning to reframe your subject knowledge in order to make it accessible to learners. For ML teachers, learning to modify your TL output both in speech and in writing is a significant part of that process.

The good news is that there are lots of different communication strategies you can use to help you get your meaning over. This includes both verbal devices, such as those illustrated in Figure 1.3, and non-verbal techniques such as use of mimes, gestures, actions and employment of pictures or objects. Pachler et al. (2014) provide further examples.

Reflective/discussion task

What potential can you see in Figure 1.3 for non-verbal communication strategies? Act out or otherwise demonstrate your ideas to a partner and ask for their feedback.

Longer term, it is worth bearing in mind that if you rely too much on non-verbal devices and limit your own TL output to routine classroom phrases, you are missing a trick. You should try to use enough non-verbal techniques so that pupils feel supported and comfortable when you use the TL, but aim to balance this with enough linguistic challenge so that they need to struggle a little to work out what you are saying. When pupils are engaged in working out the meaning of what they hear, making sense of input, they are learning. Over time you can and should aim to build progression into your TL output, making a conscious effort to gradually make the pupils rely more on the words and less on non-verbal clues and slowly extending the range of language that you use. Chambers (1991) discusses some practical starting points for incorporating the TL into classroom routines.

Good, experienced teachers intuitively know how to modify their use of the TL to suit the needs of the pupils they are teaching. For beginning teachers this process needs to start at the planning stage. In my experience, and without question, it is helpful to script key explanations and instructions in the TL before you go into the lesson. By that I mean anticipating and writing down before the lesson your own TL output for any given lesson or learning sequence. Some people like to incorporate scripting into their written lesson plan, often using colour coding to make it stand out; others prefer to use post-it notes, index cards or a separate sheet of paper. Before going into the lesson, it is helpful to rehearse not only what you anticipate saying in the TL but also how you are going to say it. Rehearsing is much easier if you have already scripted your anticipated TL output. Some people like to run through both verbal and non-verbal strategies with friends, family or other beginning teachers before using them for the first time in the classroom; others have been known to practise in private, in an empty classroom or behind a closed bathroom door!

When meeting classes for the first time, I would advise that it is better to 'over-modify' the TL that you plan to use and that you make profligate use of mime. When planning you will need to factor in extra time for this, rather than assume that pupils will understand or want to understand what you are saying in the TL. Your starting point is to make your TL output comprehensible to the pupils you are teaching. You don't need to use *much* French, German or Spanish but plan to use it *all* the time. Consider this a planning challenge; pull out all the stops to prove to the class that they can indeed understand you when you speak French, German or Spanish. This is an important way in which teachers of ML can demonstrate high expectations of all pupils they are teaching. With experience and with the help of additional reading, you will develop a fuller, deeper understanding of how your use of the TL can further enhance the learning that is possible in your lessons. Harris et al. (2001) and Jones (2002) have more practical advice on this point.

For now, Figure 1.4 has a starter list of strategies you might want to use to help pupils understand what you are saying in the TL. For maximum impact, practise using these in combination with mimes and gestures; and aim for clarity and variety of strategy use, don't just rely on speaking more slowly!

For me, paraphrasing, or circumlocution, is *the* quintessential TL modification strategy; it involves purposefully using a lot of words to say not very much, but in a way that is comprehensible and makes sense to the learners you

1. Repeat what you say
2. Speak more slowly
3. Stress particular words or phrases through intonation change
4. Stress particular words or phrases by saying them louder than the rest
5. Use shorter sentences
6. Insert longer pauses than you normally would between units of meaning- perhaps at the end of a sentence or perhaps mid-sentence build in time for pupil processing and sense making
7. Use simple rather than complex sentence structure and avoid unnecessary complication (e.g. *ouvrez vos cahiers* rather than *je veux que vous ouvriez vos cahiers*)
8. Use cognates, proper names and words that sounds similar to the English
9. **Consistently** use the same key phrases and structures to signal routine classroom events (e.g. *en parejas / vous travaillez avec un partenaire*)
10. Use examples or other words in apposition (e.g. *on va parler des matières scolaires, par exemple les mathématiques, les sciences, la géographie etc ce sont des matières scolaires*; e.g. *une semaine: c'est à dire lundi, mardi, mercredi ...*)
11. Juxtapose two ways of saying the same thing (e.g. *en parejas / en dos*; *ich beginne / ich bin dran*)
12. Contrast the target word with another (e.g. *es ist warm, es ist nicht kalt*)
13. Draw on pupils' general knowledge of the world to explain or illustrate (e.g. *David Beckham ist 44 Jahre alt. Er ist 1975 geboren*).
14. An umbrella strategy which can include all or some of the above strategies is paraphrasing (e.g. *Newcastle hat ein grosses Fussballstadion. Das Stadion heisst St James Park. St James Park ist ein grosses Stadion. Es hat ungefähr 50 000 Sitzplätze; ungefähr 50 000 Personen können sich im Stadion hinsetzen. Im Stadion kann man Fussballspiele sehen. Die Karten sind aber teuer, sie kosten viel Geld, sie sind nicht billig.)*

FIGURE 1.4 Starter list of TL modification strategies

are working with. This strategy involves the deliberate use of a combination of different strategies (especially 10–13 from the starter list in Figure 1.4) to help you illustrate or explain in different ways what you want to say. This is a case of using more language to give more clues to meaning; these increase the chance of success for more pupils and provide more opportunities for language processing. In short, using more clues augments the potential for learning.

Like all TL modification strategies, it takes much practice before paraphrasing becomes second nature. Until you reach this stage, get into the habit of scripting any planned use of paraphrasing; we will look at planned examples of this later in Chapter 2, within the context of a guessing game (Activity 8). However, there will also be times in lessons when unplanned paraphrasing is called for. For example, a pupil may ask you 'what does *Krankenhaus* mean?' There are different possible teacher responses to this question, depending on the context: you could translate for the pupil; ask the rest of the class to translate; tell the pupil to look it up in the dictionary, etc. But one option is to help the pupil (and any others who might be listening) to work out the meaning for themselves by paraphrasing in German what *Krankenhaus* means. Lesson time spent paraphrasing is not wasted time, it is learning time. Admittedly, there will be situations where you will not have the luxury of time to respond in this way. Nevertheless, whenever possible and practical, paraphrasing should be exploited as a source of additional, useful TL input. This is one way of exposing learners to rich input of the TL.

Before you take over the teaching of classes, try and arrange to observe those classes with their regular class teacher. A useful observation task is to make a note of all the routine classroom language that you hear the class teacher and pupils use, and any communication strategies (verbal or non-verbal) used by the teacher to help get her/his meaning over. This gives you a basis to build on when you take over the teaching of the class. You might find it helpful to use the observation sheet in Table 1.1.

TABLE 1.1 Target language observation sheet

Time	Activity/stage in lesson	Key TL phrases used by the teacher Write these down verbatim	Communication strategies used by teacher (verbal & non-verbal devices)	Key TL phrases used by pupils Note any routines

In my view, the ability to modify your own TL output is fundamental to good language teaching; it helps the language learning process and it models in the best possible way to pupils what it means to communicate in another language. With repeated practice, TL modification strategies will become second nature and you will be able to draw on them intuitively and spontaneously in the classroom to support learning. In the short term, however, they need to be planned for.

Checklist of key questions to guide the planning of your TL output

- At what points in the lesson do you anticipate using the TL? And for what purpose?
- What language (vocabulary and structures) will you be using at those points?
- What communication strategies (verbal and non-verbal devices) will you use to ensure that all pupils can comprehend what the words mean?

And finally ... an important point to bear in mind

We have focused here on the teacher's use of TL in the classroom, as an important condition for learning. Ultimately, however, it is the *pupils'* own use of the language that makes the bigger difference to their learning. Teacher TL use should not be at the expense of opportunities for pupils to speak in the target language, spontaneously as well as in structured tasks.

Summing up Chapter 1

Drilling sequences and TL output modification both require an eye for detail, patience and perseverance; done well, I strongly believe that they make a fundamental difference to the quality of learning that is possible in the ML classroom. The majority of experienced language teachers will use these skills most of the time without thinking about them; with experience they become almost intuitive. For beginning teachers, planning and rehearsing these skills in advance of lessons can boost self-confidence in the classroom and significantly strengthen classroom performance.

This chapter has also introduced the idea of the 'target language' as something distinct from the language content or 'content language' of individual exercises or activities. Both TL and content language are sources of learning in the ML classroom and both need to be factored into planning. Making a distinction between the two helps to analyse what language is needed for different parts of the lesson. And this can be a helpful distinction to make when learning to plan.

CHAPTER

Planning for individual activities

The aim here is to introduce a bank of activities and to suggest ways in which planning for these activities can help to establish conditions for successful language learning in the ML classroom.

Introduction to the activities

The activities which follow have been chosen for their learning potential in the ML classroom. I will be discussing the purpose of each activity, how you might squeeze as much learning as possible out of each and some key planning decisions upon which that learning is contingent. This discussion will take the PPP model as its starting point.

In the Introduction, the PPP model was introduced as a cycle. Another way of looking at PPP is more in terms of a continuum, with learners assuming increasing control or ownership over what they say and the language they use to do so. The continuum is a helpful tool for starting to map out what might be happening in the different phases of PPP. This is summarised in Figure 2.1. Please note that this is only intended as a starting point.

Teacher Control (most)   **Learner Control (least)**

Presentation

Introduction

Comprehension check

Practice

Imitation

Repetition

Manipulation

Production

Using the language for a communicative purpose

Creative language use

Independent Language Use

Teacher Control (least)   **Learner Control (most)**

FIGURE 2.1 PPP model as a continuum

During the early stages of presentation and drilling, pupils have very little choice over the language that they imitate and repeat; conversely, teacher control over content language is at its highest. It is the teacher who makes choices about what language pupils will be presented with and what language they will practise. As pupils progress along the PPP continuum, they have more choice over the language they use and the way they use it; at the same time, teacher control over the language pupils choose to use and the way they choose to use it diminishes.

The good news is that you do not need a lot of language in order to be able to start using it. An early stage might involve learners reproducing a limited number of structures within the context of a game. At a later stage, learners might start manipulating language to say things that they want to say, by integrating new language with all the other language they have learnt. Learning to use the language independently is a long process; and it does not happen all at once. Frequent bursts of guided and purposeful practice are needed along the way, repeating and practising key vocabulary and structures to ensure progress towards more independent language use. The activities discussed in this chapter are broadly organised to follow this trajectory, from drilling sequence to independent language use.

For each activity, there is a mini-plan to illustrate what the outcomes of planning might look like for a beginning teacher. I have tried to make the planning as transparent as possible. The template used for this has been kept simple; it includes a 'don't forget' column to show the sorts of reminders that beginning teachers typically write for themselves when they start planning.

For each activity, there is also a planning box. These boxes summarise key planning decisions for each of the activities. I have used the same template for each activity and I will explain in the next section the headings used.

Planning boxes

The boxes are organised under seven headings: language content, pedagogic purpose, preparing pupils for the activity, organising the activity and preparation of resources, your TL use, your backup plan and decision making in the lesson.

Language content

This heading refers to the language content of the activity. Making decisions about the language content involves thinking through what language you want pupils to be using and learning through the activity; this includes key structures and vocabulary, and any specific language points such as pronunciation. Once you have decided on the language content, write it down. You can also script exchanges that you anticipate between yourself and pupils, or between pupils. For example, typical exchanges for Activity 1 might look like this:

T: *Quiero una Coca-Cola. ¿Que número es?*
P: *Es número cinco.*
T: *Si, es número cinco. Gracias.*
T: *¿Número cinco, que desea?*
P: *Quiero una Coca-Cola.*
T: *Quiero una Coca-Cola. Es correcto.*

This sort of scripting can be a way to visualise the lesson and can help with other planning decisions. Finally, thinking through the language content is also an opportunity to identify any potential difficulties (e.g. particular aspects of pronunciation) for pupils, which you can then plan to address.

Pedagogic purpose

The pedagogic purpose covers what you are expecting pupils to achieve or learn, the learning purpose of the activity, and your reasons for choosing to 'teach' this activity. In short, this addresses the question: why have you decided to use this activity with this language content in this lesson? Thinking through your pedagogic purpose helps you to identify what is important before you go into the lesson. Being aware of what you are doing and why makes the whole pre-lesson planning process much more meaningful. It also makes it easier for you to make appropriate decisions in the lesson itself.

Preparing pupils for the activity

This heading deals with what you do and how you involve pupils before starting the activity. Typically this includes a form of warm-up exercise to revise key language and the teacher modelling the activity for the whole class. You are aiming here to prepare pupils linguistically and build up their confidence in order to maximise success when they come to do the activity. See Chapter 1 for more on planning for repetition practice.

Organising the activity and preparation of resources

The heading, Organising the activity and preparation of resources, refers to the practicalities of running the activity. This is every bit as important to think about and think through as some of the more intellectual aspects of planning. The success or otherwise of the activity may well depend on practical details. In the boxes, I have limited this to key planning decisions pertaining to specific activities.

Your TL use

Your TL use concerns how you will use the TL to introduce and manage the activity. I have tried to highlight any particular uses of the TL that should be prioritised for individual activities. As mentioned in the previous chapter, it is recommended to write down your key TL output for particular bits of the lesson. The mini-plans provide examples of what this scripting might look like. Do also give thought to any non-verbal strategies that would help you get your message over and make time to rehearse those beforehand. See Chapter 1 (teacher TL use and output modification).

Backup plan

The backup plan relates to contingency planning or what you will do if things don't go to plan. The intention here is to feel prepared, but without feeling that you need to write a second plan!

Decision making in the lesson

The heading, Decision making in the lesson, applies to those activities where it is more likely that you will need perhaps to make some planning decisions in the lesson. Where this is the case, I have tried to give some indication of what those decisions might relate to.

In short, the boxes (pp 28–60) are there to help you plan for what is important. From the outset, it is important to accept that you cannot possibly plan for every single possible eventuality before you go into the classroom. And even if you could, this would not help you. Once you have made your planning decisions, move on. Try not to overthink.

Please note that I have not included here planning for behaviour, on the assumption that beginning teachers would be at an early stage in their ITE period and would have the support of the class teacher in the room with them. I have assumed that this would allow the beginning teacher to focus in the first instance on teaching and learning. Planning for behaviour in ML will be covered later in Chapter 3.

Finally, planning decisions are presented here in linear fashion. Please do not take this to mean that planning is a linear process. Far from it! Planning is an inherently messy, iterative process and tends to involve a lot of refining along the way. It is also a task that is individual to each teacher; there is no one way to go about it. The planning box template at the end of this chapter (see Box 2.11) is intended as a simple checklist that beginning teachers can use to start to articulate key planning decisions made in relation to individual activities.

Overview of the activities that follow and how they are organised

TABLE 2.1 Overview of Chapter 2

Name of Activity	Corresponding PPP Model Stage	Focus of accompanying pedagogical narrative
1 What number is . . . ? What's number . . . ?	Early Stages	
2 What's missing?		
3 Mouthing		
4 Repeat if true	Practice Stages	Planning for pairwork
5 Noughts and crosses		Using actions to support learning
6 Listen and respond		Repeated exposure to the language
7 Listening comprehension		
8 Guessing game		
9 Spot the fib	Starting to use the language	Re-using and re-cycling familiar language
10 Mini-class survey		
	Using the language for real and letting go	Using the language for real and letting go

Planning for individual activities

FIGURE 2.2 Screen for '*En un café bar*'

PPP model: early stages

The first three activities might be included within a drilling sequence when you first present new language, or they might be used for follow-up repetition practice at a later stage once language has been introduced. These short activities provide repeated exposure to and practice of a limited body of language. In short, we are talking here about the early stages of the PPP cycle. I would refer to these as 'pre-communicative' activities (Littlewood, 1981) because they serve to prepare the learner for the production phase of PPP, which is more truly communicative.

The language content of the activities may appear quite limited, but do please bear in mind that pupils will also be exposed to other TL as used by the teacher or by themselves. I have assumed in the examples which follow that the language content has already been introduced by the class teacher and that you are building on an initial drilling sequence.

Activity 1: What number is . . .? What is number . . .?

This activity is based on a grid or screen with numbered pictures each depicting a language item. The activity involves two sorts of questioning. The first set of questions (what number is . . .?) aim to check pupil comprehension or recognition of the language items. The second set (what is number . . .?) check how well pupils can reproduce the same language from memory. The activity starts with the first set of questions before moving to the second set: comprehension before production. Once you have done that, you can mix the questions to make the activity a bit more unpredictable so that pupils have to listen more carefully to the question form.

Here are some practical ideas for maximising the learning potential of this activity. Firstly, you can hide the screen from the class (once they are familiar with or have had time to consider its contents) before asking a question. This simple strategy converts the activity into a memory game. This is likely to increase pupil motivation to answer the questions; there is now a challenge and purpose to the activity beyond demonstrating your knowledge of French, German or Spanish. By converting this into a memory game, pupils are learning the language without realising it. The game element can be further exploited by accepting multiple suggestions or ideas for each question before you reveal the answer. Do try to resist the temptation to reveal the solution after the first correct answer has been heard. Aim to enable as many pupils as possible to participate in the lesson, even if pupils are all saying the same thing! And pupils will surprise you, some have amazing memories!

Based on the screen in Figure 2.2, the mini-plan in Table 2.2 shows what your planning for this activity might look like. I have assumed that the class teacher introduced the language in the last lesson and you have been asked to revise this language at the start of this lesson.

TABLE 2.2 Mini-plan of Activity 1, What number is . . .? What is number . . .?

Topic: *En un café bar*

Language

¿Que desea? [contextualising question]   Quiero . . . [contextualising phrase]

. . . un té

un café

un vaso de agua

un vaso de vino blanco

un vaso de vino tinto

un bocadillo de chorizo

un bocadillo de jamón

un bocadillo de queso

una Fanta

una cerveza

una ración de tortilla

una ración de patatas fritas

(continued)

Planning for individual activities

TABLE 2.2 *(continued)*

Method	Don't Forget
1 Warm-up – revise pronunciation *Estamos en el café bar.* Show each item one at a time, say the Spanish *Quiero* + item and ask class to repeat each in turn.	Smile! Speak slowly!
2 Practice *¿Que número es . . .?* *Quiero una Coca-Cola, quiero una Coca-Cola - ¿Que número es . . .?* Do this to check recognition of each of the items/random order. Point to each when the correct number is given.	Paraphrase any items they have forgotten the meaning of.
3 Practice *¿Que desea?* *¿Que desea? ¿Que desea? ¿número ocho, que desea?* Start with cognates, the easier items. Do this to check memorisation of the items in Spanish. Point to each item when Spanish is given, expect *Quiero* + item. Get whole class to repeat any items that seem difficult to pronounce.	If necessary give them 2 options to choose from.
4 From memory *¿Que número es . . .?* + *¿Que desea?* Model the idea of doing this from memory, by standing with your back to screen so you cannot see the items. Elicit a number from the class and tell them the Spanish from memory. *¡Digame un número por favour! Gracias, número 2- quiero una Coca-Cola. ¿Está bien?* Once pupils have the idea, ask them the questions, remove or hide the screen with items so they have to do it from memory. (i) *Quiero una Coca-Cola, quiero una Coca-Cola - ¿Que numero es . . .?* etc. (ii) *¿Que desea? ¿Que desea? ¿número ocho, que desea?* etc. (iii) Mix of both question types – quickfire to finish.	Take MULTIPLE answers for (i) (ii)

We know from our experience of learning our first language that comprehension proceeds production. This is a useful principle to bear in mind when planning lessons and when thinking about ML teaching and learning. Before producing perfectly or imperfectly formed sentences there is a long period of taking things in, making sense of what we hear. This explains why in this mini-plan questioning starts with a focus on comprehension (what number is . . .?) before moving onto production; depending on your teaching context you may need to spend even longer on comprehension. Similarly, the drilling sequence in Chapter 1 is based on pupils hearing the language many times before they are expected to produce it. Unfortunately, in the ML classroom it can happen that learners are asked to produce language before they have had adequate time and opportunity to comprehend the meaning of what they are saying or writing. This results in pupils saying things in the TL but without knowing what it means. Production without meaning is not only a waste of learning time, it can also undermine pupils' confidence in their own abilities. Instead we should aim to ensure that learners understand the meaning of the language that we expect them to use, long before the production stage.

Box 2.1 summarises key planning decisions for Activity 1.

Box 2.1 Planning box for What number is . . .? What is number . . .?

Language content

- Plan the language that you want pupils to be using and learning through this activity.

  Have you identified a contextualising phrase to use with language items? The class teacher may well tell you what language pupils need to learn. But if not, explore and exploit any opportunity for practising language items in conjunction with a contextualising phrase.

- Plan how many items will you have on the screen.

  I would suggest no more than 12 in total. Check for visibility before making your final decision.

Once you have decided on the language content, write it down. You might also want to script a typical exchange between yourself and individual pupils.

Pedagogic purpose

- Be clear about why you are using this activity with this language content in this lesson.
    You might refer here to the PPP model to help you articulate your thinking. Try to think ahead a little bit as well, at a later stage what might pupils be using this language to do?

Preparing pupils for the activity

- Plan how you will revise pronunciation before starting the activity.
    This is also an opportunity for everyone to hear the language again before starting the activity.
- Plan how you will convey to pupils the meaning of the contextualising phase.
    This will need particular attention. For example, some teachers use a mime for *Quiero* . . . and insist that pupils repeat the mime each time they say the phrase *Quiero*.
- Plan how many pictures you will show to start with.
    You may have 12 items on the screen, but that doesn't mean you need to show all 12 at once. For this activity, and the lead up to the activity, you might want to show 6 to start with then add another 3 or 6 depending on how things go.

Organising the activity and preparation of resources

- Plan and prepare what pictures you will use to illustrate each of the items.
    If possible use the pictures pupils are familiar with (ie the same pictures used by the class teacher if those are available), otherwise go for clear, uncluttered visuals.
- Plan how you will run the activity.
    Straight activity, without concealing any of the pictures, or as a memory game? Or both?

Your TL use

- Plan how you will use the TL to introduce and manage the activity.
    Plan the key language you will use for instructions and explanations, plus any verbal or non-verbal strategies to help get the message over (see section on TL modification in Chapter 1). Once you have decided on your TL output, write it down verbatim. Rehearse key sections if you get the chance.

Backup plan

What will you do if your pictures aren't clear?
What will you do if pupils struggle to understand or say the language?
What will you do if a pupil gives an incorrect answer?

Activity 2: What's missing?

This activity involves removing one or more than one item from a screen and challenging the class to tell you what is missing. For example, you may want to do this activity in conjunction with the café bar screen used for Activity 1.
    This activity focuses on meaning, rather than the form or way in which particular language is written. For this reason I would suggest that pictures work best here. The activity aims to check how well pupils can produce the language from memory. The game element provides a context for more independent, guided production of the language. And rather like the memory game in Activity 1, there is scope here to take multiple answers in order to maximise pupil participation. You can also make this activity more challenging by removing more than one item at a time, or gradually make the missing items cumulative until nothing is left. Expect individual pupils to name each of the items that are missing. In order to maximise the benefit of this for all pupils, you might want to give pupils a

Planning for individual activities

TABLE 2.3 Mini-plan of Activity 2, What's missing?

Topic: *En un café bar*

Method	Don't Forget
1 Check prior learning: comprehension and pronunciation *Estamos en el café bar.* Show screen with all 12 items. ■ *¿Que desea? ¿Que desea?* Get pupils to name any of the items they can in Spanish, point to each as mentioned. Elicit *Quiero* + article + name of item in Spanish. *Todos juntos. Repetid, por favor.* Whole class repetition of each as mentioned. ■ What number is . . .? What is number . . .? *Quiero una Coca-Cola - ¿Que numero es?* And *¿número ocho, que desea?* - mix of both question types.	Offer alternatives if needed – *¿ una cerveza o un café?*
2 *¿Qué falta?* + individual items Close your eyes. *¡Cierre los ojos!* Remove or hide picture of Fanta. Open your eyes. *¡Abramos los ojos!* *¿Qué falta?* Elicit whole phrase *Quiero* + article + item	Take MULTIPLE answers If need be, whole class repeat the correct answer again
3 *¿Que falta?* + multiple items (gradually increase) As above but allow about 10 seconds thinking time + partner before taking answers. *Diez segundos. En parejas.* Ask 2–3 pairs to produce the Spanish before revealing the answer. Expect *Quiero* + article + item Y + article + item Finally hide all 12 items – challenge to say all 12.	Allow longer in pairs if pupils engaged – give them more time to say the Spanish together

few seconds to share ideas first with a partner before sharing more widely with the whole class. One way of organising this in the classroom is to use the 'timed, pair, share' co-operative learning strategy (Kagan and Kagan, 2015).

Table 2.3 shows what your pre-lesson planning might look like. I have based this on the same screen and 12 items that were used for *En el café bar*. And I have assumed that the class teacher has asked you to practise this language with the class.

Box 2.2 Planning box for What's missing?

Language content

■ Plan the language that you are expecting pupils to produce in this game.

Are you going to accept individual words or is this an opportunity to practise using those words in conjunction with a particular structure? I would suggest using the same phrase for each of the items, unless the class teacher has already introduced more than one. In the mini-plan, for example, the phrase would be *Quiero* + indefinite article + item. Once you have decided on the language content, write it down. It might also help to write down some sample T-P exchanges.

Pedagogic purpose

■ Be clear about why you are using this activity with this language content in this lesson.

You might refer here to the PPP model to help you articulate your thinking. Try to think ahead a little bit as well, at a later stage what might pupils be using this language to do?

Preparing for pupils for the activity

- Plan how you will check comprehension and pronunciation of the language before the activity

Pay particular attention to the contextualising phrase.

Organising the activity and preparation of resources

- See notes for Activity 1 (Box 2.1) regarding the screen that you use.
- Plan how you will run the activity.

Will you remove one item each time? Which item will you remove first? Will you allow thinking time in pairs before taking answers?

Your TL use

- Plan how you will use the TL to introduce and manage the activity.

See notes for Activity 1 (Box 2.1) regarding your TL output. Pay particular attention to the question you will use to prompt pupil answers, so that you can be consistent in using the same question. For example, are you going to ask ¿Qué falta? (what's missing?) or are you going to use a contextualising question such as ¿Qué desea? (what do you want?) to prompt the contextualising phrase *quiero* (I'd like).

Backup plan

- Plan what you will you do if pupils struggle to understand or say the language?

Decision making in the lesson

A decision about when to remove more than 1 item at a time and how gradually to remove all of the items, might need to be made in the lesson. The more confident pupils seem in their use of the language, the sooner you should challenge them to remember and say more.

Activity 3: Mouthing

The progression from comprehension to production is a gradual process. It is easy to fall into the trap of thinking that because pupils understand what words mean, and the class are confident in repeating words after the teacher, that they are ready to say them unaided. Mouthing is one way of gradually easing the transition from comprehension to production of new language. This is an activity that can be used diagnostically in short bursts, in preparation for a lengthier activity which involves producing the same language unaided. Mouthing involves reading someone's lips and then saying out loud what you think that person wants to say. It's a bit like repetition with the volume turned down. The beauty of this activity is that it can be done with the teacher and the whole class, with a partner in a pair or small group and with pupils in the role of teacher out at the front of the class. This change of focus allows for lots of practice in saying the language without it becoming boring. When pupils are mouthing in pairs, try and quickly listen in to a few of them. If you notice that some pupils are having difficulty with the pronunciation of particular items, make a point of practising those again with the whole class at the end of the activity. With experience you will learn which sounds are difficult for learners to pronounce and you will be able to focus on those more prominently in your planning.

Mouthing does not require any particular resources, but it can be helpful for some pupils to be able to see the language that is being practised. For example, within the topic of *En el café bar*, you might want to display a list of the different food and drink items. This provides a framework to guide pupils' production of the language when they are guessing and when they are mouthing themselves.

Table 2.4 shows what your pre-lesson planning might look like. Again, I have based this on the same language related to *En el café bar*.

Planning for individual activities

TABLE 2.4 Mini-plan of Activity 3, Mouthing

Topic: *En un café bar*

Method	Don't Forget
1 Check prior learning: comprehension and pronunciation *Estamos en el café bar.* Show screen with all 12 items. ■ *Quiero una Coca-Cola, quiero una Coca-Cola - ¿Que número es . . . ?* ■ *¿Qué desea? ¿Número X qué desea?* ■ Point to each item as identified, whole class repetition of each using full phrase: *Quiero una Coca-Cola. Todos juntos. Repetid, por favor.*	Hone in on any pronunciation difficulties – further drilling might be needed.
2 Mouthing to whole class (3–4 examples) Model activity, using quiero + article + item, ask question *¿Qué desea?* then mouth same sentence again. Short items first then longer. If coping well, then try longer sentences, asking for more than 1 item.	Insist on full sentence answers. Take multiple answers.
3 Mouthing in pairs *Dos minutos en parejas.*	Check all have a partner – if not, can work in a 3.
4 Mouthing with teacher clones at front of class (3–4 clones) Elicit volunteer each time *¿Hay un volontario? ¿Hay un otro volontario?*	Encourage multiple answers.

Box 2.3   Planning box for mouthing

Language content

■ Plan what language you want pupils to practise saying.

In the case of nouns will you expect pupils to use the noun plus article? Is this an opportunity to practise using words in conjunction with a particular structure? In German for example, rather than have pupils mouthing nouns plus article in the accusative case it makes better learning sense to have them practise this in conjunction with a structure that requires the accusative. For example, it is more meaningful for pupils to learn *Ich habe einen Hund* rather than *einen Hund*.

Once you have decided on the language content, write it down and highlight any items that might be particularly difficult for pupils to pronounce.

Pedagogic purpose

■ Be clear about why you are using this activity with this language content in this lesson.

You might refer here to the PPP model to help you articulate your thinking. Are there any particular pronunciations that you want to practise? Try to think ahead a little bit as well, at a later stage what will pupils be using this language to do?

Preparing pupils for the activity

■ Plan how you will you check pupil comprehension and pronunciation of the items before starting the activity.

Organising the activity and preparation of resources

■ Plan how you will you run the activity.

How will you ensure that everyone gets a chance at mouthing and at guessing? First teacher-led, then pairs, then volunteers out to the front?

Your TL use

- Plan how you will use the TL to introduce and manage the activity.
    How will you model the activity for the class? Pay particular attention to the question you will use to prompt pupil answers, so that you can be consistent in using the same question. The more consistent you are in your own use of the target language for classroom instructions and routine interactions, the more likely pupils are to pick this up and use it themselves.
- This is a good activity to rehearse before going into the classroom.

Backup plan

- Plan what you will do if pupils struggle to understand or say the language.

Reflective/discussion task

Particularly at Key Stage 3, what other topics would lend themselves to a grid or screen with numbered pictures that might be used for the activities above? For each topic, identify a contextualising phrase and question and up to 12 items that can be drawn reasonably clearly to illustrate the intended meaning.

PPP model: practice stages

Ample, repeated practice is fundamental to language learning. The three activities above might need to be repeated several times with the same content language over a series of lessons. In this case, the point of repeated practice is to keep polishing away at pronunciation and to strengthen comprehension and memorisation.

Broadly speaking, the more practice, the deeper the learning as the language becomes established in longer-term memory, and the more confident pupils will feel about using the language. Greater confidence in their abilities with the language means that the pupils will learn better. The next three activities continue the theme of repeated practice. They can be repeated over a series of lessons to provide intensive practice of the same vocabulary and structure.

Activity 4: Repeat if true

Repeat if true is a competition between teacher and class. The teacher shows or points to pictures, one at a time, and says the French, German or Spanish for what that picture represents; the class listens and repeats after the teacher but only if what they hear is 'true'. In other words, they only repeat if what they hear corresponds with the picture. If the teacher makes a mistake, then the class remains silent. The object of the game is to try and catch out the class, the teacher is trying to get the class to repeat something that is wrong; from the pupils' point of view, the point is to repeat everything that is true but to keep absolutely quiet when the teacher makes a mistake. Keeping quiet at the right time can, in itself, be quite a challenge, especially if you have a natural instinct to correct anything you know is wrong. To be successful at this activity, pupils need to listen carefully.

The standard way to use 'repeat if true' is to check comprehension, with pupils repeating what they hear if it corresponds to the meaning depicted in the picture. This can be quite challenging for the teacher, coming up with novel ways to try and catch out the class. For the class, 'repeat if true' is more challenging than mechanically repeating everything the teacher says. Pupils are challenged to think about meaning before deciding whether or not to repeat what they hear. You can further raise the cognitive level by introducing increasingly subtle changes to the language you use to try and catch out the class. For example, you might begin with quite obvious mistakes such as '*un petit café*' when holding up a picture of '*un vin rouge*', followed by the slightly

Planning for individual activities

T= teacher   P= pupils

T	*Ich spiele Tennis*		P	*Ich spiele Tennis*
T	*Ich spiele Fussball*		P	*Ich spiele Fussball*
T	*Ich spiele Tennis*			
T	*Ich spiele Gitarre*			
T	*Ich spiele Klavier*			
T	*Ich spiele Fussball*			
T	*Ich spiele Geige*		P	*Ich spiele Geige*
T	*Ich koche*		P	*Ich koche*
T	*Ich lese*		P	*Ich lese*
T	*Ich koche*		P	*Ich koche*
T	*Ich lese*			
T	*Ich höre Musik*			
T	*Ich sehe fern*			
T	*Ich fahre rad*		P	*Ich fahre rad*
T	*Ich sehe fern*		P	*Ich sehe fern*

FIGURE 2.3 Example of a 'repeat if true' transcript

less obvious such as '*un vin bleu*' when holding up a picture of '*un vin rouge*'. Pupils enjoy the challenge and they enjoy the element of competition. You can make the competitive element more prominent by using the board to keep a tally, teacher versus class.

As well as raising the cognitive level, this activity also provides a rich context for repeated exposure to the language. It is a wonderfully versatile activity for repeatedly exposing pupils to a range of language and one that is well worth rehearsing before the lesson. There is scope within this activity for pupils to hear much more language than they will actually repeat themselves. It works most effectively as a learning activity if pupils are exposed to short, snappy bits of language that they can readily repeat and if the activity is conducted at pace. Consider for example the short transcript in Figure 2.3 based on German hobbies. This short transcript shows how the activity can be exploited to increase learner exposure to particular structures.

Table 2.5 shows what your pre-lesson planning and preparation might look like, based on German hobbies and the screen in Figure 2.4. In this example, I have assumed that the class teacher has already introduced the language and asked you to practise or revise this language at the start of the next lesson.

Variations on repeat if true

Pupils can be challenged to listen very carefully not only for correct meaning but also for correct pronunciation or grammar. For example, 'repeat if true' can be a very effective way to home in on particular aspects of pronunciation or gender.

As an alternative to pictures, you can also do this activity with actions or mimes. The aim then is to repeat both the language and the action for everything that is 'true' and the double challenge is to remain silent and not to move if you hear anything that is wrong. If you think this is easy, try it!

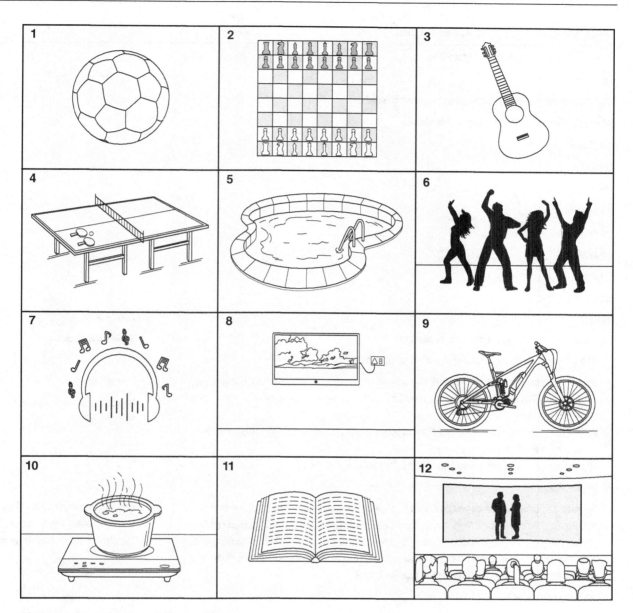

FIGURE 2.4 Screen for '*Freizeit*' (German hobbies)

TABLE 2.5 Mini-plan of Activity 4, Repeat if true

Topic: *Was machst du in deiner Freizeit?*

Language

Was machst du in deiner Freizeit? [contextualising question]

Ich spiele Fussball, Schach, Gitarre, Tischtennis

Ich schwimme

Ich tanze

Ich höre Musik

Ich sehe fern

Ich fahre rad

Ich koche

Ich lese

Ich gehe ins Kino

Method	Don't Forget
1 Warm-up – check how many they remember Show first six items on screen first – what number is . . .? ■ *Was machst du in deiner Freizeit? Hier sind einige Hobbys. Also, ich spiele Tischtennis. Ich spiele Tischtennis. Welche Nummer ist das?* Go through all six in random order, then again at speed. ■ Repeat after teacher, choral repetition of all six – *alle zusammen!* Really stress the *'e'* ending, pay attention to '*Schach*'. Then show next six items – same procedure. Pay attention to '*höre*'.	Smile! Speak slowly! Lots of praise! Do mimes of any they don't recognise.
2 Repeat if true Show all 12 items. Explain as you do it. Drill first few as normal, then make mistake with '*ich schwimme*'. *Ist das richtig? Nein, das ist falsch, das stimmt nicht. Das ist falsch. Wenn es falsch ist, sagt nichts – kein Wort! Also los!* Allow one or two mistakes until everyone has the hang of it – then introduce scoring system. Write two columns on board – *name of teacher//Klasse*. Keep a tally – *das ist ein Punkt für mich/ein Punkt für die Klasse*.	Use lots of mime and repetition to help explain, ask for pupil translation only if they seem lost.
3 *Wer hat gewonnen?* Try and engineer it so that the class win! *Wieviele Punkte hat (name of teacher)? Wieviele Punkte hat die Klasse?* Write up scores on board. *Also, wer hat gewonnen?* Whole class repeat *Wir haben gewonnen!*	Class repeat with mime.

Box 2.4   Planning Box for repeat if true

Language content

■ Plan the language items that you want to include in the activity.

Write them down and highlight any particular language points that you want to focus on (see purpose below).

Pedagogic purpose

■ Be clear about why you are using this activity with this language content in this lesson.

Which language items or formal features (such as gender, sounded verb or adjectival endings) do pupils really need to practise through this activity? Are there any particular pronunciations that you want to practise? Try to think ahead a little bit as well, at a later stage what will pupils be using this language to do?

Preparing pupils for the activity

- Plan how you will check pupil comprehension and pronunciation of the main items before starting the activity.

Organising the activity and preparation of resources

- Plan and prepare the resources you will use.
  Will you use flashcards? Or a grid with pictures? Or mimes?
- Plan how you will run the activity from the front.
  Lots of exposure and repetition before you catch them out with your first mistake? When do you plan to stop the activity?

Your TL use

- Plan how you will use the TL to introduce and manage the activity.

If pupils are not familiar with this activity, it is worth planning this in some detail– not only your TL output but also supporting actions and mimes and use of the board for scoring. The next time you do it (with the same class), this should get a bit easier. Once pupils are familiar with how the activity works, plan to organise it as an activity in pairs or small groups.

Backup plan

- Plan what you will do if pupils struggle to understand or say the language.

Decision making in the lesson

If there are any items that the class seem to be uncertain of, you might need to put the game on hold for a few seconds so that you can further drill those items in isolation, check comprehension quickly by eliciting English translation, and then provide more exposure to those items once the game resumes.

Pedagogical focus: planning for pair work

Many repetition or imitation activities can be transferred from whole class activity to short bursts of pair work. In the case of mouthing, for example, pair work can be a simple activity with thirty seconds for one partner to mouth and the other to guess, before swapping over. In the case of 'What number is . . .?', you might want to add a few seconds more for each turn.

Practising in pairs like this offers many advantages for the learner. For example, it allows learners to work at their own pace; it allows everyone the opportunity to practise speaking the language; speaking with a partner is less intimidating that speaking in front of the whole class. Another consideration is that pair work adds variety to lessons and means that attention is not on the teacher all of the time. Repeated short bursts of paired activity can be an effective strategy for pupils with a low attention span. For the teacher, pair work can be a chance to take stock and quickly monitor how pupils are progressing.

However, for pair work to be effective for learning, rather than simply a breather, it is important to set it up properly. Pairwork is done well when pupils have been thoroughly prepared for what they are asked to do and the transition from whole class to pair work is well managed. For example, it is helpful to try the activity with the whole class first, this dispenses with the need for lengthy instructions. Begin by labelling each pair of pupils A and B, so

Planning for individual activities

that they know who will start or ask the question/s, depending on your activity. This also allows you to check that everyone has a partner. Make sure that you set time limits and tell pupils to change over so that each partner gets the chance to take on different roles, as appropriate. With classes who are not used to this way of working, you can expect the transition to pair work to take extra time until the routine is established.

The next activity lends itself well to pair work and the mini-plan illustrates what planning for successful pair work might look like.

Activity 5: Noughts and crosses

Noughts and crosses is a game that most pupils are familiar with, which means that less time is needed to explain this in class and pupils can focus their attention on the content of the game rather than figuring out what to do. From a learning point of view, noughts and crosses has the further advantage that it can generate a lot of practice if done first with the teacher leading the whole class and then organised as a pair work activity. The whole class version models for pupils the language that is to be practised through the game; done well, pair work allows many more pupils to actively participate in the game and benefit from doing so.

You will need nine pictures in a 3 x 3 grid of numbered squares. Pupils either in teams or individually attempt to get a line of noughts or crosses by saying a number and matching language. If picture and language match, the teacher puts a nought or cross on the square. This game can be used for different topics to practise particular language points. For example, a grid with pictures of nine drinks may be used to practise saying the drinks plus a particular structure that you want pupils to learn; alternatively, a grid with nine hobbies might be used to reinforce first person singular verb endings.

Table 2.6 shows what your pre-lesson planning might look like. I have based this on the same screen that was used for 'repeat if true', except this time only nine numbered squares are in view.

With any game like this it is important at the planning stage to consider the learning purpose and specifically what language you want pupils to practise. This will influence, for example, the language you use to model the

TABLE 2.6 Mini-plan of Activity 5, Noughts and crosses

Topic: *Freizeit*

Method	Don't Forget
1 Check comprehension and pronunciation of 9 hobbies + question.	Might need to drill language again.
2 Noughts and Crosses – '*Tic-tac-toe*'	
Sort out the sides and who is starting.	
■ *Jetzt spielen wir 'tic- tac- toe', mit Nullen und Kreuzen.* Draw on board.	Might need to balance up sides so that same number in each.
■ *Diese Seite ihr seid Gruppe A, und diese Seite Gruppe B.* Split class into 2 groups.	
■ *Gruppe A ihr seid die Nullen, Gruppe B die Kreuze.* Clarify which group is 'O'//'X'.	
■ *Wer beginnt? Wir werfen eine Münze . . .* Toss disc with A and B on either side.	
Also gut, Gruppe A beginnt.	
Explain the game	
■ Ask what do you think you have to do to get your O or X on the square you want?	
■ Clarify	
☐ Must answer the question *Was machst du in deiner Freizeit?*	
☐ Must answer in full sentence	
☐ O or X will go on the square with matching picture.	
■ Any questions?	
3 Model the game	
Also, Gruppe A beginnt. Was machst du in deiner Freizeit?	Take first answer, be decisive!
Ask the same question each time. Confirm correct answer each time – *Ja, richtig!*	
Place O or X on appropriate square.	
Wer hat gewonnen? Gruppe A hat gewonnen. Wir haben gewonnen.	
Niemand hat gewonnen. Unentschieden.	

Planning for individual activities

4 Setting up the pair work

- Explain pair work + what needed

Jetzt spielt ihr mit einem Partner zusammen. Ihr braucht ein Stück Papier so – hold up piece of paper and draw grid for pupils to copy.

- Sort out who is A and who is B, and who is starting.

Eine Person ist Partner A, eine Person ist Partner B. Du bist A, du bist B, A, B etc. – go round room and label each pupil A or B. Then show of hands to check everyone knows – *Partner A hebt die Hand! Partner B hebt die Hand!*

Wer beginnt? Wir werfen eine Münze . . . Toss disc with A and B on either side. *Also gut, Partner A beginnt.*

- Check instructions   *Might need to drill language again.*

Ask who can explain what you are going to do?

Elicit the German (contextualising) question again *Wie ist die Frage?*

Only look in exercise books if you have to, challenge yourself!

Any questions?

5 Noughts and Crosses in pairs

Use this time to circulate. Are pupils speaking German? Without books?

6 Final Plenary

Use 3, 2, 1 signal + raised hand to stop the activity.

Quick feedback on who won – *Wer hat gewonnen? Hebt die Hand! Wer hat nicht gewonnen? Hebt die Hand! Unentshieden? Hebt die Hand! Danke.*   Check all looking at you before speaking.

activity, what will count as an acceptable answer, your approach to error correction and whether sight of the written word is likely to help or hinder the learning purpose that you have in mind. To help learners focus on meaning it is a good idea to use pictures rather than text. Please bear in mind that if all the words you want pupils to say are actually written up on the noughts and crosses grid, this will not necessarily help pupils to learn or remember what the language means.

Variations on noughts and crosses

In the Activity 5 mini-plan the point of the game is to practise using different verbs in the first person in order to reinforce the first person verb ending (which is sounded in German). However, the same grid may also be used to elicit different structures. For example, the point of the game could be to produce any sentences or questions that contain the names of the different sports or hobbies. In which case, the activity becomes an opportunity to recycle prior learning and manipulate language.

Another variation to promote language manipulation might involve having some written stimulus in each of the nine squares and the aim of the game would be to produce any grammatically correct or factually correct sentences containing said stimulus. For example, the written stimulus might be a set of nine different words, or sentence stems to complete, or it might be nine names of famous people, or nine times of the day. Using pictures, another variation is to use the game to practise the language of description. This might involve having pictures in each of the nine squares and expecting pupils to describe in one sentence what they can see. For example, the grid might contain nine faces for pupils to describe. In this case the activity allows for freer language use.

The point here is that there is no one pedagogic purpose to the game of noughts and crosses; what pupils learn or gain from playing this game will depend on what you decide to emphasise. This is something to think through carefully at the planning stage. It is also worth bearing in mind that games such as this are good opportunities to insist on correctness; in my experience, pupils tend to expect games to come with rules. A rule might be that you can only get your nought or cross on a square, provided that what you say is grammatically correct.

Planning for individual activities

Box 2.5 Planning box for noughts and crosses

Language content

- Plan the language or language points you want pupils to practise using through this game.

Which nine language items of instances of a particular language point are you going to include on the noughts and crosses game? Are you going to accept individual words or insist on sentences? Is this an opportunity to practise using words in conjunction with a particular structure? Writing down your ideas can help you to decide on the language content for the game.

Pedagogic purpose

- Be clear about why you are using this activity with this language content in this lesson.

You might refer here to the PPP model or to the 'variations' on this activity, to help you articulate your thinking. To what extent will it be important to insist on accuracy?

Preparing pupils for the activity

- Plan how you will check pupil that pupils can say the items and know what they mean, before the start of the game.

Organising the activity and preparation of resources

- Plan which item you will place in the centre of the grid.
   In my experience this is the square that is used the most, it is worth considering if there is a particular item you'd like the class to practise more than the others. Perhaps the item that is most challenging to remember?
- Plan the rules of the game.
   Pay particular attention to accuracy. To what extent will you insist on grammatical correctness?
- Plan how you will run the game.
   First teacher-led, then pairs? For teacher-led, how will you divide the class into two teams? For pair work, how will you pair pupils?
- Plan what you will be doing when pupils play the game in pairs.
   What do you want to pick up on? What do *you* want to learn from this?

Your TL use

- Plan how you will you use the TL to introduce and manage the activity.

Pay particular attention to the setting up of pair work. Decide the key language you will use, plus any mimes or actions to help get the message over. Once you have decided on your TL output, write it down.

Backup plan

- Plan what you will do if pupils struggle to understand or say the language.

It may be difficult for some pupils to participate in the game with pictures only. You can get round this by ensuring that pupils know where to find the written word if they need it – but only if they need it; with some classes, you might also write the first letter of each of the words needed on each of the squares, once pupils are confident with this challenge them to play the game without this added support.

Decision making in the lesson

Until you know your classes well, you may need to make decisions about written backup in the lesson itself rather than at the pre-lesson planning stage.

Pedagogical focus: planning to use actions to support learning

The next activity involves actions. Actions can be a powerful tool to help learners remember and recall information. Some people think that gestures and actions are a bit of a gimmick, an optional extra in the ML classroom. I would argue that as language teachers we need to be prepared to draw on as many different tools as we can to support learning. Undoubtedly there are pupils who like to be moving, and doing actions to accompany new language gets them moving and learning; they learn best if they are not sitting at a desk all lesson. Learning in this way helps learners to store new language or language items in their memory and helps them to retrieve that language when needed. For this reason, in my opinion, doing actions helps to support learning and is an opportunity that should be made available to all learners.

A surprising variety of language can be shown in mime, ranging from mimes for quite concrete meanings such as hobbies (e.g. *je joue au golf, ich spiele Fussball, juego tenis*), to the less obvious such as buildings or school subjects or food and drink, to more abstract content such as question words, verb endings, phonics, punctuation and intonation. For example, Rachel Hawkes demonstrates some gestures for questions in Spanish (YouTube, 2014). I would really encourage beginning teachers to include gestures and mimes in their basic repertoire and to plan for pupils to use them. The physical act of performing mimes and gestures seems to help with the memorisation of various linguistic content. Mimes can be used for a variety of purposes. They can be used to introduce and practise new language in advance of a topic (e.g. you might use mimes and pointing to introduce parts of the body at the beginning of a topic on health and fitness). Alternatively, as demonstrated in the drilling sequence, a simple way to check comprehension is teacher says TL, class does the mime; and a simple way to check progress in producing new language is teacher does mime, pupils say the TL. Actions are also an integral part of some activities and the next activity here is an example of this.

Activity 6: Listen and respond

Listen and respond activities are a good way of developing listening skills, especially the ability to recognise and distinguish between words. There are lots of listen and respond type activities to try in the classroom. The basic idea is that pupils respond to what they hear by doing some action or other physical response, e.g. thumbs up thumbs down, stand up when you hear a specific word or group of words, stamp your feet when you hear a mistake.

The activity I have chosen is a version of the game Simon Says. I prefer to omit the words Simon Says and simply give commands for pupils to follow, just because I feel it is a bit snappier. Rather like 'Repeat if True', the teacher is trying to catch out the class. Any pupil who falsely follows the command, copying the teacher's mime, is eliminated from the game. Done well, the game has much potential for helping learning. Done well, this is a non-threatening way of exposing learners to the language, actively involving everyone and developing confidence in comprehension.

You might want to begin with this as a teacher-led activity in one lesson, allowing plenty time to establish how it works. Some classes may not be used to doing actions and or may not be used to hearing the target language, and may think that they don't know how to do this. Be prepared to lead the activity with some mimes that you have already thought through and rehearsed. If the class is not used to hearing the language, be prepared to slow down your delivery until they get the hang of it and be prepared to give pupils second chances. Once pupils get the hang of it, the activity can then be repeated in subsequent lessons with the same language. Once pupils are confident enough in reproducing the language themselves, the game can then be played in pairs or small groups. So, in terms of the PPP model, this activity can be used early on as part of a teacher-led drilling sequence or later on for pupil-led speaking practice.

In the mini-plan in Table 2.7 I have assumed that pupils were introduced to the language in a previous lesson but not to the game. They are ready now to make the transition to more independent, less controlled practice. The game is used to practise listening and speaking, using particular structures and vocabulary related to hobbies.

TABLE 2.7 Mini-plan of Activity 6, Listen and respond

Topic: *Was machst du in deiner Freizeit?*

Method	Don't Forget
1 Warm-up – check how many they remember	
Show first 6 items on screen first – introduce mimes	Smile! Speak slowly!

(continued)

Planning for individual activities

TABLE 2.7 *(continued)*

Topic: ***Was machst du in deiner Freizeit?***

■ *Was machst du in deiner Freizeit? Ich habe viele Hobbys. Zum Beispiel* + do mime of playing table tennis. *Was ist mein Hobby?* Elicit from volunteer – *Tischtennis. Ja richtig! Tischtennis – alle zusammen Tischtennis, ich spiele Tischtennis.* Go through all 6 in this way.	Lots of praise!
■ Then show next 6 items – same procedure. Pay attention to separable verbs.	
2 Repetition with mimes	
Get class to stand up for this. *Steht auf! Steht auf!*	Switch off visualiser.
Say *Ich spiele Tischtennis. Wer kann eine Pantomime machen?* Elicit a mime from class.	
Say *Ich spiele Tischtennis* and do mime at same time. Class repeat German with mime.	Lots of praise!
Go through all 12 hobbies in this way.	
3 Listen and Respond Game (*Pantomimenspiel*)	
Hört gut zu und macht die Pantomime!	
Say *Ich spiele Tischtennis* and do mime at same time. Class do same mime.	Speak slowly and clearly – speed up a bit if this is too easy.
Do this for 4 or 5 examples, then make a deliberate mistake to try and catch them out.	
Say *Ich koche* and do mime for *Ich schwimme*. Look out for any pupils who get it right and point to them – *richtig!*	
Nochmal, hört gut zu und macht die richtigen Pantomimen!	
Do a few more examples, try to catch them out. If they look lost, ask for a pupil to explain in English.	
Do a few more examples, this time get any pupils you catch out to sit down. Get them to help you spot anyone who makes a mistake. *Kannst du mir bitte helfen?*	
Once it gets down to the last 5 or 6 pupils (or fewer) stop the game – *Applaus bitte für die Gewinner!*	
4 Listen and Respond in small groups	
Jetzt Pantomimenspiel in Gruppen. Gruppen mit 4 Personen – check pupils sitting in groups of 4. *Also, – 1, 2, 3, 4 das ist eine Gruppe* etc.	Pairs turn round and work with pair behind
Eine Person ist Gruppenleiter oder Leiterin. Der Gruppenleiter muss das Deutsch sagen **und** *Pantomime machen. Die anderen Personen hören gut zu und machen die richtigen Pantomimen. Die Pantomime muss* **richtig** *sein.*	Have list of hobbies up on screen in case needed.
Ask a pupil to explain in English.	
Give 10 seconds for each group to appoint their leader. Check all have a leader. Then start game – *Steht auf! 3, 2, 1 Los!*	
After a minute or so, groups change their leader. *Stop! Gruppenleiter wechseln – 10 Sekunden.* Check all have a leader. *Steht auf! 3, 2, 1 Los!*	
Stop again after another minute or so and get pupils to sit down again – ready for next part of lesson.	

Variations on listen and respond

The game of 'Simon Says' *(Jacques dit . . . Pumperknickel sagt . . . Simon dice . . .)* allows pupils a little breathing space before they hear each command and this might be appropriate for some classes.

Rather like 'repeat if true' this game can be used to introduce quite subtle changes to the language, which call for careful listening to detail and which make the decision to follow the teacher's action or not rather more nuanced. Consider, for example, the difference between *pliez les genoux* versus *pliez les bras*, or *Hände auf den Tisch* versus *Hände auf den Fisch*, or *abran sus libros* versus *cierren sus libros*.

Box 2.6 Planning box for listen and respond

Language content

- Plan the language items that you want to include in this activity.

Is there scope here to introduce more than a list of vocabulary? What key structure or structures do you plan to use?

Once you have decided on the language content, write it down and highlight any particular items pupils may find difficult to pronounce or remember, this might include language that is new. This will help you when you lead the activity in the classroom: you can plan to include potentially difficult items more frequently in your repertoire so that pupils hear them more often.

Pedagogic purpose

- Be clear about why you are using this activity with this language content in this lesson.

You might refer here to the PPP model or to the 'variations' on this activity, to help you articulate your thinking. Try to think ahead a little bit as well, at a later stage what will pupils be using this language to do?

Preparing pupils for the activity

- Plan how you will introduce the content language of the activity.

Will you do this separately before pupils stand up for the start of the game? Or will you do this through the game?

Organising the activity and preparation of resources

- Plan what actions you can use to go with each of the language items.
  You can also ask pupils to suggest actions but just in case they are not forthcoming (especially with a class you have not taught before), it is good to have some up your sleeve.
- Plan how you will run the activity.
  Once pupils are 'out' what do you want them to do? Plan how you are going to continue to involve them in the activity.
- If you are also planning to run this as a small group activity, plan how you will do this.
  How will you check that pupils can say all the language that they will need for the activity? How will you organise pupils into groups? How will you ensure that all pupils are involved?

Your TL use

- Plan how you will use the TL to introduce and manage the activity.
  If pupils are not familiar with this activity, it is worth planning this in some detail. Prioritise the language you will use to explain and model the activity, plus any mimes or actions to help get the message over. Once you have decided on your TL output, write it down.
- This is a good activity to rehearse before the lesson.
- If you are planning to run this also as a small group activity, pay particular attention to how you will use the TL to manage this.

Backup plan

- Plan what you will you do if things go wrong.

If you are planning to run this also as a small group activity, consider having some written backup. It might be helpful to show a list with the language items needed for the activity, so that pupils can refer to this if they need to.

> ### Decision making in the lesson
>
> You may find it takes longer than anticipated to actually set up the activity for the first time, in which case you may decide to do the game only on a whole class basis to start with. Next time you do it, it should take less time to get going and you should have time for pupils to play the game in small groups, perhaps after a short reminder game with the whole class first.

Pedagogical focus: planning for repeated exposure to the language

Repeated exposure to the language helps learning in different ways. First of all, it is important for pupils to have repeated exposure to the content language that you want them to learn. Content language is typically the language forms, consisting of vocabulary and structures, prescribed in a departmental scheme of work or an examination syllabus. In the short term, the more that learners repeatedly hear and see the same language, in both spoken and written forms, the easier it is for them to pick it up.

However, if prescribed content language was the only language that pupils were exposed to then longer-term progress would be rather limited. Repeated exposure to other language that has not been presented or drilled in accordance with the PPP model is needed in order to increase pupils' receptive language use. Such repeated exposure can also provide different pupils with another source of input. For example, pupils can quickly pick up, imitate and start using key TL classroom phrases that are used by the teacher on a regular basis, e.g. words such as '*excellent*', '*wunderbar*', '*estupendo*' and other language that is used to praise pupils. In effect, two different processes might be operating in the classroom: one involves conscious learning of content language that has been selected and formally introduced by the teacher; the other involves the acquisition, or picking up, of language that is used in the classroom.

A key point here is that we understand much more than we can say. Right from the start of their language learning experience at school, learners of all abilities are capable of comprehending or deriving meaning from language they have never met before. Long before they are capable of producing sentences or extended utterances for themselves, they are capable of understanding at least the gist of sentences that they hear. This applies at the earliest stages of language learning right through the whole course of our language learning careers. In order to progress, we need to continue to understand much more than we can say; the gap between comprehension and production typically widens as learners progress. This is a key learning principle for language teachers to exploit.

There is, however, an important caveat here. If learners are to learn and progress by making sense of the language they are exposed to, then it is important for that language to be pitched at an appropriate level. We do not help learning by restricting input of language to a level which more or less equates with the language we want the learners to produce or use for themselves; nor do we help learning by exposing learners to input that is so difficult that they fail to derive any meaning from it. These are not efficient ways to learn. As argued by Krashen and Terrell (1983) the secret is to pitch the language to which we expose learners at a level just above learners' existing level of competence, so that they need to struggle a little to arrive at meaning. In this way we are providing pupils with comprehensible input that makes a difference to learning. For more discussion of comprehensible input and its role in language learning, see Krashen (1982).

The next two activities develop the theme of comprehension precedes production and exploit the principle that we understand much more than we can say.

Activity 7: Listening comprehension

Research and experience suggest several reasons why listening needs to be taught well. Firstly, it is often perceived by learners as the most difficult of the four skills (especially in French); secondly, it is the skill which learners feel most anxious about, this anxiety may be partly due to a mistaken belief that you need to understand every single word; and thirdly, it is the skill which is least likely to be taught by the teacher. For more background on this, please see Field (2008).

Listening exercises need to be planned for, if they are to be done well. I want to focus here on listening exercises that involve either listening to the teacher or listening to recorded speech for a purpose. Providing a purpose for listening is very important if we want to help pupils develop their ability to attend to what they hear in the target language. In my view listening for a purpose needs to be planned for frequently in order to develop good listening habits. So, what is involved in planning for listening exercises?

It is always a good idea to get pupils to do something in response to what they hear, in other words give pupils an explicit purpose for listening rather than simply saying 'listen to this'. Plan to make your tasks achievable.

Remember that you are training pupils to listen, not testing all the time. You want all the concentration to go on the listening, so keep the task itself simple. Avoid tasks which involve a lot of reading or writing. Good devices to use are pictures, grids, tick boxes or one word answers; these help to reduce time needed for reading and writing and maximise time available for attending to what is heard.

The setting up of listening tasks, even simple ones, can be notoriously complicated. This is neither helpful to pupils nor to the teacher. Aim to make the preparation and administration of the task as easy as possible. It is useful to help pupils visualise what the completed task will look like in their books; for example, a grid with ticks in it, a list of words, a list of ticks and crosses, a drawing. This can help listeners to feel in control of their learning and this in turn goes some way towards allaying fears and anxieties. Linked to this, I strongly recommend doing the task yourself first, rather than just relying on the transcript or answers in the teachers' book. Listening to the recording and completing the task yourself first means that you can go into the lesson with the answers worked out and having pre-empted any possible controversy or ambiguity.

How often to let pupils hear the recording or text is a moot point. As a default I would suggest twice but there are no hard or fast rules on this. Much might depend on the quality of the recording, if you are using one, or on the actual task. However, if pupils really struggle to cope with the task, you will need to be flexible. Sometimes, the most helpful solution is to let pupils hear the recording or text again and again if need be. Sometimes the quickest and most efficient way to support a group of learners, who are genuinely struggling to make sense of what they are listening to, is to play the recording with pauses or to slowly read out the transcript yourself. However, this tactic should be reserved for those very few instances when the listening material or task is genuinely too difficult for the class. Longer term, the more time spent listening and relistening the better, as this helps learners to develop their listening skills, and especially if this is coupled with listening strategy instruction. For more on this point and on listening strategies, please see Graham et al. (2011).

Administration of the task also includes checking answers at the end. Checking answers can be an opportunity for pupils to use the TL to tell you what they have heard and understood. However, this may not always be the best use of lesson time, especially if pupil delivery is laboured and barely comprehensible. In some cases, the most time effective way is to show pupils the answers on a pre-prepared slide or screen and allow a short time for pupils to check their own or their partner's work. Feedback to pupils should be immediate, and should include some indication of how well they have done.

Every now and again, it is worth eliciting feedback from pupils themselves, for example: How did they find the task? What helped them with the task? What did they find difficult? Rather than leaving this to chance, plan to build in opportunities for pupils to share with you and with each other any difficulties they have experienced with particular listening tasks and strategies for getting round those. This is a good idea because it means that over time teacher and pupils can gain a sense of getting better at listening.

Finally, planning for listening exercises should also consider how the listening will feed into further language work. This theme will be discussed more fully later in the book. For now, it is worth considering whether the listening task can lead to a follow-up speaking, reading or writing task. A simple speaking task would be to act out an interview or dialogue that was heard in the listening task; transcripts of recorded listening material can be exploited in lots of ways to support literacy development, one simple way to do this is to read the transcript together with the class and ask pupils to highlight what they understand. A simple writing task would be to write a few sentences to describe what they have drawn or to sum up the information they have noted.

In short, listening exercises can initially take a lot of planning. Done well, they are a staple of the language learning diet.

Table 2.8 shows what your pre-lesson planning might look like.

TABLE 2.8 Mini-plan of Activity 7, Listening comprehension

Topic: Things you can do at the leisure centre

Key Language (introduced and drilled last lesson)

Qu'est-ce qu'on peut faire au centre de loisirs? [contextualising question]

On peut + . . . [contextualising phrase]

. . . jouer au basket, au badminton, au tennis de table, au mini-golf

. . . jouer d'un instrument de musique

. . . faire de la natation, de la peinture, de l'escalade, du bricolage, du trampoline

(continued)

Planning for individual activities

TABLE 2.8 *(continued)*

Method	Don't Forget
1 Practise language needed for listening – *On peut* + infinitive Use same pictures as in text book, numbered 1–10 on Smartboard *Répétez après moi* *Jeu de mémoire – une minute pour mémoriser des phrases* *OK, qu'est-ce qu'on peut fair au centre de loisirs? On peut . . . Avec ton partenaire, écrivez une liste des activités – vous avez une minute.* Use this time to give out grids to use for the listening. *Arretez! Stop! Regardez-moi!* *Vous avez 10 sécondes pour comparer votre liste avec celle-ci* – show list on board. *Qui a 10 sur 10? lève la main! Excellente mémoire!*	 Put grids face down on tables. Wait for all eyes on teacher before explaining.
2 Instructions for listening *Posez les stylos! Regardez-moi!* *On va faire un excercice d'écoute. On va écouter une conversation dans un centre de loisirs en France. Vous, vous avez une liste avec des activités – comme ça* (hold up). *Vous écoutez la conversation et vous cochez toutes les activités qu'on peut faire. Toutes les activités qui sont possibles, vous cochez- comme ça.* *Et les activités qu'on ne peut pas faire, vous marquez avec un X – comme ça.* *Qui peut expliquer en anglais? Y a-t-il des questions?*	 Wait for pens down, all eyes on teacher. Demonstrate 'cocher' by writing on board, same for X.
3 Listening Do example first and check it. Stop after first activity is mentioned. *Alors, est-ce qu'on peut faire de la natation, oui or non? Lève la main si tu penses 'oui'! Lève la main si tu penses 'non'! La réponse correcte est 'oui'- on peut faire de la natation.* *Y a-t-il des questions?* *On écoute deux fois.* Play the whole recording twice.	 Tick grid on Smartboard.
4 Checking answers – pupils read out activities in French *Alors, quelles sont les activités qu'on peut faire au centre de loisirs? On peut . . . Et quelles sont les activités qu'on ne peut pas faire? On ne peut pas . . . .* *Alors, c'est fini. Comptez les réponses correctes. Qui a 7 sur 10? Lève la main! 8 sur 10? 9 sur 10? 10 sur 10?*	Tick and cross as mentioned . Lots of praise!

Box 2.7 Planning box for listening comprehension

Language content

■ Plan what key language you will revise with pupils before they do the listening.

What key structures and or salient vocabulary will need to be pre-taught or revised in preparation for the task? E.g. if the listening text contains numbers (especially larger numbers or dates) and these are important for the task, then it is well worth spending a few minutes revising those first in the lesson. Are there any specific cultural differences that might interfere with comprehension? E.g. are there any proper names that it would be helpful to explain?

Pedagogic purpose

■ Be clear about why you are using this listening with this language content in this lesson.

Apart from practising listening skills, and beyond comprehension, do you have any other learning purpose in mind? Try to think ahead as well to a possible follow-up; after the listening, is there any language in the text that pupils could practise using themselves? What could they be using this language to do?

- Plan what form the task will take.

What will the completed task look like? What purpose do you want pupils to see in this task?

Preparing pupils for the activity

- Plan how you will revise or preteach any language identified above.
- Plan to do an example first to demonstrate.

How will you check that everyone knows what to do? And how to do it?

Organising the activity and organisation of resources

- Decide on the source of the listening material.

Before the lesson, check that any audio recording you plan to use is audible enough for whole class use. If not, do not use it. Instead you might read out monologues yourself or read out dialogues with the class teacher.

- Plan how you will run the listening task.

How many times will pupils hear the recording? As a default I would suggest twice but there are no hard or fast rules on this.

- Plan how answers/responses will be checked.

Will you simply show the correct answers on the screen for pupils to self or peer assess? Or will you elicit answers from individual pupils? If so, are you expecting a response in English or the TL?

Will those answers also be written up on the board or shown on the screen?

- Plan feedback to pupils.

How will pupils know how they have done? Do you need a mark scheme? If so, keep it simple!

Your TL use

- Plan how you will use the TL to introduce and manage the activity.

Pay particular attention to how you will explain the activity. Keep your TL output simple and to the point. Break instructions down into chunks, rather than giving them all at once.

Backup plan

- Plan what you will you do if things go wrong.

If technical problems arise, do not waste lesson time trying to sort them out. As appropriate, check that the electricity is switched on, the machine is switched on, volume is on and that the CD is in the machine or that you have the correct web link. If this doesn't solve the problem, adopt Plan B – read out the text.

Decision making in the lesson

You may need to make a decision about how often to let pupils hear the recording or text in the lesson itself.

Follow-up reflective/discussion task

The grid below (Figure 2.5) can be used for a listening task on the topic of hobbies. The idea is for pupils to draw or write the names of the hobbies of these French speakers; there is also a column where they can note any extra information they hear, as per example given.

Based on the grid, plan how you would explain the listening task to a mixed ability class you are teaching. Aim to do this as far as possible in the TL of your choice. Consider the following:

Planning for individual activities

- *Will pupils hear monologues or dialogues?*
- *How would you prepare the ground for the listening task? Is there any key language that you would practise first?*
- *What instructions would you give pupils? And how would you do this?*
- *How would you check answers?*
- *What follow-up task might you set?*

Discuss your ideas with someone else.

Activity 8: Guessing game

The next activity pulls together all the advantages of repeated exposure to the language. In this activity the language is used to describe or explain what an item is but without mentioning the name of that item. This is a great way for teachers to use their skills in paraphrasing in order to support learning. Essentially pupils are involved in working out what the teacher is talking about; they are listening for clues to help them identify the name of the item that is being described. For example, you might describe to pupils an object that you have in your hand and which they cannot see. You might further refine this by limiting the objects you describe to one lexical group; for example, items you can buy in the supermarket, fruit and vegetables or items of clothing.

This activity is rich in learning potential. First of all, from a linguistic point of view, paraphrasing exploits the principle that we understand much more than we can say; it also models the language in use and provides learners with repeated exposure to the language in use. These are all important ingredients for successful language learning. Secondly, pupils should find this activity challenging, it will make them think. But with appropriately selected language, they should not find it unnecessarily difficult. The key thing to remember here is that there is no need to always understand every word.

The secret to planning a successful guessing game is to start with language that pupils are already familiar with. Use a limited range of structures, as appropriate to the class you are teaching, build in constant repetition of those. Aim to use structures that can be used with a variety of different vocabulary to generate a variety of information about any given entity. The rich exposure that is provided by constant repetition of key patterns and high frequency words and structures in a meaningful context creates optimal conditions for language learning.

It is helpful to script in advance the language you will use so that you can develop your own understanding of the learning potential of this activity. Having a script to read for this activity will not only help your own confidence in the classroom, especially in the early stages of learning to teach, it will also help you to ensure that the language to which pupils are exposed is pitched at an appropriate level. Another advantage is that you can use the written version afterwards as a further teaching resource.

Most of your planning time for this activity will be taken up with linguistic considerations; the logistics of the game itself are not difficult to think through. Table 2.9 shows what pre-lesson planning might look like, based on the screen in Figure 2.6 and the guessing game script in Figure 2.7.

Nom	Sports	Sports	Sports	Musique	Musique	Infos Supp.
Martin	⚽	🎾		Guitarre		12 ans
Elizabeth						
Philippe						
Chantal						

FIGURE 2.5 Listening grid

Planning for individual activities

FIGURE 2.6 Screen for guessing game with jobs (*les métiers*)

49

Qu'est-ce que tu fais comme métier? Qu'est-ce que je fais comme métier?

Exemples

- *Je travaille dans la cuisine d'un grand restaurant. Je ne gagne pas beaucoup d'argent et je travaille de longues heures, surtout le soir et le weekend. Je travaille avec les mains et je porte un tablier blanc pour protéger mes vêtements.* [chef]
- *Je voyage beaucoup dans mon métier, je voyage en Angleterre et aussi à l'étranger, par exemple je voyage en France, en Italie et aux États Unis. Je voyage en avion. Je porte un uniforme et je gagne beaucoup d'argent.* [pilot]

1. *Je fais un métier très important. Je travaille dans un hôpital, je ne travaille pas dans un bureau. Je porte un uniforme, un uniforme bleu ou blanc. Et j'aide des gens, je parle avec des gens et je travaille avec les mains. Je travaille le weekend, et je travaille de longues heures, c'est à dire que je travaille le matin, l'après-midi et le soir. Je ne voyage pas beaucoup dans mon métier et je ne gagne pas beaucoup d'argent.* [nurse]

2. *Je fais un métier très pratique. Je travaille avec les mains mais ce n'est pas un métier dangereux. Je travaille avec des voitures, des motos et des véhicules motorisées. Je porte une salopette pour protéger mes vêtements. Je travaille avec des collègues dans un atelier dans un grand garage. Je ne travaille pas le soir, normalement je finis le travail vers 5 heures du soir.* [mechanic]

3. *Je fais un métier dangereux. Je porte un uniforme, par exemple je porte une veste, un pantalon, des gants noirs et un casque. Je porte un uniforme pour me protéger contre le feu. J'aide des gens et des animaux qui se trouvent en difficulté. Je travaille le matin, l'après-midi, le soir et aussi pendant la nuit; je travaille le weekend et tous les jours de la semaine.* [firefighter]

4. *Je travaille en plein air, je ne travaille pas dans un bureau. Je travaille avec les mains et je travaille avec des plantes et des fleurs. Je ne travaille pas avec les animaux et je ne travaille pas avec les enfants. Je ne gagne pas beaucoup d'argent. Je porte un jean et un t-shirt pour mon travail.* [gardener]

5. *Je fais un métier très important. Je ne porte pas d'uniforme. Je travaille avec les enfants et avec les ados. J'aide des gens, je parle beaucoup dans mon métier. Je ne travaille pas en plein air, je travaille dans une salle de classe, dans un collège. Je gagne assez beaucoup d'argent mais je ne voyage pas beaucoup dans mon métier.* [teacher]

6. *Je gagne beaucoup, beaucoup d'argent. Je travaille en plein air, surtout le samedi et le dimanche. Je ne travaille pas avec les mains, je travaille avec les pieds. Je voyage assez souvent avec mes collègues, normalement on voyage en Angleterre en autocar, mais quelquefois on voyage en Europe. Je porte un short, un maillot et des chaussures de foot, les chaussures sont très importantes pour mon travail.* [footballer]

FIGURE 2.7 Sample guessing game script in French (*les métiers*)

TABLE 2.9 Mini-plan of Activity 8, Guessing game

Topic: Jobs (*les métiers*)

Method	Don't Forget
1 Recap on names of jobs + screen	
Check comprehension of '*métiers*'. *Regardez les images, ce sont des métiers. En anglais les métiers?*	Smile!
Check comprehension of individual jobs + what number is . . .?	Don't rush it.
Je suis professeur, c'est mon metier, je suis professeur. C'est quel numéro? Etc.	
Check they can say individual jobs + number X is what job?	
Numéro 6 – c'est quel métier? Etc. choral repetition of each job as mentioned	
Quick practice of all 10 jobs + partner	
30 sécondes avec un partenaire – C'est quel métier? Numéros 1–10	
Quick check – ask for volunteers to say all 10	
Des volontaire s'il vous plait – qui peut dire tous les metiers, numéros 1–10?	
2 Guessing Game – example to model	Speak slowly and clearly – use
Read out example for pupils to guess– read out twice. Elicit the clues – keywords.	mimes if they look stuck.
Ecoutez bien. C'est quel métier? Et pourquoi? Quels sont les mots clés?	
Do a second example if not many get the idea.	Write keywords on board as mentioned.
3 Guessing Game – *C'est quel métier?*	
■ Pupils write 1–6 and the name of the job in French.	
Écrivez 1–6. Écoutez bien, c'est quel metier? Écrivez les réponses en français.	Write 1–6 on board.
Read out descriptions.	
■ Check answers with partner	
Allow 1 minute to compare answers with partner.	
■ Read out descriptions again – pupils write down keywords.	Use board to refer back to example + keywords.
Écoutez bien, c'est quel metier? Écrivez les mots clés.	
4 Checking answers	
For each one elicit the job and the clues.	Don't labour it – move on once some keywords have been suggested.
Numéro 1, c'est quel metier? Et pourquoi? Quels sont les mots clés?	
5 Feedback	
Hands up those who got all 6 jobs?	
What helped you to work them out? Do you always need to understand every word?	
Well done!	

Variations on the guessing game

- Reuse the same language in a reading exercise. Once you have completed the game as a listening exercise, give out copies of the script. Read through together as a class. Pupils work in pairs, one reads out the description for their partner to guess.
- The structures and vocabulary used to paraphrase can often be recycled as yes/no questions and form the basis of a game of 20 questions. This would lend itself well to the topic of jobs; a limited number of question stems can generate lots of relevant questions, for example: *Est-ce que tu travailles. . . .? Est-ce que tu portes . . . .? Est-ce que tu voyages . . . .? Est-ce que tu gagnes . . . ?*

Planning for individual activities

> ## Box 2.8 Planning box for guessing game
>
> ### Language content
>
> - Decide on your topic and how many different items you are going to describe.
>   Probably 5 to 8 items are fine.
> - Plan what TL modification strategies you will use to feed in plenty of clues.
>   What frequently used structures are you going to use? Keep it simple and try not to include too many different structures. Be conscious of including a generous quantity of cognates, close cognates, proper names and other wider world references.
> - Once you have decided, write your script and rehearse this a few times before the lesson.
>   Pay particular attention to your pace of delivery and to particular words you want to stress.
>
> ### Pedagogic purpose
>
> - Be clear about why you are using this activity with this language content in this lesson.
>
> Are there any particular structures that you want pupils to encounter through this game? Or any particular chunks of language? Try to think ahead as well to any language in the text that pupils might be using at a later date. What could they be using this language to do?
>
> ### Preparing pupils for the activity
>
> - Plan how you will revise the key language needed to make a guess.
>
> Before the activity, how will you check pupil knowledge of the group of items you are going to describe? How will you check that pupils can say those and know what they mean? It is a good idea to revise a larger pool of possible items (as exemplified in the mini-plan), rather than limiting revision to the subgroup that you will be describing.
>
> ### Organising the activity and preparation of resources
>
> - Plan how you will run the activity.
>
> How many times will you read out each description? What form will the task take? Do you want pupils to write anything down as they listen? Do you want pupils to be looking at anything as they listen? (for example, you might want pupils to have a list of possible answers to choose from). What will the completed task look like?
>
> ### Your TL use
>
> - Plan how you will use the TL to introduce and manage the activity.
>
> This activity lends itself well to modelling rather than lengthy instructions. Plan to do an example first to model the activity. How will you do this?
>
> ### Backup plan
>
> - Plan what you will do if pupils struggle to understand the clues that they hear.
>
> ### Decision making in the lesson
>
> Be prepared to be flexible in the classroom, pupils may need to hear the descriptions more often than you had originally planned.

> **Follow-up reflective/discussion task**
>
> *Write a similar script in French, German or Spanish for a guessing game based on: places in town, fruits and vegetables, drinks or based on another topic of your choice. Challenge yourself to keep the language simple and to give as many clues as you can to the meaning. You might find it helpful to refer back to the list of TL modification strategies in Figure 1.4.*
>
> *Once you have produced about six examples, try out your ideas with a friend or colleague, not necessarily another French, German or Spanish speaker.*
>
> *Reflect on what you have learnt from this experience for your own practice.*

PPP model: starting to use the language

The final activities in this chapter involve progression beyond the practice stage. In each case, learners are starting to use the language for a more truly communicative purpose: to take part in a game of bluff, to find out about each other and to take part in a discussion. These activities exemplify learning a language by using it to do things.

Activity 9: Spot the fib

This activity involves saying or writing a few sentences one of which is a deliberate 'fib'; the idea is for others to spot which sentence that is. It provides a purpose for generating different sentences using a limited number of structures with a variety of different language. And because the sentences don't all have to be true, the 'fib' element encourages creativity. Even with beginners it is quite amazing how many different sentences can be created, with limited preparation or thinking time. For example, when beginners in China were challenged to say three sentences about themselves in English (one of which was a fib), they would come up with sentences such as the following:

1   *My favourite colour is red.*
2   *My favourite day is Thursday.*
3   *My favourite food is chicken.*

1   *My favourite month is October.*
2   *My favourite animal is panda.*
3   *My favourite ice-cream is tiramisu.*

1   *My favourite subject is History.*
2   *My favourite number is five.*
3   *My favourite drink is water.*

In terms of content, I have found that sentences about yourself work well, based on structures that pupils are familiar with. I would normally suggest no more than five sentences, one of which is a fib. Depending on the class, you might need to provide pupils with a framework to scaffold the activity. For example, the following framework could be used to write five sentences about what you were like when you were a child.

1   *Quand j'avais cinq ans, j' habitais . . . .*
2   *J'aimais . . . .*
3   *Je faisais . . . .*
4   *J'étais . . . .*
5   *Je jouais . . . .*

The activity can be organised in different ways. If the activity is organised on a whole class basis with one individual pupil performing at a time, this can generate a sense of suspense; the rest of the class are involved in listening for a purpose and at the end can participate with a show of hands to indicate which of the sentences they think is not true. If organised as a pair work activity, everyone can have a chance to speak and practise the language; once initial 'fibs' have been spotted, pupils can do the activity again with different sentences or with slight changes to what they originally said. If organised as a milling exercise, it will generate much repeated practice of the same sentences as pupils move round the room. Either way, I strongly recommend that the teacher models the activity first with different examples, so that the idea of 'spotting the fib' is established in pupils' minds before they do their own examples. When preparing their own examples, it is a good idea to give everyone just a few minutes thinking time first and in most cases it is probably helpful for pupils to note down what they are going to say.

Once the activity has been exploited orally, it can be followed up with a written exercise. Done well, the speaking part helps to scaffold or support the writing. If pupils know what they are writing, because they have practised it and re-practised it orally first, the act of writing in another language is meaningful and pupils can now focus their attention on formal aspects of the language, such as spelling. If pupils are instructed to write carefully, with due attention to spelling, grammar and presentation, the writing helps to reinforce and consolidate what has been learnt from doing the activity as a speaking exercise first. Another important reason for the written follow-up is so that pupils can have a record of the structures and language they have been practising. Without that written record, learning may well disappear.

It is also worthwhile to write up an example together with the class on the board in order to show pupils what to do. Even if most of the class don't actually need this to know what to do, do it for the minority who stand to benefit most. This is an ideal opportunity for the teacher to model for pupils the process of 'writing carefully'. Plan to use the board to explicitly demonstrate this for pupils (especially beginners). Primary school teachers are very skilled at doing this. For example, they write slowly and clearly in non-cursive script; they say the words out loud as they write them on the board; they spell out any difficult words; they read aloud what they have written when they get to the end of the sentence; they correct themselves. Learning to write in another language is demanding, time spent modelling the process is not wasted time.

Table 2.10 shows what the outcomes of your pre-lesson planning might look like, I have assumed here that you have not taught the class before and plan to use 'spot the fib' to tell the class a little bit about yourself and to find out a little about them.

TABLE 2.10 Mini-plan of Activity 9, Spot the fib

Topic: Personal Information

Sample sentences to model the activity – numbered 1–5 on slide, following this structure

J'habite à Chester le Street.

J'ai 21 ans.

Ma couleur préférée est le jaune.

J'adore Kylie.

Je déteste Harry Potter.

Method	Don't Forget
1 Introduce yourself to class *Bonjour la classe, je m'appelle M/Mme/Mlle* . . . . . Write name on board, spell out for class and repeat *je m'appelle M/Mme/Mlle* . . . . *Alors, je me présente* . . . read out 5 sample sentences. Repeat, this time show each sentence as you read it out.	Write name up on board.
2 Model the game Once all 5 sentences are up, *C'est vrai ou c'est faux? Numéro un, c'est vrai ou c'est faux? Lève la main, si tu penses que c'est vrai/faux.* Confirm each time – *très bien, c'est vrai/faux.*	If stuck use board to draw a tick for 'vrai' and a cross for 'faux'
3 Do another example Read out another 5 sentences. This time say *Une phrase est fausse. Quelle phrase?* Pupils can say the sentence number. *C'est numéro un* etc.	
4 Pupils play Spot the Fib Show slide with model to follow in case needed. Invite volunteers to come up with sentences about themselves. *A vous maintenant. Est-ce qu'il y a un volontaire? Cinq phrases, une phrase est fausse.*	If difficult give option of 3 or 4 sentences with 1x fib.
Show of hands from rest of class to indicate which one is the fib.	
After 4 or 5 volunteers, move onto same activity in pairs. *Avec ton partenaire!*	Try and listen in to a few – maybe get another volunteer to say theirs for rest of class?
Use countdown to get quiet again – *5, 4, 3, 2, 1 – silence!*	

5 Write up an example together
Ouvrez vos cahiers. Copiez la date et le titre – C'est vrai ou c'est faux? Elicit a volunteer to provide sample sentences, if not – use your own one again. Write those up on board for pupils to copy.

Exemple

Je m'appelle . . .

J'habite à Chester le Street.

J'ai 21 ans. Etc.

Pupils mark each sentence with a tick or cross in margin – model on board – and write either *C'est vrai.* or *C'est faux.*

Then write up their own sentences.

Write clearly and slowly – read out loud.

Variations on spot the fib

'Spot the fib' also works well as a reading and writing activity. Pupils write sentences for others to read and spot the fib. This works well with factual statements; for example, statements about your school timetable. Organising 'spot the fib' as a written activity provides pupils with a communicative purpose for reading and writing. The key point here is that there is an audience for pupils' writing. Others will be reading what has been written, not to correct or check spelling or grammar, but to spot the fib. Writing for an audience provides a purpose for writing; how we write for an audience is different from how we write when making notes for ourselves.

With more advanced learners, who have more language at their disposal, 'spot the fib' also provides opportunities for freer expression. You might want to use this activity as a fluency exercise, or ice breaker, just to get pupils talking and interacting with each other.

Box 2.9 Planning box for spot the fib (with class of beginners)

Language content

- Plan which key structure or structures pupils will be practising through this activity.

Choose structures which can be used with a variety of different vocabulary to generate multiple sentences. Check that there is enough scope for pupils to draw on language they are familiar with and be a little creative or playful with language. Writing down examples yourself can help you to explore this point. It also means you have some examples that you can use in the classroom to model the activity and its creative potential.

Pedagogic purpose

- Be clear about why you are using this activity with this language content in this lesson.

You might refer here to the PPP model or to the 'variations' on this activity, to help you articulate your thinking. As well as the speaking part, you might also want to incorporate a written follow-up. In which case, bear in mind that this will have implications for how your prioritise the lesson time available. Try to think ahead a little bit as well, at a later stage what will pupils be using this language to do?

Preparing pupils for the activity

- Plan how you will model the activity.
    What examples will you use? And how will you model the activity? I would tend to do this without the written word, so that pupils can focus on listening to the TL. Once pupils have guessed the fib, then perhaps show the written version on a slide to consolidate understanding.
- Plan how you want pupils to indicate what fib they spotted.

Organising the activity and preparation of resources

- Plan how you will organise the speaking part.
    Volunteers with the rest of the class listening? Pair work with pupils seated? Pair work with pupils circulating? A combination of these?
- Depending on how important the writing part is, plan how long you can spend on the speaking part.
- If doing pair work, plan how you will signal the end of the activity and how you will regain class attention.
- Plan how you will organise the writing part.

If you are planning to write up some examples together with the class, allow at least ten minutes for this.

Your TL use

- Plan how you will use the TL to introduce and manage the activity.

Pay particular attention to the TL and mimes you will use when modelling the activity.

Backup plan

Prepare a few different sets of examples to use when modelling the activity, just in case pupils struggle to understand the procedure. Have a written version of those on different slides, in the event pupils really find it hard to understand you when you say the sentences; you can then gradually reveal and read out each sentence in turn for pupils to follow.

Decision making in the lesson

Be prepared to be flexible in the classroom, pupils may need to hear a few examples before they understand what to do. If pupils are engaged and getting lots of listening and speaking practice you might allow a bit longer than originally planned for the speaking activity itself, and curtail the writing part.

Pedagogical focus: reusing and recycling familiar language

An important aspect of planning is to create opportunities for learners to use familiar language, vocabulary and structures, for new purposes and in different contexts. This is what I mean by 'recycling'. Recycling is an opportunity for learners to transfer language learnt in one context to another context in order to create new meanings for themselves.

Consider, for example, what was happening with the Chinese pupils cited above. Given the opportunity to do so, pupils were able to transfer words learnt in different contexts to create new sentences. Their sentences are simple but nevertheless valid examples of independent language use. For example, the juxtaposition of 'my favourite' + 'number' had not been taught before. I suspect that the pupil who said 'my favourite number is five' said so for the first time in his English learning career; and it is possible that other pupils who heard him using it were also hearing this for the first time. Other learners quickly followed suit, and made up their own sentences using 'my favourite number is . . .'. Learning to manipulate and use structures for yourself like this is key to learner progress.

When you observe lessons, be conscious of opportunities that exist for pupils to recycle what they have previously learnt. Notice also anything that the class teacher does to support this; for example, notice how the teacher explicitly reminds pupils and helps them to recall language they have already been taught.

Activity 10: Mini-class survey

Class surveys are an opportunity for pupils to use the language they have been learning to find out and record information about others in their class. Typically this involves pupils getting up out of their seats and circulating round the classroom, interviewing their classmates. If you have the resources, a prepared survey sheet for pupils to complete and then stick in their exercise books or work folders can look professional and add authenticity to the task. If this is not possible, then use a very simple format for collating answers that pupils can neatly copy down in two or three minutes. Try not to waste lesson time with excessive copying, keep the format simple.

In learning terms, a survey provides repeated opportunities for pupils to use the TL needed to ask and answer questions on a given topic. This functions as a learning opportunity if pupils are confident in using the language of the task. If pupils are not confident, there is the very real possibility that at best they will resort to English in order to complete the task, at worst they will use this as an opportunity to chat in English. In order to maximise pupils' preparedness for this task, there are two vital ingredients. Before doing the survey, pupils need to have had adequate exposure to the language of the task, both question and answer forms, and adequate repetition practice of this language.

Prior to embarking on the survey, it helps if the teacher can model the task with a pupil or pupils in the class, this involves demonstrating to the class what you want them to do. If the modelling is clear and backed up visually, perhaps with a copy of the survey sheet that everyone can see, there should not be the need for you to also give instructions. Once the task has been modelled, a simple way to find out if pupils have understood the task is to get them to tell you what to do; for example, by asking a pupil to explain to the rest of the class. In some cases, it may be necessary to model another example to help more pupils understand what is involved. As a rule of thumb it is a better use of lesson time to model two or three examples, if need be, rather than spend a long time explaining the task in English. Don't talk about it, do it!

Finally, decisions need to be made about what will happen at the end of the survey period, when pupils return to their seats. Having used the survey to practise key structures, it would be a wasted opportunity not to follow this up in some way in order to squeeze even more learning out of the task and in order to add value to the task in pupils' eyes. There are different ways to do this. One possibility would be to follow up the survey with some questions in the TL relating to the survey results; this might be an opportunity to introduce and use the third person of key verbs, or an opportunity to collate all the results on the board. Another possibility would be for individual pupils to draw up a bar or pie chart showing the results of their survey; this might also be an opportunity to use the written form of the third person, or to write up some sample dialogues.

Depending on the extent of language needed for task completion and on the needs of the learners, a survey can be part of a longer-term plan covering a sequence of lessons leading up to and including the survey itself. We will look at the long term planning implications later in the book. For now, I would like to focus on a mini-class survey, a short learning activity that does not necessarily depend on long term planning, yet which still illustrates some of the key principles that underpin the planning of any successful survey in the ML classroom.

A mini-class survey is limited in scope. Each pupil is given one or two questions which they will ask to at least six others in the class, within a limited length of time. This works well with simple 'yes/no' type questions and with structures which can be used with a variety of different vocabulary or can be used with proper nouns and names. A good example is 'likes and dislikes'. A mini-class survey may be limited in scope and not involve much language, but it is still an opportunity for learners to use French, German or Spanish to find out and record information about their classmates. If pupils can achieve that politely in the TL, without relying on notes, without recourse to English and within the given time limit, then you have done a good job of teaching them. However, it might take you longer than you imagine to achieve this.

Assuming that you are doing a mini-class survey with a class you are unfamiliar with, Table 2.11 shows what the outcomes of your pre-lesson planning might look like. I have deliberately chosen proper names, in this case the names of celebrities, to keep this as simple as possible.

TABLE 2.11 Mini-plan of activity 10, Mini-survey

Topic: Likes and Dislikes

Key language

Est-ce que tu aimes + name of celebrity?

Oui, j'aime . . . j'aime beaucoup . . . j'adore . . .

Non, je n'aime pas . . . je n'aime pas beaucoup . . . je déteste . . . .

(continued)

TABLE 2.11 *(continued)*

Method	Don't Forget
1 *Est-ce que tu aimes Elvis Presley?* Hold up picture of Elvis. Ask *Il s'appelle comment? Oui, il s'appelle Elvis Presley.* *Moi, j'aime beaucoup Elvis. Et toi? Est-ce que tu aimes Elvis Presley?* Take as many answers as possible before drilling.	Show enthusiasm. Take multiple answers.
2 Drill key language + screen Show symbols (1–6) first, one at a time, and elicit the French first then choral repetition of each. Then repeat if true.	
3 *Est-ce que tu aimes Beyonce?* Hold up picture of Beyonce. *Elle s'appelle comment? Oui, Elle s'appelle Beyonce.* *Moi, je n'aime pas Beyonce. Et toi? Est-ce que tu aimes Beyonce?*	Show enthusiasm. Take multiple answers.
4 Practise the question form Use mouthing to introduce further questions plus different celebs. *Regardez- moi. C'est quelle question?* Choral repetition of question each time it is guessed. Pupils do same mouthing activity in pairs *30 secondes avec ton partenaire*	Use *Est-ce que tu aimes...?* each time. Take multiple answers.
5 Modelling the Mini-survey *On va faire un petit sondage. On va poser les questions aux autres dans la classe.* Par exemple, *Est-ce que tu aimes* Elvis? *Est-ce que tu aimes* Beyonce? Etc *On va posez des questions en français et on va noter les réponses.* *Par exemple* (show example on board) *Je voudrais des volontaires svp.* Ask a few volunteers 2x questions and use board to record the answers – using ticks and crosses or faces, next to the name of the celeb.	Elvis ☺ ☺ Beyonce ☹ ☺
6 Instructions for Mini-survey *Je vais vous donner un morceau de papier* – hold up – *comme ça. Vous avez une minute pour écrire le titre (un petit sondage), la question (est-ce que tu aimes . . .?) et deux noms* – point to this information on slide, pupils can choose their own celebs from suggested names. *Y a-t-il des questions? Qui peut expliquer?* *Vous avez trois minutes pour faire le sondage. Trois minutes. Il faut demander à six personnes au minimum. Très important – il faut poser des questions en français!*	
7 Follow-up to survey Use countdown to signal to pupils to return to their seats. *5, 4, 3, 2, 1 – c'est fini. Asseyez-vous!* Return to list of possible celebs on slide. *Qui a demandé à six personnes? Excellent!* Encourage pupils to feedback in French– the 2 questions that they asked and how many people said they did//did not like each of their 2 celebs.	

If pupils are not used to surveys or talking to each other in the TL, you might need to be quite flexible about the actual time you allow for this in the lesson. At the planning stage, it is a good idea to identify a minimum and maximum time; in the lesson itself you will need to make a decision about the cut-off time. As indicated above, this decision might be contingent upon what you want pupils to do with survey information at the end of the task. It will be important to allow quality lesson time for any write up. You might decide to set the write-up as a homework task, in which case it will be important to model and clarify expectations in the lesson itself. Alternatively, you may find that pupils are enjoying the survey and using a lot of TL. In such a case, you may decide to extend the time allowed for the survey or even to continue with it next lesson. If you find there is just enough lesson time to complete the survey task, postpone the write-up until the start of the next lesson; finish the lesson with some quick hands-up feedback that everyone can take part in, e.g. you might ask the class who was able to ask six people?

Or who was able to speak only French, German or Spanish? The key thing here is to try and think this through a little bit before you go into the lesson. Essentially you are trying to pre-empt any likely decisions that will be needed in the lesson.

When pupils are doing the survey, it is a good idea for you to circulate, observing and listening in to their conversations. In the first instance, this is an opportunity for you to pre-empt any pupil difficulties or problems with the task, e.g. pupils might bunch together in one area of the room. This is also an opportunity for beginning teachers to know more about individual pupils. Who seem to be the ones who are most confident in speaking in another language? Who seem to struggle?

> ### Variations on mini-class survey
>
> In the case of classes who need a very structured approach to their learning, or classes who currently present challenging behaviours when let out of their seats, a mini-class survey can be conducted with the class remaining seated. This would involve one person speaking at a time, that person would either be the interviewer or the interviewee, with the rest of the class listening and keeping a written tally of answers. The interviewer might be the teacher each time or this role might alternate amongst pupils.

Once classes are familiar and confident with the format of surveys you might think about introducing further key language to be used for successful task completion. After all, a survey is not just a literal matter of asking questions, it is also an opportunity to practise some of the niceties usually associated with such an event. In real life for example, it is unusual to launch straight into a survey or an interview without some sort of greeting or salutation, and it is usual at the end of an interview to thank the interviewee. Even with a simple mini-survey there is scope for pupils to draw on and recycle prior learning in order to make their language use as authentic as possible. In the case of the mini-survey exemplified in Table 2.11, this might involve exchanges such as the following, where part A is the interviewer and part B the interviewee:

A *Salut. Ça va?*

B *Salut. Oui, ça va bien.*

A *Est-ce que tu aimes Elvis Presley?*

B *Non, je n'aime pas Elvis.*

A *Est-ce que tu aimes Beyoncé?*

B *Oui, j'adore Beyoncé.*

A *Merci, au revoir.*

B *Au revoir.*

Presenting a sample dialogue such as this is the first step in modelling for pupils how they might conduct a survey using French, German or Spanish. You may choose to do this with the dialogue written up on a slide, or use cues to represent the written word or a mixture of both. Assuming that pupils are already familiar with the different elements of the dialogue, here are some steps you might follow to prepare pupils well for conducting mini-surveys independently of the teacher. This is based on the ideas of Wendy Phipps; please see her book *Pairwork, interaction in the modern languages classroom* (1999) for more on the transition from whole class to pair work.

1. Read out part of interviewer, whole class reads out part of interviewee
2. Read out part of interviewer, vary the questions with other names of celebrities and ask individual pupils to answer your questions
3. Reverse roles, whole class reads out part of interviewer and you answer questions
4. Select individual pupils to read out part of interviewer with other names of celebrities and you answer their questions
5. Pupils practise the dialogue in pairs – substituting their own information

Having worked through steps 1–5, pupils are now ready to work to start work on their mini-surveys in pairs. You might want to keep up a copy of the sample dialogue that pupils can see, just in case that extra support is needed.

Box 2.10 Planning box for mini-class survey

Language content

- Decide on a minimum of language that all pupils will need to complete the survey in the TL.

What would a sample dialogue or survey exchange look like? Identify a key structure for the question form and for the answer, as appropriate. Within the minimum framework is there also scope for some pupils to bring in other language that they know? Write up some sample dialogue to help you plan this.

Pedagogic purpose

- Be clear about why you are using this activity with this language content in this lesson.

You might refer here to the PPP model or to some of the ideas above to help you articulate your thinking. Try to think ahead a little bit as well, at a later stage what will pupils be using this language to do?

Lead up to the activity

- Plan how you will revise the language needed to complete the survey
  Even if most or all of the language needed has already been taught in previous lessons, still plan to revise it before the survey. Pay particular attention to the question form or forms to be used. Build in explicit practice of those. Pay particular attention to non-topic specific language such as numbers or alphabet which might be needed to answer survey questions. Plan how you will revise such items, as needed.
- Plan how you will model the survey task so that pupils know what to do and how to do it.
  Plan how you will elicit a pupil to help you model the survey. How will you check that everyone has understood what to do? And how to do it?

Organising the activity itself

- Plan when you will give out the survey sheets.
  Do you want pupils to have a copy of the survey sheet in front of them when the task is being modelled? Or would it be better to project a copy of the sheet onto the screen and to use this when modelling the task? Or would both of these be helpful?
- Plan a minimum and maximum time for pupils to do the survey.
  Will you need to stop it after a specific time? What is the minimum number of interviews that you expect all pupils to have achieved in that time?
- Plan what you will be doing when pupils are engaged in the mini-survey.
  What do you want to pick up on? What do *you* want to learn from this?

Your TL output

How will you use the TL to introduce and manage the activity?
Pay particular attention to the language you will use when modelling the survey. Also, to how you will signal to pupils the end of the activity and let them know that they need to return to their seats. Prioritise the key language you will use, plus any mimes or actions to help get the message over. Once you have decided on your TL output, write it down.

Follow-up to activity

- Plan how you want to follow up the survey.
  Is there any information you can quickly collect through a show of hands? What will happen to the results? Do you want pupils to keep a written record of the mini-survey?
- Plan how you will model the writing of the written report for pupils
  Plan how you will involve pupils in this process. Will some pupils need a simple writing frame to support any written follow-up? If you are planning to set the write-up as a homework, then allow at least ten minutes to model and clarify expectations.

Backup plan

- Plan what you will do if some pupils struggle to do the survey in the TL.
    Where can some pupils get linguistic support if needed? Is the key language written down somewhere they can refer to? Can you use the screen to project that key language?

Decision making in the lesson

You might need to be quite flexible about the actual time you allow for this activity in the lesson.

PPP model: using the language for real and letting go

In both of these last two activities, learners have the opportunity to use the language for the purpose for which it is intended: communication. The better we prepare the ground for those activities which are less controlled, the more confident learners will feel and the better able they will be to use the language independently. To a large extent, the first two 'Ps' in the PPP model are about preparing the ground for those moments in lessons when the teacher steps back and lets the pupils talk and actually use the language that they have been learning to say things that they choose to say. The rewards of getting this right are what make it all worthwhile both for pupils and teacher.

In order to illustrate what is possible, I'll refer here to the work of Wendy Ward, Head of Languages at Sir James Smith's School in Cornwall. In this example, Wendy exploits a 'True/False' activity for speaking purposes. This is an activity that can be used when learners are quite confident with the language and you just want them to use it for real. The core idea of the activity is that pupils are presented with a list of related statements and need to work out which of them are true, which are false and why. Wendy refers to 'true/false' as a 'letting go' type activity; she exploits it as an opportunity for pupils to use the language of discussion, especially agreeing, disagreeing and forming an argument based on reasons. Wendy explains how it works:

> The true//false facts idea always works well. Students work in pairs as a team, they discuss each 'fact' and they MUST both put the same answer. If they disagree they must argue and argue until one backs down. This works well after holidays. I do a list of 'facts' about my holiday and they have to speculate about what is true//false, but again they have to write the same as their partner. It can run for 10-15 mins and the teacher can just stand back. BUT of course students have to be very confident with the language of agreement// disagreement before you start! When it is running I usually listen out for words causing problems and just quietly write a list of tips on the board for them to refer to.
>
> (Wendy Ward, 2018, personal communication)

This activity is also good for at the start of a topic when pupils don't necessarily know the answers, for example, facts about schools in Germany, Easter in Spain or New Year celebrations in France. It is important to bear in mind that the actual language content of the statements should be relatively simple, carefully selected by the teacher to recycle previously taught language as far as possible. If the language of the statements is too complex or contains too much unfamiliar language, it will prevent pupils from getting as much as they might out of the activity, the main purpose of which is to stimulate and provide a context for discussion and spontaneous language use.

Finally, don't be disheartened by how long it might take you to reach this stage with classes that you teach. In a sense, Wendy has been preparing her pupils for this activity over a period of years, carefully building up a classroom culture that promotes spontaneous language use by pupils. To find out more about promoting spontaneous learner talk and what is involved in creating an atmosphere in the classroom where the use of the TL is seen as the normal mode of communication by both teacher and pupils, please see Christie (2016) or Crichton (2009).

Reflective//discussion task

To what extent do you think that the pupils in Wendy's example are using the language spontaneously?

Draw up a list of possible discussion phrases that pupils might use for activities such as 'true/false' and 'spot the fib'. For example, a good starting point might be phrases for agreeing or disagreeing with each other in the TL. Plan how you could introduce and teach a few discussion phrases to classes that you teach. Plan how you would progressively introduce, drill and practise these phrases, and discuss possible contexts you could create in the classroom for pupils to use them spontaneously. You might want to use the planning box template below to help you (BOX 2.11).

Box 2.11 Planning box template

Language content

Pedagogic purpose

Preparing pupils for the activity

Organising the activity and preparation of resources

Your TL use

Possible follow-up

Backup plan

Decision making in the lesson

TABLE 2.12 PPP model and the role of the teacher

Phase	Purpose	Teacher's role
Presentation (pre-communicative phase)	■ To present new language in context so that meaning is clear ■ To present the new form in a natural spoken or written text so that learners can experience language in use ■ To link new input to what learners already know ■ To make meanings clear ■ To check comprehension	**Instructor**, corrector
Practice (quasi-communicative phase)	■ To help learners memorize the form and meaning of new input ■ To help learners produce the word order ■ To give practice in pronouncing the new forms ■ To give intensive practice through repetition ■ To provide opportunities for feedback and error correction ■ To help learners re-produce the language from memory ■ To support pupils in manipulating the new language ■ To develop confidence	**Manager**, evaluator, corrector
Production (more truly communicative, independent phase)	■ To reduce control and encourage learners to find out what they can do ■ To encourage learners to make the language their own, to express meaning that matter to them ■ To help learners see the usefulness of what they have learned ■ To assess what has been learned and progress made ■ To diagnose problems	**Assessor**, resource, facilitator, diagnoser

Reflecting on the activities in Chapter 2

We have focused here on the different phases of the PPP model presented at the start of this chapter, and the implications for planning. We have considered a range of activities and seen the progression from highly controlled to freer language use, from pre-communicative to more truly communicative language use. In this, the role of the teacher changes commensurate with the purpose of each phase of the PPP model; in practice, this means that teachers can often play different pedagogic roles within the course of one lesson. Table 2.12 brings together key points.

Reflective/discussion task

Activities have deliberately been omitted from Table 2.12. Consider the pedagogic purpose of activities that have been introduced in this part of the book, where in the model would you locate each of them? Can any activities be located in more than one part of the model depending on how they are used? To what extent are you able to locate activities you observe in school in this model? What different teaching roles can you discern in the lessons that you observe?

A final word about learning to plan

Planning is a complex process. It has been deconstructed here in an attempt to highlight some of the elements that might usefully be thought through when planning for individual activities at an early stage in the ITE period. This planning process becomes smoother and less time consuming with experience and as you develop your own approaches to planning (Deane, 2002). The other thing that makes a difference is evaluation. Even at an early stage in your ITE when you are planning for individual activities, it is good to get into the habit of evaluating your experience of teaching to help you learn from it.

In the early stages of learning to teach, lesson evaluation can help us to review in general terms what went well and what could be improved. It is important to give equal attention to both and to accept that there will always be ways in which you might teach even better. As a teacher, there is a sense in which you are never the 'finished product', but that does not mean that you are not a good teacher. On the contrary, one of the hallmarks of the best teachers is a disposition to continue to learn and to improve. We will consider lesson evaluation further in Part II.

For now, a simple format for lesson evaluation might include the following headings; beginning teachers have found these useful during the early stages of the ITE period:

- **This is what I/we did in the lesson . . . .**
- **This is how I thought it went . . .**
- **This is how the class teacher thought it went . . .**
- **Lessons learnt . . .**

Please note, the comments of the class teacher might be written during the lesson or written up after the lesson.

Conclusion to Part I

The planning decisions we make can help us to establish conditions for successful language learning. Planning allows us to identify key language that we want to model for pupils in use; it allows us to teach language in chunks of meaning rather than decontextualised lists of words; and to ensure that exposure to the language in use is repeated, comprehensible and pitched at an appropriate level for pupils to make sense of the language for themselves. You can plan how you will maximise pupil participation in oral work, exploiting multiple answers, organising whole class activities to be repeated in pairs and with teacher clones. You can plan drilling sequences so that pupils learn chunks of language, building blocks which lay foundations for interaction. You can plan opportunities for pupils to use the language they have learnt for communicative purposes. Motivation to learn is rather more difficult to plan for. But a useful starting place is to think about what you are planning from the learners' point of view and to ask yourself: what purpose or relevance will they see in doing this? And what sense of achievement might they feel once they have done it?

Chapter 1 introduced two fundamental teaching skills for any ML teacher: drilling and TL use, especially TL output modification. In my view, these fundamental skills are part of the Pedagogic Content Knowledge needed to teach ML. Get those right and you have an excellent basis for fostering ML learning in your classroom. But getting them right is not a simple matter. Technically, it is possible to develop excellent skills in drilling language and in modifying the TL to which pupils are exposed. But learning to teach is about much more than developing technical ability. Good teachers are not only technically good, they are also able to use technical ability to promote learning. In order to help pupils learn and progress, it is vital that planning decisions are informed by an understanding of what you are seeking to achieve and why. We have started to consider what this might mean in relation to individual activities; in Part II, we consider the implications for planning whole lessons.

References for Part I

Chambers, F. (1991) Promoting use of the target language in the classroom. *The Language Learning Journal*, 4(1), pp27–31.

Christie, C. (2016) Speaking spontaneously in the modern foreign languages classroom: tools for supporting successful target language conversation. *The Language Learning Journal*, 44(1), pp74–89.

Crichton, H. (2009) 'Value added' modern languages teaching in the classroom: an investigation into how teachers' use of classroom target language can aid pupils' communication skills. *The Language Learning Journal*, 37(1), pp19–34.

Deane, M. (2002) Planning MFL learning. In A. Swarbrick (ed.) *Aspects of teaching secondary modern foreign languages*. Routledge/Falmer: London, pp147–165.

Field, J. (2008) *Listening in the language classroom*. Cambridge University Press: Cambridge.

Graham, S., Santos, D. and Vanderplank, R. (2011) Exploring the relationship between listening development and strategy use. *Language Teaching Research*, 15(4), pp 435–456.

Harris, V., Burch, J., Jones, B. and Darcy, J. (2001) *Something to say? Promoting spontaneous classroom talk*. CILT: London.

Hedge, T. (2000) *Teaching and learning in the language classroom*. Oxford University Press: Oxford.

Jones, B. (2002) *You speak, they speak: focus on target language use*. Classic Pathfinder 1. CILT: London. Available from The Barry Jones Archive at: https://www.all-languages.org.uk/student/barry-jones-archive/ [accessed November 2018].

Kagan, S. and Kagan, M. (2015) *Cooperative learning*. Revised edition. Kagan Publishing: San Clemente, CA.

Krashen, S.D. (1982) *Principles and practice in second language acquisition*. Pergamon Press: Oxford.

Krashen, S.D. and Terrell, T.D. (1983) *The natural approach: language acquisition in the classroom*. Pergamon Press: Oxford.

Littlewood, W. (1981) *Communicative language teaching*. Cambridge University Press: Cambridge.

Macaro, E. (2000) Issues in target language teaching. In K. Field (ed.) *Issues in modern foreign languages teaching*. Routledge/Falmer: London, pp171–189.

Mitchell, R. and Myles, F. (1998) *Second language learning theories*. Arnold: London.

Pachler, N., Evans, M., Redondo, A. and Fisher, L. (2014) *Learning to teach foreign languages in the secondary school*. Fourth edition. Routledge: London

Phipps, W. (1999) *Pairwork, interaction in the modern languages classroom*. Pathfinder 38. CILT: London.

YouTube (2014) Gestures for questions, performed by Rachel Hawkes. Available at https://www.youtube.com/watch?v=iqCvE258vY0 (accessed February 2019).

PART

Well-planned lessons

Aims of Part II

The overriding aim of Part II is to build on elements of planning introduced in Part I and to develop understanding of the concept of 'well-planned language lessons'. Chapter 3 looks at concrete examples of ML lessons based on the lesson plans of beginning teachers, identifying and discussing particular features of the plans which, in my view, are integral to promoting learning. In so doing, I will also introduce and briefly discuss further layers of decision making that are integral to lesson planning, such as assessment, differentiation and behaviour. Chapter 4 then steps back from this and considers the process of lesson planning, including the writing of lesson plans.

CHAPTER

Planning whole lessons

Introduction

Planning a whole lesson extends the decision making involved in planning a standalone activity. Similar planning decisions are made in relation to the headings which were introduced in Part I:

Language content

Pedagogic purpose

Preparing pupils for activities

Organising activities and preparation of resources

Your TL use

Backup plan

Follow-up

Planning for whole lessons builds on these and extends your thinking to consider the bigger picture. For example, decisions about the linguistic content and pedagogic purpose of a single lesson need to take into account how the lesson fits into medium-term plans for the class. This can help the teacher to decide what learning will be important in this lesson and why. Decisions made about a possible follow-up to the lesson are likely to include planning for homework and perhaps some tentative thoughts about how the next lesson will follow on from this one.

Looking ahead to longer-term plans for the class can increase awareness of intended progress over time and how a single lesson might contribute to these plans. Lesson planning will also involve building on prior learning. When planning individual lessons, for example, it is good idea to try to include time and opportunity for pupils to practise or revise what they did in the last lesson, rather than planning each lesson in isolation. Similarly, you might plan to present and teach new items of vocabulary within the context of a familiar structure or use well-known vocabulary to introduce and practise a new structure. This is an example of 'teaching the new within the context of the familiar', a useful principle to follow.

I would also like to stress that thinking through the practicalities is every bit as important as the more intellectual aspects of lesson planning. Compared to planning an individual activity, there will be more things for you to take into account when making decisions on the organisation of the lesson and the required resources. Good lesson organisation ensures that lessons run smoothly. For example, it will be important to plan how you will ensure a prompt and organised start to the lesson, provide clear instructions, manage transitions between activities, give out and take in books and resources, organise pupils into pairs or groups, make seating arrangements, use technology and see to an orderly and punctual end to the lesson. Learning to teach smoothly run, well–organised lessons is an important, early priority for beginning teachers. This helps you to establish yourself as the teacher in the classroom and it can help to minimise the likelihood of unwanted pupil behaviour. There are many books offering practical advice on generic aspects of good lesson organisation and class management; a good place to start might be *Essential Teaching Skills* (Kyriacou, 2018).

These points illustrate just some ways in which planning whole lessons can build on and extend the decision making needed for planning individual activities. I would like to focus now on lesson structure, an important difference between the two situations, and discuss some of the implications for planning whole lessons.

Planning whole lessons

Lesson structure

Lessons last for a finite length of time and lesson planning needs to include decisions about how best to use that time. A key consideration here is which activities to include and in what order; there may also be non-ML specific issues that need to be factored into lesson time. This has implications for how we organise the time available and, more significantly, how we structure the lesson so that pupils can progress in their learning.

Developing a clear lesson structure depends upon having a clear sense of where you are heading. Typically, lessons are structured with particular outcomes or learning intentions in mind. Well-structured lessons facilitate progression. This is a crucially important element of lesson planning: if there is no progression, there is no learning. A starting point in planning for progression might be to think through what we expect pupils to demonstrate by the end of the lesson that they couldn't do at the start.

There follows an example of a clearly structured language lesson that I recently observed (Table 3.1a). This example is based on notes I made whilst observing, it is not a lesson plan as such. In a sense I did not need to see the lesson plan to know that the lesson had been well planned. From observing I was able to see how learning was progressing; it was clear that the structure had been well-thought through to enable a particular group of people to progress and fill gaps in their learning. The text used in the lesson is shown in Figure 3.1:

What is the name of the sport?

1. This sport is played outdoors. Players compete individually, rather than as part of a team. Each player uses a long metal club to hit a small round ball; the ball is about the size of small egg. The aim is to hit the ball into a hole.

2. This sport is played indoors. It is a team sport. Players use a large round ball, about the size of a watermelon. The aim is to throw the ball through a metal hoop.

3. This sport is played outdoors. It is a team sport. Players use a round ball about the size of a large melon. They are not allowed to touch the ball with their hands. The aim is to kick or head the ball into a large net.

4. This sport is usually played outdoors. Players usually compete individually, rather than as part of a team. The aim is to run faster than your opponents.

5. This sport is played outdoors. It is a team sport. Players use a large oval shaped ball. They can kick the ball or throw it backwards; they are not allowed to throw the ball forwards. The aim is to take the ball down to the opponents' end of the field and to touch the ground with it.

6. This sport is played indoors or on a beach. It is a team sport. Players use a large round ball, about the size of large melon. The aim is to punch the ball over a net, so that the opponents cannot return it.

7. This sport is played outdoors. It is a team sport. Players use a hard ball, about the size of a large apple. A player from one team throws the ball towards a wooden wicket and a player from the other team tries to hit the ball with a long wooden bat.

FIGURE 3.1 Text used in English conversation group lesson

TABLE 3.1A Example of a clearly structured lesson

The lesson took place in a voluntary conversation group for refugees and asylum seekers who want to practise their English in a friendly, informal setting. The participants in this lesson did not share a common first language, they had a very wide range of English proficiency, and had formed a group for the purposes of the lesson. There were about eight men and women in the group and a volunteer native English speaker who led the lesson. It was a standalone lesson about sport, planned to coincide with the start of the Premier League football season in England.

Here is an outline of what happened.

1. Setting the scene - T started by asking P if they knew about the English football Premier League. Those who did know explained to those who didn't. This information was repeated again for late arrivals. Having established what the Premier League is, T asked P if they knew the names of any football clubs in the Premier League.
2. T showed a blank map of England and Wales and distributed amongst the group pieces of card, each with the name of one of the clubs already mentioned. P worked in pairs, read the name of the club and then placed it on the map. The group then discussed if all the names were placed correctly.
3. T then gave out copies of a map of England and Wales which had all 20 Premier League clubs marked on it. P had a few minutes to digest the implications of this in pairs and to ask any questions.
4. T then focused on Newcastle United Football Club (NUFC) – the local club. T showed two slides with pictures to stimulate the sharing of information about the club and to provide a backdrop to questions about the club, e.g. What nationality is the manager? What about the players – how many different countries are represented in the team? What are those countries? NUFC also has a women's team, what do you think about that?
5. T showed further slides to illustrate other sports that are popular in Newcastle. Questioning was used to elicit the name and key features of each sport and how it works. New vocabulary was introduced within this context, e.g. words such as 'net' and 'backwards' which would be needed for the next task.
6. Guided reading task – based on seven short texts (see Figure 3.1) to describe different sports but without mentioning the name of that sport. Texts used a limited range of language and structures, lots of recycling and repetition. T gave out copies and then read out each text in turn. P followed the written word and at the end of each text wrote down the name of the sport described.
7. Checking answers – T went through each of the texts in turn. For each one, the correct answer was elicited and why? P said which keywords had given them a clue to the answer. During this time, there was a chance for P to ask questions about any unknown vocabulary e.g. one person asked the meaning of 'hoop', another the meaning of 'golf club'.
8. Further practice in reading and listening – in pairs, one P read out a sport description at random for their partner, who could not see the written version, to guess.

Participants enjoyed the lesson, they were finding out and talking about something that interested them. But at the same time they were learning English and growing in confidence.

TABLE 3.1B Commentary on the example of a clearly structured lesson

At the start of the lesson, the teacher establishes what the participants already know. This is an important point. It informs the teacher, who wants to identify what the different participants have already learnt, so as not to waste learning time teaching things the class already knows. It also helps participants to revise what they have previously learnt and to feel part of the lesson.

The teacher then builds on the participants's pre-existing knowledge of firstly the names of the football clubs and secondly of the language used to describe particular sports. In effect, this is teaching the new within the context of the familiar. This is a useful principle to bear in mind when planning for learning in any subject. This assists learners to make connections and helps the teacher to ensure progression in learning from one lesson to the next

The lesson has been broken down into small steps which help learners gain as much benefit as possible out of the activities and resources that the teacher has prepared for them. Consider, for example, the steps leading up to point 3 when the participants see the completed map for the first time. They were able to make sense of and engage with that map because of what had led up to that point. Consider also how the participants are prepared for the guided reading task. They are familiar with the names of possible sports, they have looked at pictures of each, talked about key features and been introduced to some new vocabulary that will come up in the reading task. In turn, the guided reading task itself and the checking of answers help prepare participants for the final paired reading and listening task.

The structure of the lesson facilitates progression, enabling the participants to advance their learning and use of the English language and increase their knowledge of cultural aspects. It is structured to lead up to a final activity involving listening, reading and speaking, which the participants carried out independently of the teacher. Other activities have been sequenced to help the participants progress towards the last activity. Planning lessons with a sequence of activities which progressively prepare learners for the end activity is one way to conceptualise planning for progression.

(continued)

TABLE 3.1B *(continued)*

There is an obvious progression from the start of the lesson where the focus is on names of football clubs and simple sentences to the end of the lesson where participants are using and engaging with a range of different structures and vocabulary. Progression also takes other forms: in learner independence, from teacher-led to participant-led activity; from the spoken word to the written word; from the familiar to the new; from words to sentences to text.

Follow-up Reflective Task/Points to discuss

This was a clearly structured standalone lesson leading up to a substantial end activity. What learning intentions do you think the teacher had in mind when he planned this lesson? What do you think might have been the main lesson aim or objective?

The commentary in Table 3.1b discusses salient features of how the lesson was structured: breaking the lesson down into steps and sequencing those to lead progressively to a substantial end activity.

To sum up so far, lessons do not usually occur in a vacuum; well-planned lessons are part of a medium- or longer-term plan. They build on prior learning and help prepare for future learning and progress over time. Well-planned lessons are clearly structured to promote learning and facilitate progression. It is this latter point, planning for progression within the lesson, that concerns us in Part II; medium- and longer-term planning and progression across lessons will be covered in more detail in Part III.

A word about lesson objectives

On the plans that follow, I have used lesson objective/s (LO) throughout to refer in general terms to the teacher's learning intentions for the lesson. This is what the teacher expects pupils to learn by the end of the lesson, or where the lesson is heading. The clearer and more specific you can be about learning intentions, not just what pupils are learning but also why, the better you will be able to think through how learning might develop in the lesson and the better planned your lessons will be. Typically learning intentions fall into knowledge, skills and understanding. Key questions to help identify your LOs are:

- **What contribution does the lesson aim make to pupils' knowledge, skills or understanding?**
- **If all goes to plan, by the end of the lesson, what will pupils know, understand or be able to do that they could not do or could not do so well before the lesson?**

Further discussion of LOs and how they are developed is to be found in Chapters 5 and 6 in Part III.

The lesson plans which follow

The lesson plans which follow are based on plans written by beginning teachers. In my view, they are indicative of well-planned lessons for teachers at that stage in their professional learning. That does not necessarily mean that the lessons themselves were all equally successful. In my experience, good lessons are by their very nature well planned; but unfortunately good lesson planning is no guarantee of a great lesson. The relationship between planning and learning is not straightforward.

I have chosen these lesson plans because in each case I think there are clear links between the teacher's learning intentions and the learning experience, or activities, that have been planned for pupils in the lesson. In other words, the choice of pupil activity is appropriate for the stated LO of that lesson. For example, if the LO is to learn how to take part in a conversation talking about hobbies, then we might reasonably expect pupils to spend most of the lesson practising this orally and to have the opportunity to hear what a conversation about hobbies sounds like. Conversely, we would not anticipate pupils spending most of the lesson reading and writing in silence or talking about how to form questions in the TL. This is a key point to check when planning your own lessons:

- **Are the activities I am planning relevant and appropriate for the LO for this lesson?**

Finally, a word about the format used here for presenting lesson plans. I have deliberately kept this as simple and clutter-free as possible so that attention can focus on how the lesson was structured. For practical reasons, scripting of the teacher's TL output has been reduced to key phrases only. I have purposely not included timings on all the lesson plans, but have assumed in each case that the lesson is 60 minutes long. The intention here is to give beginning teachers some sense of what they might reasonably expect to cover over a 60 minute period. Different points in the lesson are numbered for ease of reference in the comments page which follows each plan.

Overview of the lessons that follow and accompanying narrative

TABLE 3.2 Overview of Chapter 3

Class	Main Lesson Objective	Focus of the accompanying narrative
Year 11 French	To be able to describe physical appearance of others.	Assessment
Year 7 French	To ask and answer questions about how many brothers and sisters you have and their names.	
Year 8 Spanish	To be able to ask and answer questions about whether you like/ don't like drinks.	Differentiation
Year 8 Spanish	To be able to order something in a café/ bar and understand what the waiter/ waitress says.	
Year 7 German	Use sentences to talk about your school timetable, using the verb as second idea.	Timing
Year 7 German	Use sentences to talk about your school timetable	Support and Challenge Scaffolding
Year 8 Spanish	To begin forming sentences which combine vocabulary for presents with family member.	Planning for behaviour

Two French lessons: Year 11 and Year 7

The first two lesson plans highlight the range of abilities that you might come across in secondary schools. These lessons were taught in different schools; however, you may well find this same range of abilities within one year group at a single school.

TABLE 3.3A Year 11 French lesson plan: *'Comment est-il/elle?'*

Year 11 French class with 12 pupils. Bottom set class, most of them have poor attention spans and are rather disaffected with French. This was the first lesson on the topic of descriptions.

LO: To be able to describe physical appearance of others.

Key language needed	Extras
C'est un homme/une femme	*Il/elle a . . . . un grand/petit visage,*
Il/elle s'appelle . . .	*un grand/petit nez, une grande/petite bouche,*
Il/elle a . . . ans (Numbers 1–60)	*de grandes oreilles/de petites oreilles,*
Il/elle a les cheveux + colour	*une moustache, une barbe, des lunettes*
Il/elle a les yeux + colour	

1. Presentation of key language + 4x flashcards with photos of male personalities.

   C'est un homme. Il s'appelle . . . . Il a . . . ans. Il a les cheveux . . . Il a les yeux . . .

   Hold up flashcards, one at a time, stick face down on board and label 1–4.

   Rick il est quel numéro? Etc

   C'est un homme. Il a 15 ans. Il a les cheveux bruns et les yeux marron. Il s'appelle comment?

2. Presentation of key language + 4x flashcards with photos of female personalities

   C'est une femme. Elle s'appelle . . . . Elle a . . . ans. Elle a les cheveux . . . Elle a les yeux . . .

   Hold up flashcards, one at a time, stick face down on board and label 5–8

   Same procedure as for males.

3. Mix of both male and female [masculine and feminine forms]

   Faites attention! Repeat questions but with mixture of male and female personalities.

4. Practice + Identikit (cut-outs on visualiser)

   On va dessiner Rick (male personality). *Comment est-il?*

   Elicit sentences from pupils – and show relevant piece on visualiser. If they don't know, give them a choice and point to flashcard to help. Feed in extras + either/or questions.

   On va dessiner quelqu'un d'autre. Qui? Quel numéro? (point to flashcards)

5. *On va dessiner une personne imaginaire*

   Still using Identikit to get the idea, this time pupils suggest ideas.

   Describe a face for pupils to draw (give out coloured pencils) – *montrez moi les cahiers.*

   Then in pairs + vocab list backup on screen. Monitor!

6. Introduction of written word + handout

   Match short written description to photo of personality.

   Check answers orally by getting pupils to read out the text.

7. Writing practice + small cards

   On card write 4x sentences about one of the personalities – do not write the name of person. Language needed is on handout. Collect in cards and read out descriptions for class to guess.

8. Written consolidation

   Pupils copy into their books a description of 1x male and 1x female. Encourage to check for spelling – swap with partner.

Copyright material from Cheryl Mackay (2019), *Learning to Plan Modern Languages Lessons*, Routledge

TABLE 3.3B Commentary on Year 11 French lesson: '*Comment est-il/elle?*'

This lesson was planned by a beginning teacher early in her first teaching placement. I have chosen this lesson to show how even limited language content can be used to engage pupils for a whole lesson through a variety of activity. There are several points in the thinking behind this plan that made this a well-planned lesson, especially for someone at an early stage in her PGCE year.

The first point to note is the linguistic progression within the lesson. The introduction of key language is chunked, masculine forms are introduced before feminine forms and key language is introduced and practised before the introduction of extra vocabulary.

Linked to the above, each chunk of language is practised before the next is added on. Breaking down the language into manageable chunks that are progressively practised like this scaffolds the learning process.

At point 4 on the plan, there is scope for the teacher to input extra vocabulary within the context of the same structures. Using the device of 'either. . . or. . .' questions, the teacher can offer pupils a choice of two possible options; all pupils need to do is repeat the option of their choice. This is a useful way to simultaneously present and practise new language. There is also scope here to go beyond what is already written on the lesson plan. For example, there is scope to introduce intensifiers [*il a un très grand nez ou un assez grand nez? un tout petit nez ou un assez petit nez?*] and colour adjectives agreeing with feminine nouns [*il a une moustache grise ou une moustache blanche?*].

At point 7 on the plan, pupils are not simply copying key language they are copying for a purpose. Once they have written the cards, the teacher has a resource that can be used for listening practice – both in this lesson and for future lessons. The cards also help the teacher to diagnose possible difficulties or misconceptions which she can correct when reading out and which she might also want to pick up on before pupils write up sentences in their books.

<u>Follow-up Reflective Task/Points to discuss</u>

At point 5 on the plan there is explicit mention of monitoring pupils during the pair work activity. What do you think would be monitored at this stage in the lesson? If you were teaching this lesson what would you need to know at this stage? What other opportunities for monitoring can you identify in the lesson plan?

TABLE 3.4A Year 7 French lesson plan: '*Tu as des frères ou des sœurs?*'

Mixed ability Year 7 French class in a large, high achieving comprehensive school. This was the first lesson on the topic of family. Pupils know *j'ai/je n'ai pas de/tu as. . .?* from other contexts.

LO: To ask and answer questions about how many brothers and sisters you have and their names.

Key language needed

Tu as des frères ou des sœurs?

Oui, j'ai . . . un frère/un demi-frère/   *Non, je n'ai pas de . . . frères/sœurs*
       une sœur/une demi-sœur   *Je suis enfant unique*

Il s'appelle . . . elle s'appelle .. ils/elles s'appellent . . . . . . et . . . .

---

1. State objectives for lesson + *Tu as des frères ou des sœurs?* up on board, read out together check comprehension – *en anglais? Comment dit-on . . . en français ?* Insist on silent 's'

2. Presentation of new language + flashcards with drawings

    Qui, j'ai . . . x4 options, choral repetition of each; *Non, je n'ai pas de . . .* x 2 options, choral repetition of each; mix of both, *vrai/faux*.

    Final card *Je n'ai pas de frères et sœurs. Je suis enfant unique.* Choral repetition.

    Final mix of all options + repeat if true (introduce different numbers of siblings)

3. Listen and respond

    Pupils stand up if the statement applies to them. *Lève-toi si c'est vrai pour toi* routine. *J'ai une sœur/j'ai un demi-frère et une demi-sœur/j'ai six frères/je n'ai pas de frères* etc.

    Ecrivez les numéros 1–10, faites des notes ou dessins. Par exemple, j'ai un frère – use board to demo. Check answers in French – use stick people to draw correct answers on board. *Qui a 10 sur 10?* Etc.

4. Individual repetition – chain game

    Check question on board, read out together. Check brothers *en français?* Sisters *en français? Ecoutez bien!* Ask Pupil 1 *Tu as des frères ou des sœurs?* Pupil 1 replies and asks pupil 2. Pupil 2 replies and asks pupil 3 etc

5. Quick check to incorporate 3rd person

    Alors Paul – sshh – dis-moi – il a des frères ou des sœurs? Qui sait? Paul, il a . . .

    Alors Katy – sshh – dis-moi – elle a des frères ou des sœurs? Qui sait? Katy, elle a . . .

6. Presentation of language to ask about names

    Pin 6 name cards + 6 drawings of my family on board. *Voici mon père. Il s'appelle comment? Devinez.* Pupil guesses correctly, places name next to picture. Choral repetition *Il s'appelle John.* Same for all 6 family members. *Père – il s'appelle/mère – elle s'appelle/frères – ils s'appellent/ sœurs elles s'appellent.* Remove names *Voici mon père. Il s'appelle comment?* Etc.

7. Questionnaire

    On va faire un questionnaire. Hand out worksheet. Use visualiser to go through vocab needed. Point to question on sheet. Choral repetition. Demonstrate on visualiser + 2 pupils. Check question again. *5 minutes pour demander à 5 personnes minimum. Levez-vous.*

8. Writing up the results

    Ecrivez les résultats- écrivez en phrases complètes. Utilisez les boîtes de clé à la page 91.

    Exemple: Madame Smith, tu as des frères ou des sœurs?

        Oui, j'ai une sœur. Elle s'appelle Paula. Je n'ai pas de frères.

    Extra (write up on board) Reading exercises from textbook, p90 no. 1 and p91 no.3

Copyright material from Cheryl Mackay (2019), *Learning to Plan Modern Languages Lessons*, Routledge

TABLE 3.4B Commentary on Year 7 French lesson: '*Tu as des frères ou des soeurs?*'

This lesson was planned by a beginning teacher towards the end of her second teaching placement, she has been teaching the class for about 8 weeks. I have chosen this plan to demonstrate clear linguistic progression within a lesson, also to show how activities have been well chosen to help pupils achieve the teacher's learning intentions for this lesson. This is a well-planned lesson, the teacher has given careful and detailed thought to how learning might develop.

Pupils are systematically introduced to the key language for this lesson. This key language covers all the language pupils will need for the questionnaire. This includes different structures which are gradually introduced and built up. For example, affirmative answers are covered before negatives and *je suis enfant unique* is only introduced after that as a synonym for language that pupils are familiar with. All of this is then intensively drilled and practised before the chain game at point 4 which brings together the question and answer. At point 6 vocabulary from the first part of the lesson is used to create a context for introducing further key structures.

I particularly like the way that the key question, that pupils will need for the questionnaire, is introduced right at the start of the lesson. This helps pupils to start to think about what they are learning today, they can start to anticipate what language they might be using. Having it up on the board enables the teacher to refer back to it at different stages in the lesson, leading up to the questionnaire. There is an example of this at point 4. This helps preparation for the questionnaire at point 7. By this stage pupils are quite familiar with the question they need to use and more of them might be inclined to use it.

Assessment opportunities are built into the lesson plan. These are not always explicitly mentioned on the plan but they are integral to the different activities. Activities not only help the pupils to progress in their learning, following the PPP model, they also assist the teacher by providing feedback on pupil progress as the lesson unfolds. The teacher plans to constantly assess pupil progress, and not just at point 7 when there is the opportunity to listen in to different pupils. She aims to use a range of question forms, including for example incidental use of the third person at point 5; she also envisages using different practice activities which will provide feedback, for example at points 2 and 3.

<u>Follow-up Reflective Task/Points to discuss</u>

This is the first lesson on the topic of family. What would you plan to do in the next lesson if you were teaching this class? What opportunities would you plan to revise or practise the learning from the first lesson? How would you plan to build on the first lesson? And why – what learning would you want to foster?

Copyright material from Cheryl Mackay (2019), *Learning to Plan Modern Languages Lessons*, Routledge

Despite the different teaching contexts, the planning of both these lessons shows remarkably similar thinking. What is evident from both these lesson plans is clear linguistic progression. In both plans the key language to be learnt is gradually built up, giving both lessons a clear structure. At the same time, the two plans include scope for using further incidental language that is relevant to the topic. Another similarity is that assessment opportunities are integrated into both plans. Both teachers have planned lessons which allow them to assess or monitor pupil progress and learning as the lesson unfolds, as an integral part of their teaching. Planning for assessment is the theme of the next subsection.

Planning for assessment

It is important that we don't just assess after teaching; we also need to assess whilst teaching. That is because there is little point in teaching the pupils what they already know and it is unproductive to stick rigidly to the lesson plan if pupils are clearly struggling.

Assessment opportunities in the lesson, or continuous assessment, serve a useful diagnostic purpose. The information we gather in this way informs decisions we make in the classroom. For example, based on what you hear or see in the classroom, you might decide to spend longer or shorter than planned on a particular activity. In a way, diagnostic assessment provides a snapshot of pupil performance at any given time. You may decide that pupils are progressing pretty much as expected at that point in the lesson, and proceed with the lesson as planned. You may, however, conclude that the lesson is not proceeding as well as planned, in which case you may decide to revert to further drilling or more intensive repetition of key language before checking again. When planning lessons, remember to build in opportunities for diagnostic assessment; try not to plan lesson time too tightly because – if you do – you may not have time in the lesson to think on your feet and adjust your planning if need be.

A useful planning device is to write down on your lesson plan questions that you will be asking yourself at key points in the lesson. Try and think through at the planning stage what you will want to know at particular points in the lesson. Here are examples of such questions taken from lesson plans of beginning teachers:

- Can pupils apply the rule themselves?
- Can they say the French, German or Spanish from memory?
- Can most of the class recognise the French, German or Spanish?
- Can they perform the dialogue without notes?
- Are they all participating?

Feedback from continuous assessment is also helpful to the learner. For example, this might take the form of a mark out of ten for a short listening exercise to check comprehension (based perhaps on What number is …?), or feedback on the quality of their pronunciation or encouragement for their ideas, etc. Feedback like this can be motivating and provide a sense of achievement. However, corrective feedback (or error correction) needs to be managed with caution. This will be discussed in greater detail in Part III.

There are many different strategies that you can use to assess the extent of pupil progress and learning and it is a good idea to develop and use a variety of those in your teaching. In particular, it is important in ML lessons to develop a bank of different tools to help you check pupil comprehension. There are lots of ways for pupils to demonstrate comprehension without needing to use English: actions and mimes, drawing, yes/no responses, thumbs up and thumbs down, what number is …?, repeat if true, point to, show me, multiple choice questions, etc. Increasingly, as pupils acquire more language that they can draw upon, they can be expected to express their understanding in the TL; indeed, this is in itself an opportunity for real language use. Of course there will also be times when the quickest and most expedient way to check comprehension is to ask for an English translation. However, reliance on translation as the sole way of checking comprehension can create a stop-start effect which shifts the attention of the lesson from learning to use the ML to learning in English about the ML. When you are planning to check comprehension, challenge yourself to use translation only as a last resort.

Here are some other helpful strategies you might plan to use for assessment purposes.

- Mini whiteboards. It is worth planning your mini whiteboard routine and then sticking to it. Usually when pupils have written on their boards you will want to be able to see what *everyone* has written. A routine (such as *3-2-1 montrez!*) helps everyone hold up their mini board at the same time. Avoid asking pupils to write too much information, remember you need to be able to read it easily and quickly from the front of the classroom. Short one word answers, symbols or numbers work best.
- Listening in to pupils when they are working in pairs or in groups. Over time, plan to listen in to different pupils. You might find yourself giving pupils feedback, providing support, modelling for them how to improve. Or you might collate any common errors that you hear and go through those later with the whole class.

- Questions to individual pupils when they are working independently. Over time target different pupils, possibly starting with those pupils who are most likely to need extra support or challenge.
- Before and after. This involves starting the lesson with an activity that you repeat at the end of the lesson, in order to assess any difference in pupil performance. For example, talk to your partner about where you live for one minute.
- Plan to make strategic use of random or targeted questioning with the whole class, rather than always relying on volunteers (Jones and Wiliam, 2008).
- Plan to make strategic use of opportunities for multiple answers.

For more on assessment and planning for assessment opportunities in ML, please see Barnes and Hunt (2003). To sum up, here are key questions to prompt planning for assessment:

- **At what points or stages in the lesson do you plan to build in opportunities for diagnostic assessment?**
- **What learning or progress do you plan to monitor at those points in the lesson? How will you go about doing so?**

Two contrasting Year 8 Spanish lessons

These lesson plans were written for different teaching contexts in different schools. They illustrate two distinct approaches to teaching similar content.

TABLE 3.5A Year 8 Spanish lesson plan 1: 'Spanish drinks'

Large and lively Year 8 Spanish class, plenty of willingness to learn languages. They have been learning Spanish for just over a year and know Spanish phonics. In the previous lesson they learnt the names of drinks in Spanish and they know '*me gusta*' etc from other topics. The teacher had a specific professional development target for this lesson: to insist on good pupil pronunciation.

LO: To be able to ask and answer questions about whether you like/don't like drinks.

Key language needed	Names of drinks in Spanish
Me gusta . . .	12x drinks recapped from previous lesson
No me gusta . . .	6x new drinks introduced + article
¿Te gusta . . .?	Extra language
+ *el/la* + drink	*es/no es* . . . *una fruta, masculino, feminino, caliente/frío* etc

1 Recap on drinks + Odd One Out on Powerpoint (ppt) [10mins]

Pupils are familiar with the OOO format. Repeat words together first. Pupils do OOO in their heads during register, then in pairs. Model activity, do first one as example together (*¿Cual es diferente?*) Questioning (*¿Cual es diferente? ¿Por qué? ¿qué significa. . .?*). Then in pairs on mini whiteboards, feedback after each one.

2 Learning Objectives [2mins]

Pupil to read out. Stress importance of building on what we know + getting more confident.

3 Drilling of drinks + ppt [5mins]

Choral repetition + rhythms – picture only, then picture + written word. Watch *zumo*.

Repeat if true – picture only, check comprehension of new drinks. Mouthing if needed.

4 Pronunciation Practice + ppt slide then grids *La pronunciación* [15mins]

Go through the sounds together with volunteers, then whole class, then again with volunteers.

Give out grids, in pairs – how many drinks can they find in the grid? Model first and write up example on board. (*Tenéis 5 minutos. Buscáis las palabras, por ejemplo una coca cola.*)

Feedback – how many did each pair find? Go through correct pronunciation and gender.

5 Survey Preparation: recap on *me gusta* etc. [5mins]

Show faces ☺ ☹ on ppt and elicit the Spanish *¿Que es esto?*

Ask a few questions *¿Te gusta la Fanta de limón?* expect full sentence responses/take multiple answers.

Choral questioning of individuals to practise saying the question together.

6 Mini-survey + Spanish background music [10 mins]

Each pupil allocated a drink and will ask 6 people if they like that drink or not. Model it. (*Tengo esta carta. Voy a preguntar a 6 personas ¿Te gusta el . . .? Sí* – note down, *No* – note down.) Use board to show tally. Get pupils to explain. 5 minutes moving around the room, asking questions. Use music as signal to find next person, when music stops start asking. Monitor- correct pronunciation?

Survey results. Ask a few pupils to feedback. *¿Cuántas personas dicen si me gusta . . .?* Etc.

7 Written consolidation [5 mins]

Write up sample survey dialogues on board. Pupils tell T what to write – elicit.

8 Review objectives [2 mins]

Copyright material from Cheryl Mackay (2019), *Learning to Plan Modern Languages Lessons*, Routledge

TABLE 3.5B Commentary on Year 8 Spanish lesson: 'Spanish drinks'

This lesson was planned by a beginning teacher early in her first teaching placement. This is an example of a lesson planned to build on what pupils already know, especially pronunciation.

The first point to note is just how much time is planned for a recap on previous learning of vocabulary and structures (see points 1, 3 and 5), also knowledge of Spanish pronunciation (see especially point 4) in order to more firmly establish these points in pupils' memory and give them the confidence needed to successfully complete the survey in Spanish independently of the teacher.

An important aspect of preparation leading up to the survey is pronunciation of key vocabulary and structures needed. For example, at point 1, the words are repeated together before pupils start the activity; at point 3 different repetition techniques are used to hone pronunciation and potential difficulties are pre-empted; at point 4 there is substantial revision of Spanish sound-spelling links (phonics). The lesson is planned to help pupils improve their pronunciation and the teacher is aware of when she might monitor how well this is achieved (see point 6). Here is the pronunciation grid (not to scale) from the lesson, showing 30 different Spanish sounds and their spellings:

na	un	ran	té	te
ba	fan	a	da	fe
con	ca	lo	ti	do
sa	li	ja	so	la
co	fre	de	zu	ta
món	che	mo	cho	le

The teacher has anticipated what language pupils might need to justify their Odd One Out answers in Spanish (point 1). She has chosen simple vocabulary and structures that pupils can play around a little with, especially *es . . .* and *no es . . .* This anticipation of incidental language helps the teacher to respond quickly and appropriately to pupils' needs as they arise in the lesson.

Another feature of her planning is that time limits are written into the lesson plan. When pupils are given tasks to do in pairs or independently of the teacher, they are given time limits or deadlines to work within. In the actual lesson, an electronic timer was used as a visible reminder to pupils of how much time they had. This seemed to help the pace of the lesson and keep pupils focused.

Finally I think that point 7 is significant. Adequate time had been planned for pupils to be able to go away from the lesson with a written record of their work. Involving the pupils in telling her what to write gives the teacher a useful insight into pupils' learning at the end of the lesson.

<u>Follow-up Reflective Task/Points to discuss</u>

At point 6 on the plan the teacher wants to ask a few pupils to feedback their survey results in Spanish. If you were teaching this lesson, how would you select which pupils to ask? And why?

At different points in the lesson, the teacher plans to model for the class what she wants them to do. How do you think this helped the lesson run smoothly? Are there any other advantages?

Copyright material from Cheryl Mackay (2019), *Learning to Plan Modern Languages Lessons*, Routledge

TABLE 3.6A Year 8 Spanish lesson plan 2: '*En un café bar*'

Mixed ability Year 8 Spanish class. Pupils have been learning Spanish for just over a year. In the previous lesson they learnt the names of nine items of food and drink in Spanish.

LO: To be able to attract the attention of the waiter/waitress in a café bar, order something to eat and drink; to understand questions/ responses of waiter/waitress.

Key language needed	Items of food and drink from last lesson
¡Oiga camarero! ¡Oiga camarera!	un té, café, bocadillo de chorizo, bocadillo de
¿Qué desea?	queso, vaso de vino blanco
Quiero + name of item	una Fanta, cerveza, ración de tortilla, ración de
Lo siento, no hay.	patatas fritas

1 Get class organised as soon as possible. Countdown to *silencio*.

2 Recap vocab from last lesson + pictures with labels on visualiser

   Mirad e estudiad el vocabulario. Teneís un minuto para revisarlo. Turn off visualiser. *Un minuto para escribir los 9 artículos.* Turn back on to check. *¿Cuántos tienes Sarah, Leon etc.? Dame uno . . . otra persona . . .* Uncover and repeat with whole class as each item is suggested. Follow up with either/or questions. Repetition in pairs, *entonces en parejas, 30 segundos*. Then pictures only – *dame uno, dame dos, dame tres etc*.

3 Introduce *¿Qué desea?* and *quiero* + flashcards (f/c)

   Estamos en el café bar. Estoy camarera . Hold up f/c *¿Qué desea?* – ask individual, drill *qui-er-o* + action with whole class. Pupil to say whole phrase to get f/c. Repeat with different f/c whole class repeat whole phrase each time.

   Pair Practice + visualiser with pictures of items and new words. Point to new words and drill *¿Qué desea?* and *quiero. Estamos en el café bar. En parejas pedís en turno algo del camarero. 2 minutos para pedirlo todo.* Pick a pair to demo. *¿Qué desea?* and *quiero* for each item.

4 Introduce *no hay* + flashcards

   Choose f/c and hide, ask pupil *¿Qué desea?*, insist on full phrase + *quiero*, respond with *lo siento, no hay* 3–4 times with different pupils. Check comprehension, whole class repeat *lo siento, no hay* + actions. Do again with volunteer waiter at front, if waiter has the item, gives card to pupil who asked for it, if not *lo siento, no hay*.

5 The waiters game + key vocab up on visualiser if needed

   Aquí estamos en el café bar. Estoy esperando 10 minutos. Hay muchas pesonas aquí. Tengo hambre (rub stomach). *Quiero algo para beber y algo para comer. ¡Oiga camarero! ¡Oiga camarera!* – drill + choral repetition, *camarerooo . . .camareraaa*

   4x voluntarios – 2x camareros, 2x camareras – give a tray to each + mini-cue cards of café items.

   Explain + check understood after each stage, pupil interpreter/any questions:

   (i) *Vais a servir a nuestros clientes. Aquí en el café bar lo que quieren del menu* – menu on visualiser. (ii) *Lo voy a demonstrar* + class teacher in role of customer – hand out the item asked for, wait for *gracias. Si no lo tienes, dices "Lo siento, no hay." Y sirves a otra persona.* (iii) *Atención los clientes – 2 equipos, el que tiene más cartas al fin gana.*

   Allow about 5 mins for game. Countdown to *silencio. Pase las cartas al frente* – collect in two piles at front. *Vamos a contar* – whole class to count cards with me. Write score on board.

6 Written consolidation

Copyright material from Cheryl Mackay (2019), *Learning to Plan Modern Languages Lessons*, Routledge

TABLE 3.6B Commentary on Year 8 Spanish lesson: '*En un café bar*'

This lesson was planned by a beginning teacher halfway through her first teaching placement. I chose this plan because of its attention to detail. It exemplifies the sort of detail that we might reasonably expect beginning teachers to think through in the early stages of their ITE period.

Firstly, the language content of the lesson has been thought through in detail. This applies to the language that pupils are expected to produce at different points in the lesson. For example, at point 3 pairs are expected to practise both the question and full sentence answers, at point 4 pupils are expected to use full sentences.

The language that the teacher herself intends to use is also planned in detail. Significant parts of the lesson are scripted, such as instructions and explanations, also the use of the TL to contextualise or set the scene, see for example how she plans to introduce the idea of *no hay* at point 4. Care has been taken to modify her own TL in order to expose pupils to comprehensible input; I really like the repeated use of *estamos en el café bar*, for example. Also mimes and actions have been planned to support TL use. This scripting of predictable TL use and attention to detail in the early stages of the training year will reap benefits as the year progresses and we can start to use the TL in the classroom more automatically, without the same need for scripting.

Secondly, the practical organisation of the lesson has been planned in detail. For example, careful thought has been given to the start of the lesson, including the signal for quiet and what pupils will be doing as soon as they arrive in the lesson. At point 5 she has outlined how to organise the results of the game and how to involve pupils in this process. By the end of point 5 everyone will know which team has won, they will know the score, and all the cue cards will also be collected in. Instructions have been planned very thoroughly in the TL, especially instructions for the waiters game at point 5. As well as chunking the instructions, the teacher also plans to demonstrate what to do with the class teacher. Class teachers, or fellow trainees, or other observers, are usually more than willing to help in this way! Finally, an aspect of organisation, not apparent from the lesson plan, is what the teacher planned to do just before the lesson. There were three things: set out the mini-cue cards on four trays; put a clock in the classroom where it could be seen; display café items on the visualiser ready for the first activity.

Thirdly, the recap of vocabulary at point 2 is planned in commendable detail. The scaffolding of the written word is removed after the one minute revision time, and subsequent short activities scaffold the process of learning to name the items from memory. Timed, short bursts of activity (7 short activities in total) based on the same vocabulary provide intensive practice for the whole class and this in turn creates learning momentum right from the start of the lesson. It is true that such momentum takes skill to manage in the classroom, but it is only possible as the result of detailed planning. This is a model that could be replicated at the start of other lessons.

Follow-up Reflective Task/Points to discuss

The teacher has planned ten minutes at the end of the lesson for written consolidation of pupils' learning. If you were teaching this lesson, what different forms might this written consolidation take? What might you ask pupils to write down, how might you set it up and why?

In both lesson plans, what pupils are asked to do is relevant to the LO for the lesson; both explicitly build on prior learning; and each includes revision of relevant prior learning. Both are well organised and clearly structured to support or scaffold progression in pupils' learning; and assessment opportunities have been integrated into relevant stages of both lesson plans.

Neither of the plans makes explicit reference to 'differentiation'. But does that necessarily mean that differentiation didn't take place?

Planning for differentiation

For the purposes of this book, I have taken differentiation to mean what the teacher does to ensure that every pupil in the class is able to learn to the best of their ability. This is based on an understanding that all pupils are different; every pupil comes to the classroom with differences in experiences and attitudes, ability and interests, and prior learning. And the belief that all pupils are capable of learning; all pupils need to be challenged and supported if each is to reach their full potential. Regardless of whether you are teaching a large mixed ability class, a top or bottom set class or a small A level group, you still need to differentiate.

One of the hallmarks of a well-planned lesson is that it is sufficiently differentiated to support and challenge all of the pupils you are teaching. In my experience, this is the element of planning that beginning teachers take longest to develop. This is simply because they lack the detailed knowledge of their pupils that experienced teachers draw on in their daily practice. Indeed, Mutton et al. refer to this detailed knowledge of pupils themselves as 'the most crucial element of a teacher's knowledge' (2011, p408). Such knowledge is a prerequisite for differentiation; the better you know your classes, the better you will be able to tailor lessons to their needs.

In the short term, there are different steps you can take to start developing your knowledge of the pupils you will be teaching.

- Ask the school to provide you with computer generated pupil data; this will at least give you some insight into the range of attainment within the classes you are teaching. However, pupil data is only a starting point and can be a poor substitute for the knowledge of class teachers.
- Talk to class teachers about how you might make your lessons appropriate to the classes you will be teaching. For example, class teachers might be able to comment on levels of maturity, attitudes towards language learning and relative strengths or otherwise in listening, speaking, reading and writing.
- Before you take over the teaching of specific classes, make arrangements to observe the classes being taught. Note down information that will be useful to you when planning lessons, such as: key TL phrases used by the class teacher; strategies used by the teacher to support TL use; established classroom routines; any particular strengths or areas of difficulty that you become aware of. This will help you start to plan lessons for those classes.

Learning about the diversity of ways in which pupils can differ, and how best to respond to those differences, will extend beyond your ITE period. What I would like to highlight here are a few simple but important ways in which you can start to incorporate differentiation into your planning. Please bear in mind when you read this that it is difficult – if not impossible – to differentiate *all* of the time.

The first thing you can do is to plan how you will cater for any particular learning needs of individual pupils, especially pupils with Special Educational Needs (SEN), pupils with disabilities or pupils who may need to be particularly stretched. In any given class there may be at least a few pupils with particular learning needs. At the planning stage it is important to think through any changes that might be required in order to cater for the needs of those pupils. For example, it might be necessary to provide written materials in larger font size for some pupils; or if there is a native speaker in your ML class, careful thought will need to be given to how that pupil might best benefit the lesson and benefit from the lesson. Schools should be able to provide you with information about individual pupils with particular learning needs. Talk to the class teacher about strategies for meeting the particular needs of any individual pupils or groups of pupils in the classes you are teaching.

A second strand is planning to ensure that *all* pupils in the class are able to participate and make progress in lessons, not just the high attainers, fast learners, those who love learning or those who love learning in a particular way. As a teacher you have a responsibility to help *every* pupil reach their full potential. A good starting point is to build up a repertoire or bank of activities and techniques that allow you to vary what you do in the classroom. It is important to bear in mind that the way that you like to learn languages may not be the best way for all of your pupils to learn. Equally it is important to realise that you cannot possibly plan to meet the needs of every single learner in every single lesson you teach. But *over a series of lessons* you can reasonably plan to achieve this. Over a series of lessons, you can plan to:

- Cover a variety of ways of presenting new material (e.g. flashcards, visualiser or PowerPoint + pictures, video, written text, song, mime, dialogue acted out with class teacher or audio recorded)
- Practise different skills (e.g. listening, speaking, reading and writing)
- Cover a variety of task types (e.g. role-play, games, competitions, information gap, survey)
- Include a variety of groupings (e.g. seated pair work, milling activities, group work, whole class, individual)
- Include a variety of resources (i.e. not always the text book or PowerPoint!)
- Try to build an element of open-endedness into at least some tasks, i.e. veer away from having one and only one correct or possible answer. Some examples of simple open-ended tasks are: listen to the text and write down what you understand; how many different sentences can you write about this? How many sentences can you say about this picture? Or using these words?; how long can you and your partner sustain a conversation about . . .?
- Find time for learners' own input and ideas (e.g. ask pupils for feedback on what helps them learn/ what activities they like to do/ suggestions for activities) and use those to inform your lesson planning.

As a ML teacher, your most versatile differentiation tool is probably questioning. Planning what questions you will ask at key stages in the lesson and writing those down verbatim in your lesson plan is time well spent. Here are some of the ways that you can plan to use questions to support differentiation.

Plan to use questions to help diagnose pupils' strengths and weaknesses; in particular, aim to include:

- A variety of question types and strategic use of open and closed questions;
- Plenty of open and open-ended questions where different answers are possible and there is no single correct answer; plan to use this as an opportunity to accept multiple answers;
- Random questioning (e.g. use lollipop sticks with names of pupils), rather than always relying on volunteers.

Once you get to know individual pupils better and as you gain more insight into what they are capable of, you can be more strategic in your approach to differentiation:

- Plan to expect various types of answer from different pupils (e.g. longer/ more detailed/ more complex/ more accurate answers);
- Plan to target different types of question at different pupils (e.g. yes/no or either/or questions are easier than other questions, especially questions which require pupils to give reasons);
- In the lesson, be prepared to scaffold a pupil's response if needed. This is differentiation by support (e.g. offer possible answers or alternatives for the pupil to choose from, mouth the language needed so that the pupil can lip read what you say, provide a gapped answer to help pupils self-correct before repeating the complete answer). Decisions about whether this scaffolding is necessary might need to be made in the lesson itself.

Finally, in my opinion, the biggest single thing you can do to differentiate as ML teacher is to make strategic and plentiful use of the TL. To my mind this is a natural differentiator. The trick here is to think in terms of creating a language acquisition environment that is rich enough to stretch everyone, yet supported enough to ensure that no one feels excluded. Pupils will pick up and notice different things in what they hear. For example, some pupils might only just get the gist of what is said, relying heavily on teacher's mimes and other non-verbal clues; others might get the message, loud and clear, and pick up new language used by the teacher; in addition to this, others might also be noticing and possibly thinking about the formal qualities of the language itself. The point is that you cannot know in advance of the lesson which pupils will pick up what, but you can plan and prepare for different potentialities. This for me is the essence of open-endedness.

Let's return now to the two Spanish lesson plans in Tables 3.5a and 3.6a. It is true that neither plan makes explicit reference to 'differentiation', but in both cases the planning does provide scope for different pupils to learn as much as they can. I should point out here that it is probably most difficult to differentiate during the presentation and drilling phases of the PPP model, especially with beginners. And this is precisely the context of both Spanish lessons. Nevertheless, both lessons provide lots of planned exposure to the TL and a good variety of paired and whole class activity, with opportunities for pupils to work at their own pace; in addition, there are planned open-ended activities in lesson one (e.g. Odd One Out and the pronunciation practice activity) and the waiters game in lesson two is an opportunity for pupils to take on different roles. All of these are examples of differentiation.

For further practical ideas and subject-specific advice on differentiation in ML, please see Convery and Coyle (2000); and Pachler et al. (2014) for more on pupil differences and differentiation.

To sum up, here are key questions to prompt planning for differentiation:

- Have you catered for any particular learning needs?
- What difficulties do you think some pupils might have this lesson? How have you planned to address those?
- Is extension work appropriate for some pupils? Which pupils? What extension have you planned?
- Have you included a variety of activities to involve pupils in different ways in the lesson?

Year 7 German lesson with a top set class

The next two lesson plans cover the same topic taught to different ability sets in the same year group. The first of these was written for a high ability Year 7 set.

TABLE 3.7A Year 7 German top set lesson plan: '*Mein Stundenplan*'

Chatty, top set Year 7 German class in a large comprehensive school. Pupils have been learning German for one term and have one lesson a week. This is the second lesson on the topic of school. Pupils have a workbook which contains key language for the topic. The lesson is 2.30– 3.30pm.

LO: Use sentences to talk about your school timetable, using the verb as second idea

Key language needed	From last lesson
Was hast du am + day of week?	Names of 14 school subjects
Am + day of week *habe ich* + subject.	*Was ist dein Lieblingsfach in der Schule?*
Montag, Dienstag, Mittwoch,	*Mein Lieblingsfach ist . . .*
Donnerstag, Freitag	*Ich habe kein Lieblingsfach.*
Am + day Stunde X *habe ich* + subject.	*Wie findest du . . . ? . . . ist interessant/ langweilig.*

1 Revision of School Subjects + slide with numbered pictures of school subjects [max 10 mins]

 Instructions + paper on arrival *Schreibt a-h. Guten Tag die Klasse! Welche Nummer ist das*? Read out sentences (*Mein Lieblingsfach ist Musik; Erdkunde ist interessant* etc.) Pupils identify subject and write its numbers. Check answers. Drill subjects/ repeat if true/revise Q&A from last lesson + ball.

2 LO – *Lernziele* – pupil reads out, explain *Stundenplan* + show example on ppt, *auf Englisch*?

3 Introduce days/ model word order + *Mein Stundenplan* on ppt   [10 – 12 mins]

 Also hier sind die Schultage: Montag, Dienstag, etc. Choral repetition of days. Individual repetition + fingers. Concept check – *Was ist heute für ein Tag? Und morgen? Und gestern, was war gestern für ein Tag? Was ist der erste Schultag?*   [max 4 mins for days]

 Und hier sind die Schulfächer. Also was hast du am Montag? Wer kann mir ein Schulfach nennen? Elicit name of subject and put into sentence *Am Montag habe ich . . .* write up on board. Build up chain, add on another subject each time. Go through other days in turn (*Was hast du am . . .?*) few seconds thinking time in pairs, choose a pair to say a sentence with all the subjects for that day. If sluggish, use true/false using '*Am . . . habe ich . . .*'

4 Listening Exercise + German Stundenplan   [10 mins]

 Dieter is going to tell us about his school timetable. Hand out blank timetables – partially filled in. Listen to Dieter and fill in the missing lessons. Use visualiser to help explain – play 2x times, listen and check. Show completed timetable on visualiser, pupils self assess – *eine Minute.*

5 Cultural background + German Stundenplan   [max 5 mins]

 Also hier ist Dieters Stundenplan. Hier sind die Schultage. . . und hier sind die Schulfächer . . . Wie lang ist eine Stunde in Dieters Schule? Wieviele Minuten? Ist das besser als dein Stundenplan? Ja- heb die Hand. Nein – heb die Hand. Wann ist Dieters Schule aus? Ist das besser etc.? Wie findest du Dieters Stundenplan? Was ist gut? Was ist nicht so gut? Wer hat eine Frage?

6 Oral practice of Q&A- substitution dialogue (*Was hast du am Freitag Stunde 1? . . .*)   [6 mins]
 Guided reading with whole class then in pairs replace underlined words and pictures.

7 Give out cards + timetable for Friday, find someone with same timetable as you. Challenge to do Q&A from memory.   [6 mins]
 Was hast du am Freitag Stunde 1? Am Freitag Stunde 1 habe ich . . . etc.

8 Homework   [start by 3.20 at latest]

 Stick *Mein Stundenplan* sheets in books. Write model dialogue on board- **Was hast du am Mittwoch Stunde fünf? Am Mittwoch Stunde fünf habe ich Deutsch**. At least 5x dialogues about *Mein Stundenplan* + at least 5x about *Mein idealer Stundenplan* – use what you know.

Copyright material from Cheryl Mackay (2019), *Learning to Plan Modern Languages Lessons*, Routledge

TABLE 3.7B Commentary on Year 7 German top set lesson: '*Mein Stundenplan*'

This lesson was planned by a beginning teacher during her first teaching placement. This is her third lesson teaching this class. The context of one lesson a week brings particular challenges for lesson planning, especially (as was the case here) when there is pressure to cover a given amount of content in each lesson. Nevertheless, this was the situation that this beginning teacher found herself in. I would like to look at how she planned to make the most of limited lesson time and what learning was prioritised.

First of all, the teacher is planning to use limited lesson time to prioritise learning experiences which would be difficult to replicate outside of school. The plan is to use most of the lesson for speaking and listening practice, especially using the verb as second idea in the sentence. Interaction in the TL, including the opportunity to ask and answer questions, and to listen to a native speaker (Dieter is a German assistant at the school) are difficult to set as homework tasks. Homework time is used for written consolidation of the new structure that pupils will practise orally; and homework is supported with a model to guide them.

Right from the start of the lesson, pupils are working at sentence level, picking out keywords and then identifying those on the slide. This is more challenging that conducting the whole activity at word level. This level of pace and challenge is maintained through intensive bursts of teacher questioning and through high expectations of pupils; for example, at point 3, the concept check involving days of the week is done entirely in the TL and uses a range of question forms to stretch and challenge this top set class; at point 4, pupils are given one minute to check their answers and at point 7 they are challenged to complete the final activity from memory.

The plan identifies specific parts of the lesson where only a limited time can be spent. Timings for revision of last week's lesson and cultural background have been limited, see points 1 and 5. Both of these points are desirable learning experiences. Strictly speaking, however, neither is essential for the achievement of the LO for this lesson and this might be why the teacher has limited the time available for those. Time limits, when appropriate, help to prioritise lesson time and maintain pace.

The total time allowance for the introduction of new language (point 3) is kept quite flexible. Within that allowance, there is a maximum amount of time to be spent on the days of the week. In fact, introducing the days of the week is quite straightforward and can be done relatively quickly, compared to the introduction of a new sentence structure. The teacher has planned more time for the latter, and she has also planned an extra true/false activity if needed.

Essentially the lesson has been well-structured to enable pupils to achieve the LO.

Follow-up Reflective Task/Points to discuss

A possible issue when classes have just one lesson a week is that coverage of content takes precedence over deeper learning. To what extent do you think that this lesson plan manages to prioritise learning over coverage of content?

Using the TL, how would you explain the LO for this lesson? How would you explain 'Stundenplan' (emploi du temps/horario escolar) to a top set Year 7 class? And to a bottom set Year 7 class? And to a Year 10 class?

Copyright material from Cheryl Mackay (2019), *Learning to Plan Modern Languages Lessons*, Routledge

The context in which this lesson was planned presented particular challenges with regard to timing. Before looking at the next lesson plan, we will look more closely at timing.

Timing

Time was tight in the Year 7 German top set lesson. Teaching is difficult when you feel rushed. On the one hand, you need to allow pupils enough time to learn from the activities that you have planned for them; on the other, you might feel under pressure to cover a given amount of content within a set amount of time and especially if there is a formal assessment looming.

Thinking through how best to use lesson time is a crucially important element of lesson planning. I think most teachers would agree that it's not a good idea to try and cram too much into the lesson. It is more important that pupils learn something than attempting to teach them everything in one lesson. So, it is important to prioritise activities which help pupils to learn rather than simply keep them busy.

Much depends here on your learning intentions for the lesson; the activities that you plan should be relevant to the LO for the lesson. But perhaps even more significant is the need to ensure that adequate time is spent on learning activity that will enable pupils to make progress. It can be helpful to identify on your lesson plan the one activity that you consider most important to progress learning in that lesson. Your aim then is to ensure that adequate time is planned for that activity and that you prepare pupils for it as best you can to maximise success and achievement. Conversely, try not to spend too long on activities which are low in learning value – regardless of how much pupils like them! Drilling, for example, is of relatively low learning value; it might be better to spend a few minutes on this every lesson than to let this dominate whole lessons.

Another aspect of prioritising lesson time is to privilege those activities in the lesson that cannot or cannot easily be replicated in a typical homework situation. Interaction with the teacher, especially through the TL, the opportunity to ask questions, listening to the language and learning to read aloud in the TL all have high learning value and are not always easy or possible to do outside of the classroom. By contrast, learning vocabulary, especially spellings, doing written grammar drills (provided pupils can find the spellings) and learning grammar rules by heart are examples of activities that can quite easily be set as homework rather than take up lesson time.

Planning how long to allow for an activity is tricky. It can be easy to underestimate the amount of time a lesson activity might take. As well as the activity itself, you might also need to factor in time for modelling what to do and or giving instructions and time for checking answers. How long you spend checking answers and how you go about doing this might depend on what happens next. If the answers are important for the rest of the lesson, then you might want to spend some time on this; if not, your priority might be to get those checked as quickly as possible.

Some activities are quite elastic, so you can be quite flexible about the finishing time, e.g. repeat if true. A good rule of thumb with flexible activities is to leave pupils wanting more, avoid letting the activity overrun. Other, more substantial activities need a minimum amount of time if pupils are to learn from them and gain a sense of achievement; to cut them short could be self-defeating, e.g. a class survey or a debrief at the end of the lesson. If pupils are working independently of the teacher, a good rule of thumb is to give pupils a time limit for task completion and to clarify a minimum that all pupils are expected to achieve within that period, e.g. you have five minutes to write at least three examples.

To sum up, here are some key planning questions to help manage timing and pace:

- **What is the most important thing that pupils need to spend time doing this lesson? What is the minimum length of time needed for this? When is the latest time you can start this in the lesson?**
- **Is there any part of the lesson that might be omitted or shortened if time runs out?**
- **What is your plan for early finishers? And what if the whole class finishes their work early?**

The next lesson plan provides a basis for comparison with the previous lesson plan. Both lessons are about *Mein Stundenplan* (my school timetable) but the teaching contexts are quite different. The previous lesson was with a top set class who had one lesson of German per week; the following lesson plan was written for a bottom set class who have three lessons of German per week.

Year 7 German lesson with a bottom set class

TABLE 3.8A Year 7 German bottom set lesson plan: '*Mein Stundenplan 2*'

The context is a bottom set Year 7 German class in a large comprehensive school. Pupils have been learning German for one term, three lessons a week. In previous lessons they have been taught school subjects, expressing opinions of those . The lesson is 2.30–3.30pm.

LO: Use sentences to talk about your school timetable

Key language needed	From previous lessons
Am + *Montag, Dienstag, Mittwoch,*	Names of 14 school subjects
Donnerstag, Freitag,	*Was ist dein Lieblingsfach in der Schule?*
Was hast du am + day of week?	*Mein Lieblingsfach ist . . .*
Am + day of week *habe ich* + subject.	*Ich habe kein Lieblingsfach.*
	Wie findest du . . .? . . . ist interessant/ langweilig.

1 Revision of School Subjects + activity on desks and slide with numbered pictures [10–12 mins]

   Match up names of subjects + numbered pictures. Check answers, pupils read out the German. *Wer hat 14/14? Heb die Hand!* Choral repetition of each / repeat if true pictures only. Q&A + ball routine to revise *Was ist dein Lieblingsfach in der Schule? Wie findest du . . .?* Q&A practice in pairs A+B (*Eine Minute dann wechseln. Achtung fertig los!*)

2 LO – *Lernziele* – paraphrase *Stundenplan* + show example on ppt, get pupil to translate LO

3 Introduce days of week + *Stundenplan für Klasse 7C* [5 mins]

   Also hier ist der Stundenplan für diese Klasse. Hier sind die Schultage. . . . Montag, Dienstag, etc. Choral repetition of days of week- careful with '*ie*' and '*ei*'. What's missing? Show days on board – random order. Pair work – read out the days in order.

4 Introduce new structure + *Stundenplan für Klasse 7C* [6–7 mins]

   Also, hier sind die Schultage . . . und hier sind die Schulfächer. Also was hast du am Montag? Wer kann mir ein Schulfach nennen? Take different answers and put into sentence. *Richtig! Am Montag habe ich . . .* Repetition + Mexican wave – *Was hast du am Montag? Am Montag habe ich Deutsch* – stand up on *am*. Same with other days (*Was hast du am . . .? Am habe ich . . .*) .

5 True false sentences about *Stundenplan für Klasse 7C* [10 mins]

   Pupils write 1–8, (*schreibt 1 bis 8*). Read out sentences, pupils write R or F – do example on board first. Check answers and ask pupils to correct what is false, ask *warum*? (why?). *Wer hat 8/8? Heb die Hand!* Etc. 7/8? Same activity in pairs A+B (*eine Minute*). If time, volunteer teacher clone at front.

6 *Was hast du am Freitag?* – oral practice [12–15 mins- start by 3.05 at latest]

   Sample dialogue on ppt – whole class reading. Then in pairs A+B, replace underlined words. Choose a pair to read out their version, rest of class to notice the replacements. *Was ist anders?*

   Give out cue cards + different combinations of school subjects, find the others in your group by asking *Was hast du am Freitag?* – keep question up on board if needed. Pupils circulate- once found their group call out *Fertig!* All listen to a few. *Setzt euch!* 5–4–3–2–1

7 Homework [10 mins]

   Stick *der Stundenplan für Klasse 7C* sheets in books and write mini dialogues based on this model – **Was hast du am Montag? Am Montag habe ich Deutsch.** – pupils copy from board. At least 5x mini dialogues about *Mein Stundenplan*. Check instructions in planners before packing away.

Copyright material from Cheryl Mackay (2019), *Learning to Plan Modern Languages Lessons*, Routledge

TABLE 3.8B Commentary on Year 7 German bottom set lesson: '*Mein Stundenplan 2*'

I would like to focus here on the thinking behind the lesson structure and decisions made about how best to prioritise learning time.

Overall, this lesson is structured to help pupils progress to point 6 on the lesson plan where they are able to conduct short cued conversations with each other. Each point of the lesson is linked to what has gone before and this includes the homework which arises naturally out of what has been learnt and practised in the lesson. In other words, the lesson is structured to scaffold the speaking activity and maximise pupil success and achievement. There are some particular points to note.

First of all, a substantial amount of time has been earmarked for revision of previous learning on this topic, especially the school subjects. Looking ahead to points 5 and 6 it will be important for pupils to feel confident in their knowledge of school subjects in German and how to say them. It is worth noting, that the extent of revision and practising needed can vary considerably from class to class.

Secondly, the new language content is broken down rather than presented all at once: first days of the school week then the new structure and question. There is plentiful controlled practice with pupils hearing and repeating the new language in different activities (see Points 3–5) before they see the sample dialogue, this is supporting them and scaffolding their progress.

Thirdly, the sample dialogue brings together all the language so far practised and models for pupils the sort of conversations they will have themselves. Again, this modelling helps to scaffold the speaking activity. And guided reading with the whole class helps to scaffold the transition to independent reading in pairs. Guided reading helps pupils to learn what the written word sounds like and enables the teacher to pick up on any difficulties. It is important for any class of beginners to spend ample time learning how the sounds of the TL are represented in writing, and this is most meaningfully done if pupils are familiar with the words they are reading. This not only helps pupils to learn the language for the topic, it also is aids them in developing their German literacy skills. This will be a priority with classes, like this one, who have low literacy levels in their first language.

Finally, there is a well-planned homework routine at the end of the lesson. Ample time is planned for this and includes: time for pupils to write down a worked example of what is expected (the example is written on the lesson plan), time for instructions (which have also been planned) and for checking those, time for pupils to complete their homework planners and for those to be checked.

All in all, the lesson has been well planned to prioritise learning over simply keeping pupils busy or entertained.

<u>Follow-up Reflective Task/Points to discuss</u>

If you were planning to teach this lesson to a bottom set Year 7 class in term one, what activity or part of the lesson might you be prepared to drop if the lesson goes slower than anticipated? And why? Conversely, how might you plan to 'fill in' should the lesson go quicker than anticipated?

Assuming things do go to plan, how might you plan to revise what has been learnt with the same class in the next lesson? How might you develop the lesson further? What might your priorities be?

Copyright material from Cheryl Mackay (2019), *Learning to Plan Modern Languages Lessons*, Routledge

Let us now consider the two contrasting Year 7 German lessons. The commentary for the top set lesson plan refers to challenge; the commentary for the bottom set refers to scaffolding and support. This does not mean, however, that only top sets need to be challenged nor that only bottom sets need to be supported. Planning for challenge and support is the focus of the next subsection.

Planning for challenge and support

All pupils need to be challenged *and* feel supported if each is to reach their full potential. And this doesn't only apply to pupils; we all need to be challenged to leave our comfort zone if we are to learn. But equally too much challenge can be counter-productive, resulting in panic, feelings of helplessness or worse.

The nature of challenge within the context of ML learning is quite distinctive. First of all, learning a language is cognitively challenging, it makes you think; for example, pupils might be challenged to write a sentence including a particular keyword with exactly ten words in it, to sort nouns (without articles) into gender columns or to generate different possible answers in an Odd One Out activity. Each of these examples presents pupils with a cognitive challenge. For further practical examples and more on challenging pupils to think in ML, please see Jones and Swarbrick (2004).

However, in my opinion, what is distinctive about ML is the challenge to communicate and express yourself in another language and this calls for more than intellect or cognitive skills. Personality, attitude and emotions all play a role in spontaneous use of another language, along with thinking on your feet and generally making an effort to connect with other speakers of the ML you are learning. These variables are described in the literature as 'affective', they relate to feelings and emotions and they play a significant role in language learning. For example, Stern writes that 'the affective component contributes at least as much as and often more to language learning than the cognitive skills' (1983, p386). This helps to explain why it is not always the pupils, who are most academically able or who cope best with the cognitive demands of the subject, who manage most successfully with the challenge of conversing or performing in another language.

Language teachers have different options for creating challenges that they can draw upon; here are just a few examples:

- perform or complete a task from memory;
- complete a task within a time limit;
- understand or make sense of the written word without using a dictionary;
- listen and learn when the teacher is speaking the TL;
- only speak in the TL.

Returning to the lesson plan for the German bottom set class, the word 'challenge' is not explicitly mentioned on the plan; yet, I would argue, the lesson was clearly planned with challenge in mind. Throughout the lesson the extent of the teacher's use of the TL sets high expectations and challenges pupils; of particular note is the teacher's use of the TL to explain today's LO including the idea of '*Stundenplan*', challenging pupils to listen and work out for themselves what this means. There are also particular challenges at different points in the lesson; bear in mind that this is a bottom set class in their first term of learning German. Pupils are challenged firstly to recognise the school subjects from memory (without looking in their books) and seconds later to then repeat if true, which requires pupils to think about meaning before deciding whether or not to repeat;

The true/ false activity later challenges pupils to attend to sentences that are read out in the TL and to relate this to a version of their own school timetable. The key point to remember here is that bottom sets, like all other sets, *need* to be challenged.

You might want to focus on challenge and involvement of pupils when observing the lessons of experienced ML teachers. Make a note of any strategies you observe that seem to raise the level of challenge for all pupils. You might also like to consider what the teacher does or could do to encourage individual pupils to raise their game.

In well-planned lessons, pupils are not only appropriately challenged, according to their current level of proficiency in the language; they are also well supported to help them meet those challenges, learn from them and make progress as a result. Due to the cognitive and affective demands of our subject, it is important to think through how best to support pupils in different ways.

In the typical ML lesson, emotional or affective support might include the following:

- opportunities for paired practice before expecting individual pupils to use the TL in teacher-led oral work or to perform in the TL in front of their peers;
- heaping praise and encouragement on pupils who make the effort to try to use the language;

- providing clear examples of what is expected and giving pupils the chance to do an example together in preparation for more independent work away from the teacher.

This sort of support serves to increase learner confidence, especially their confidence in using the language and belief in their own abilities to do so. As confidence grows, levels of pupil motivation and engagement are also likely to rise and this in turn can have a noticeable impact on the pace of lessons, not to mention pupil progress. For more on supporting pupils to use the TL, please see Christie (2016).

Hand in hand with this affective support goes linguistic and cognitive support for learning. Support of this sort is designed to help pupils make progress in their language learning, especially their abilities to use the language with increasing accuracy and independence. It draws on a teacher's subject knowledge and might include, for example:

- providing clear linguistic frameworks and models to support speaking and writing tasks;
- giving clear points of reference for specific grammar points;
- setting exercises which help learners to manipulate the language.

Scaffolding

Building on what was said above about linguistic and cognitive support for learning, scaffolding is a useful concept for describing the process of supporting learning in this way. In particular I'll be referring here to Bruner's definition, as cited in Gibbons, when he refers to scaffolding as:

> the steps taken to reduce the degrees of freedom in carrying out some task so that the child can concentrate on the difficult skill she is in the process of acquiring.
>
> (Gibbons, 2014, p16)

In other words, scaffolding refer to the steps we take in order to reduce the demands that the learner might face in a given situation, so that the learner can focus their attention only on acquiring the knowledge or skill that is required.

Well-scaffolded ML lessons break down the intended learning into small steps or stages, thereby reducing linguistic and cognitive demands on pupils at any one time. This makes the learning more accessible. For example, writing in the TL is much more achievable if it is based on language that pupils have already been practising and are familiar with from oral tasks. Similarly, paired speaking tasks are easier if preceded by adequate whole class practice and modelling. In my experience, if planned well, scaffolding not only has a positive impact on the quality of ML learning but also on the pace of the lesson. Conversely, the absence of scaffolding can have a negative impact on motivation to learn and the pace of the lesson.

Returning to the lesson plan for the German top set class, we can identify points in the lesson where, I would argue, the teacher has clearly planned to scaffold the learning in order to support learners. Bear in mind that this class has just one lesson of German a week; if ever a class needed support it was this one! At point 3, for example, the introduction of new language is broken down into two parts: first days of the week, then the new structure. The days of the week are intensively drilled before pupils are expected to produce those with the new structure (*Am Montag habe ich . . .*) and the structure is written up on the board to support memory. Also, pupils are given thinking time in pairs before being expected to contribute orally in front of the rest of the class (this supports pupils in both an affective and a learning sense); and there is a contingency plan in case pupils need even more practice.

Having introduced the general idea of scaffolding to support learning in the ML classroom, the next subsection will concentrate on some examples of linguistic scaffolding and implications for planning.

Examples of Linguistic Scaffolding

The Year 7 German lesson plans use a substitution dialogue to scaffold the progression from recognition of the new language forms to using them within the context of a communicative activity. A substitution dialogue is a controlled and simple way for learners to practise manipulating the language in order to make different sentences. The framework provided is an example of linguistic scaffolding. The ability to produce appropriate writing or speaking frames for the classes you teach is a very useful language teaching skill and an important aspect of learning to plan ML lessons.

I want now to look at some examples of substitution dialogues. In the case of the bottom set German class, Figure 3.2 shows what the substitution dialogue might look like.

Planning whole lessons

Person A	Was hast du am **Freitag**?
Person B	Am **Freitag** habe ich **Mathe** und **Englisch**.
	Und du? Was hast du am **Freitag**?
Person A	Ich auch! Am **Freitag** habe ich **Mathe** und **Englisch**.
Person B	Was hast du am **Montag**?
Person A	Am **Montag** habe ich **Sport**.
	Und du? Hast du auch **Sport** am **Montag**?
Person B	Nein! Am **Montag** habe ich **Deutsch**.

FIGURE 3.2 German substitution dialogue for bottom set Year 7 lesson

The dialogue is kept deliberately simple to focus on the new language points for this lesson. It has been designed to model particular language in use; just a few words have been underlined for pupils to substitute with alternatives so that they are able to produce different sentences.

The dialogue contains limited vocabulary and structure but those are used repeatedly. In total, the dialogue contains seven instances of *am+* day of the week and four instances of inverted word order. In addition to these language points, the dialogue also includes a couple of very simple extras (e.g. *ich auch!* – me too!); these are there to make the dialogue sound a bit more authentic but without distracting from the main point. There are six turns in the dialogue but you might plan to break this down, so that you focus on just the first three turns to begin with.

With another class you might replace the names of school subjects with picture cues. This makes the reading of the dialogue more challenging, in the sense that pupils are having to do two things within the same exercise: read out words, and recall vocabulary.

The next example was written by a trainee teacher for use with a Year 10 Spanish lesson on the topic of films (see Figure 3.3). It follows the same format as the German example; in this case it makes more sense to keep together the words '*las películas de ciencia-ficción*' and '*las películas del Oeste*' as interchangeable units of meaning. The intention was for pupils to use the dialogue as a basis for controlled speaking practice – see instructions in the TL.

The final example is a substitution table, used to scaffold the process of language manipulation (see Figure 3.4). The language included in the table has been selected and presented by the teacher so that pupils can concentrate on the key components needed to form sentences talking about where they went on holiday. The key phrase '*je suis allé(e)*' is presented as one unit of meaning; at this stage pupils do not need to make decisions about conjugating the verb, they can focus instead on selecting different complements to the verb. One possibility would be to invite pupils to use the table to write (and possibly translate) as many different sentences as they can within a given time

Con tu compañero/a, haz diálogos cambiando los datos subrayados.

Persona A	¿Qué tipo de películas te gustan?
Persona B	Me gustan **las películas de ciencia-ficción**.
Persona A	¿Qué tipo de películas no te gustan?
Persona B	No me gustan **las películas del Oeste**.
Persona A	¿Por qué prefieres **las películas de ciencia-ficción**?
Persona B	Porque son más **interesantes** que **las películas del Oeste**.

FIGURE 3.3 Spanish substitution dialogue for Year 10 lesson

Je suis allé (e)	en Australie	avec	ma famille.
	en Espagne		ma sœur.
	en France		mon frère.
	en Grèce		mon oncle.
	en Italie		mes amis.
	au Portugal		mes grands-parents.
	aux Etats Unis		Alan Shearer.
	à Londres		Kylie.

FIGURE 3.4 French substitution table for Year 9 lesson

limit; writing some of the examples from memory would make this more challenging. As a follow-up, pupils might be asked to use the same structure or pattern to make up other sentences of their own; inviting pupils to act out their own examples for others to guess would provide a communicative purpose for using the new structure.

Substitution dialogues and tables such as those shown here have served language learners well for generations. In my opinion, they are an effective way of scaffolding the process of language learning, helping pupils to internalise key structures and patterns, bridging the transition from 'pre-communicative' to 'communicative activity' (Littlewood, 1981, p92).

Finally, please bear in mind that vital though scaffolding is for progressing learning, the role of scaffolding is strictly temporary. Over time, it does need to be removed as appropriate, so that pupils have regular opportunities to show and know what they can achieve independently and without support. At the end of the day, scaffolding is there to help pupils move to more independent language production; it is not an end in itself. For more theoretical perspectives relating to scaffolding and language learning, see Gibbons (2014).

Year 8 Spanish lesson

In theory, it is LOs or subject-specific learning intentions that inform planning decisions about how to prioritise lesson time, what activities to include and in what order. In practice, other factors might also have a bearing on those planning decisions. One such factor, especially for beginning teachers, is pupil behaviour. The following lesson was planned to avoid unwanted behaviour getting in the way of learning.

TABLE 3.9A Year 8 Spanish lesson plan: 'Spanish presents'

All the pupils in this class were identified as having behavioural issues and or a range of SEN. It is a challenge to keep all of the class on track. This is their second year of learning Spanish and their third lesson on the topic of 'Buying Presents'. In previous lessons they had been introduced to presents and family vocabulary. The teacher's professional development target for this lesson was to incorporate differentiation into his teaching so as to ensure and improve pupil progress.

LO: To continue learning presents vocabulary, not just meaning and pronunciation but also spelling; to begin forming sentences which combine vocabulary for presents with family members.

Key question + answer	Los regalos
¿Qué compras para tu familia?	Una gorra, camiseta, caja de bombones,
Para mi . . . compro . . .	caja de galletas, foto
Mi familia	Un CD, poster, llavero
Padre, madre, hermano, hermana, tío, tía,	
abuelo, abuela	

1 Revise names of presents + matching activity on desks [10mins]

   Match up names of presents with numbered pictures, instructions on ppt. Can use exercise books if need to. Hands up to check answers – pupil says the Spanish, whole class repeat.

   Learning Objectives + success criteria (must, should, could)

   Pupil to read out. Stress importance of accuracy when writing in today's lesson. Reminder about behavioural expectations + why elicit from class, reminder of consequences.

2 Spelling names of presents from memory + ppt   [5mins]

   Identify the presents by filling in the missing letters. Pupils use Spanish alphabet from previous lessons to supply missing letters, and read out the word. Watch 'll', 'j','rr'.

3 Family members recap + ppt with pictures of Simpson family [7–8 mins]

   ¿Que número es mi madre? etc Drill vocab. Repeat if true. Stress 'o' and 'a' endings

4 ¿Qué compras para tu familia? + Para mi . . . compro . . . [10 mins]

   Soy Bart Simpson. Estoy en España . . . Shopping list to introduce new structure, use mime and board to write up presents in list – keep repeating 'para mi . . . compro. . .'

   Write up sample sentence Para mi hermana compro un CD. As a full group, pupils create 2–3 sentences on the board.

   Create a chain using 'Para mi . . . . compro . . .' each time adding on another family member and present. First with whole class + volunteers, then in pairs/small groups. Remind about behaviour for learning. Check who is starting. Depending on behaviour [2–5 mins]

5 Writing practice [15 mins]

   As a class write up together sentences created as whole group – pupils copy down.

   Differentiated Writing Activity Sheets. 10 minutes to write at least three accurate sentences using Para mi . . . compro using differentiated written support to help them as appropriate.

   Go through first 3 answers in class + ppt, pupils check own work, clarify any points.

6 Review objectives + success criteria [5 mins]

   How well did pupils do? (success criteria for Spanish) Reflections + feedback on behaviour.

   Backup

   Tres en raya! Split class into two teams and play noughts and crosses

Copyright material from Cheryl Mackay (2019), *Learning to Plan Modern Languages Lessons*, Routledge

TABLE 3.9B Commentary on Year 8 Spanish lesson: 'Spanish presents'

This lesson was planned by a beginning teacher halfway through his second teaching placement. He has been teaching this challenging class for about five weeks. Careful lesson planning, specifically with this class in mind, helped the teacher keep most pupils on track for most of the lesson. As an additional planning prompt he had written on his lesson plan to continue to monitor pupils carefully in order to try and prevent behavioural issues.

The teacher has a clear idea of what he wants pupils to achieve in the lesson. This is encapsulated within the learning objectives themselves and at point 1 when key learning expectations are made explicit. Previous learning within the topic is consolidated and systematically linked up. Prior learning of the Spanish alphabet and phonics is practised, this helps to scaffold the transition to the written word and focus on spelling; teacher-directed oral work also helps prepare the ground for writing sentences.

An important aspect of planning for this lesson is the promotion of behaviour for learning. I'd like to highlight four particular points. The first is that pupils have a task on their desks as soon as they arrive in the lesson; it is a simple task that everyone should be able to do. Next, time has been factored into point 1 for an explicit reminder about behavioural expectations. Eliciting those from the class means that the teacher can check and pick up on any misconceptions at the start of the lesson. Most of the interaction in the lesson is mediated through the teacher. It is only at point 4 that there is scope for pupils to talk with each other in pairs. The teacher has planned a reminder about behaviour for learning at this stage; and has pre-empted that pair work might need to be curtailed if appropriate behaviour for learning is not forthcoming. Finally, at point 6, behaviour is reviewed. Helping pupils to reflect on their own behaviour (either as individuals or as a class) and discussing with them possible areas for improvement, is enabling them to be responsible for their behaviour. This can make a powerful difference to how pupils approach their learning. However, to be effective, this needs to be done on successive occasions rather than as a one-off experiment.

In terms of differentiation, the first part of the lesson involves a variety of core activities mostly led and controlled by the teacher; at point 5, pupils work independently of the teacher and of each other. At this point they can work at their own pace and with differing levels of written support; the teacher has decided at which level each pupil will work. He uses this time to target pupils who might need extra support.

Finally point 6 refers to 'success criteria'. These were shared with the class at the start of the lesson:

By the end of the lesson I . . .

MUST have written one accurate sentence about a present I am buying for a family member.

SHOULD have written three accurate sentences about a present I am buying for a family member.

COULD have written more than five accurate sentences about a present I am buying for a family member.

<u>Follow-up Reflective Task/Points to discuss</u>

At point 4, pupils are reminded about behaviour for learning. What key messages would you plan to elicit from pupils at this stage?

What are advantages and disadvantages of using differentiated success criteria? In what sort of context do you think they might they be most effective?

Copyright material from Cheryl Mackay (2019), *Learning to Plan Modern Languages Lessons*, Routledge

The context in which this lesson was planned presented particular challenges with regard to pupil behaviour, attention span and learning needs. The lesson still followed a typical PPP pattern but it is tightly structured to promote behaviour for learning. This is one example of how planning for pupil behaviour can be integrated into lesson planning and was appropriate for the teaching context in question. Planning for behaviour is the subject of the next subsection.

Planning for behaviour

Numerous factors can influence pupil behaviour in the classroom and not all of them are under the control of the teacher. The focus here will be on identifying some practical ways in which beginning teachers of ML can plan to reduce the likelihood of unwanted behaviour arising in their lessons. There are, of course, no guarantees in this. However, I think most educationalists or teachers would agree that badly-planned lessons have a detrimental effect on behaviour.

Stirrers and settlers

The activities that we choose to ask pupils to do in the classroom may impact on behaviour in different ways. One way of thinking about this is in terms of in terms of 'stirrers' and 'settlers'. All other things being equal, some activities tend to have a more settling or calming affect on pupils; others are the opposite, they tend to make pupils excitable or wind them up. The term 'settlers and stirrers', as discussed in Alison and Halliwell (2002, p66), refers to this difference.

I think this is a useful idea to be aware of when planning lessons. The trick here is to plan for balance. For example, the lesson plan above for the bottom set German class (Table 3.8a) has a good balance of stirring and settling activity, this helps the teacher to manage potential restlessness. Probably the two most stirring activities are the Mexican wave (point 4) and the cue card activity (point 6). The plan is to follow each of these with a more settling, heads down activity (see points 5 and 7). The more you get to know your classes and how they tend to be at different times in the day or week, the better placed you will be to tailor your planning to the classes you are teaching.

Figure 3.5 shows some ideas to help you plan balanced lessons, adapted from Alison and Halliwell (2002).

Contingency planning

In any lesson you never know what's going to happen, so it's always important to plan a backup just in case things go wrong. Sometimes, the reason for things going wrong is behaviour and this is perhaps more likely to happen with some classes than with others. What happens, for example, if the planned balance of stirrers and settlers goes badly wrong? You will need a contingency plan to help pupils calm down and return to a 'teachable state'. A helpful strategy can be to put the planned lesson on hold, ask the class to 'write down what you have learnt so far this lesson...' and expect them to do this in silence. Alternatively, a short dictation, with pupils writing in silence, can also be very effective in helping the teacher to restore calm and order. These strategies buy you some time to consider your next step. You may decide to return to the lesson as planned or in an amended form; or you may decide to take advantage of the situation (you should have a captive audience) to remind pupils of behavioural expectations.

Discipline plan

The idea of a discipline plan is credited to Bill Rogers, the Australian behaviour guru. In my experience, this is a helpful device for helping beginning teachers to think through the behaviours they want to see in their classrooms.

A discipline plan involves thinking through your behavioural expectations, what you will do to positively reinforce those, what routines you will have in your classroom and what action you will take in response to distracting and disruptive behaviour. This last point will involve considering how you will respond if such behaviour arises, and what the consequences of 'poor behaviour' will be for the pupil/s concerned, including the use of sanctions. Rogers (2012; 2015) argues that being proactive in planning for behaviour in this way enables the teacher to focus in the classroom on the core business of teaching and learning rather than pupil behaviour. Figure 3.6 summarises some key areas to think through, based on the ideas of Bill Rogers. Please note, it is very important that any discipline plan, and planning for behaviour generally, is consistent with school and departmental policy. Please make time to know and understand the systems in place in your school so they can be integrated into your plan and planning, and so you can apply those with confidence, consistency and fairness.

- Be aware of ways of making activities more 'stirring'
    - Base it on the visualiser, PowerPoint or whiteboard with you directing it, rather than on a desk resource
    - Select teams and award points or prizes
    - Get pupils to work against the clock
    - Get your pupils to work in competition with you
    - Put your pupils into larger groups to work
    - Become excited yourself!

- Be aware of ways of making activities more 'settling'
    - Take away any element of competition
    - Let pupils work at their own pace
    - Base resources and tasks on pupils' desks
    - Cut down the noise, excitement and movement
    - Get your pupils reading, writing and manipulating text rather than communicating orally
    - Allow pupils to work in peace and quiet

- Look at each activity that you have planned for your lesson and decide whether it is likely to be a stirrer or a settler.
- Look closely at what pupils will be doing first when they arrive in the lesson and knowing what you know about the class and their typical emotional state at that time of day - decide whether a stirrer or settler is going to be most helpful.
- Look closely at what pupils will be doing last before they leave the lesson and ensure that when they leave your classroom they will be suitably settled for their next lesson.
- Look critically at the amount of time you expect pupils to work as a whole class, all at the same pace, or concentrating on you.

Adapted from Alison and Halliwell (2002)

FIGURE 3.5 Planning for a balance of stirrers and settlers

In my experience, planning what your expectations are going to be for the context you are teaching in is a useful starting point for beginning teachers. That way you can go into the classroom with the confidence of knowing what you want and be consistent in your approach. On the whole, classes like teachers to know what they are doing so this is an important point to plan for.

Of course, beginning teachers will encounter some classes and some pupils who present seriously challenging behaviours. And in some cases, such classes or pupils will also be every bit as challenging for more experienced teachers to teach. It is, however, outwith the scope of this book to address issues of more serious behaviour management. I would only advise any beginning teacher who finds themself in such a situation to seek help and advice from experienced colleagues in school and to do so without hesitation. It is entirely normal to encounter challenging behaviour in the classroom, very often for reasons that are outside your control, so don't feel bad about asking for help.

To sum up, here are some key questions to prompt planning for behaviour:

- **Have you anticipated any likely behaviour challenges and how to address those?**
- **Are you clear about the behaviour you expect to see in the classroom?**
- **Are you clear about possible sanctions or consequences that might be needed?**

Summing up Chapter 3

We have now looked at seven ML lesson plans, structured to follow the PPP model; the PPP model may not account for all aspects of ML teaching and learning, but it can be a helpful starting point for learning to plan clearly structured lessons that build on prior learning. We have also considered simple, limited aspects of other planning issues that need to be factored into lesson planning. Again, what has been covered here is intended as a starting point.

1. What do you mean by 'good behaviour' or behaviour for learning in your classroom? Identify a few fundamental expectations you will have for learning, respect and manners and safety. Here is one example used by a beginning teacher:
   - Arrive on time
   - Come prepared
   - Do the work
   - Respect others

2. What essential routines are going to ensure the smooth running of classroom life? And what rules will need to be followed?
   Routines might include:
       Entry to classroom
       Appropriate seating plans
       Giving out and collecting in resources needed
       Appropriate noise levels in class learning time
       How to fairly get teacher attention and support
       Engagement in whole class questions and discussions
       Packing up and tidying classroom
       Exit from classroom

3. How you will reward or positively reinforce 'good behaviour' in your lessons? What sanctions or consequences will apply for 'poor behaviour'?

4. Where and when and how will you share and discuss key expectations with the classes that you teach? Even if your expectations and routines mirror what is already in place, it is worth taking some time during your first lesson with classes to explain and discuss with pupils why those are essential for learning. This is a very important aspect to plan for. For example, you might want to make pupils aware that learning is a basic human right, to which everyone is entitled without undue distraction or disruption; you might want to highlight to pupils the responsibility they have for their own learning and progress. Most pupils are usually willing to accept rules, especially if the rules are seen as part of routines and the rationale is made clear.

Based on the ideas of Bill Rogers (2012, 2015)

FIGURE 3.6 Thinking through your discipline plan

In the early days it can be helpful to prioritise and focus your planning on just one or two particular issues when lesson planning, rather than trying to cover every possible issue all of the time. The planning prompts in Table 3.10 might be helpful to you. They are based on a checklist of questions first devised in 2007 by Vivienne Baumfield and myself at Newcastle University and subsequently used by different cohorts of PGCE students. It includes key questions highlighted in this chapter and in Chapter 2. Please don't be put off by the length of this checklist! Not all of these questions will apply to every lesson you plan and your priorities are likely to change as you gain in experience and knowledge of planning. As you progress in your planning and teaching, you will no doubt find yourself tackling increasingly more complex aspects of these issues and be able to add further prompts of your own.

Finally, the checklist may also be useful to you when you are evaluating your lessons, especially if you are uncertain about the factors that contributed to the success (or otherwise) of the lesson. Lesson evaluation is covered in the next chapter.

TABLE 3.10 Learning to teach: lesson planning prompts

Lesson aims and objectives

Are your aims and objectives expressed with reference to what pupils should have learnt or learnt to do by the end of the lesson?

Structuring the lesson

What are the different stages of the lesson? Are they relevant and appropriate to your LO?

Have these been sequenced in a logical order?

Is there a purpose to the activities that pupils are asked to do?

Have you built diagnostic assessment opportunities into the lesson?

Progression

Have you identified the main language you want pupils to be using/learning in the lesson?

Have you planned for opportunities to practise or recycle previously learnt language?

Have you planned homework and if so does it flow naturally from the lesson?

Timing and pace

Have you decided how long to spend on each stage of the lesson?

Have you identified any activity that might be omitted or shortened if time runs short?

Do you have a plan for early finishers? If a pupil or the class finishes their work early?

Dealing with the practicalities

Have you considered how pupils will know what to do at each stage of the lesson?

Are your instructions clear? Have you rehearsed or simplified any complicated instructions?

Have you considered what resources you will need and the availability of those?

Have you considered the groupings you want pupils to work within? And how you will organise this?

Assessment

How will you know that the LOs have been met? And how well they have been met?

Do the activities you have planned provide opportunities to assess learning and its outcomes?

Differentiation

Have you catered for the range of ability within the class and any particular pupil needs?

Have you anticipated likely learning difficulties and how to address those?

Are your expectations high yet realistic for all the pupils you are teaching?

Have you included a variety of activities to involve pupils in different ways in the lesson?

Is extension work appropriate for some pupils in the lesson? Which ones? What will it consist of?

Behaviour for learning

Have you anticipated any likely behaviour challenges and how to address those?

Are you clear about the behaviour you expect to see in the classroom?

Are you clear about possible sanctions or consequences that might be needed?

Target language

Have you identified the TL you will use to introduce and manage activities?

Have you included opportunities in the lesson for pupils to use the TL?

Links to wider curriculum

Have you established how the lesson plan relates to departmental medium- and long-term plans?

Have you used the National Curriculum Programme of Study to inform your planning?

CHAPTER

Lesson planning process

Introduction

This short chapter steps back from the nitty-gritty of planning for different elements of individual ML lessons, to look at the planning process in more generic terms. The aim is here is to consider how particular elements fit in to that process. These are:

- Lesson evaluation;
- Learning intentions;
- Writing lesson plans.

But first of all a few words about the process itself.

Lesson planning

Lesson planning is a much messier and more complex process than neatly organised formal lesson plans might suggest. What is formally written up as a lesson plan is the outcome of much thinking and re-thinking, not all of which can be captured in writing and not all of which is necessarily relevant to the final product! I would suggest that a lesson plan records key decisions made during the lesson planning stage.

Lesson planning is also an individual process. I take the view that neither I nor anyone else can tell you *how* to plan; to do so would be like telling you how to think – it's a no-brainer! You will find that teachers approach lesson planning in different ways. There is no single way to plan a lesson and part of learning to teach is finding a way that helps you to plan efficiently and effectively. Planning efficiently means making good use of the time available to you for planning; planning effectively means planning lessons that lead to learning, specifically the intended learning for that lesson.

Lesson planning may be an individual process but it does not need to be a solitary one. On the contrary, I take the view that lesson planning can be a highly interactive process. Talking with others, thinking out loud, can help you to get your own head round what you want to achieve in the classroom or the learning that you want to foster. So, please don't feel that you need to plan in your head away from other people; and please don't think that planning needs to make perfect sense in your head before you start talking with others or making rough notes.

However, even with the best planning and preparation in the world, there is no guarantee that the plan 'will work' nor that the learning experience that you set up and provide in the lesson will achieve what you want it to achieve. Teaching is not an exact science and not all learning is predictable! Pupils do not always engage or respond in ways that we had anticipated; for example, they might respond in ways that exceed your expectations, they might also react in ways that highlight unforeseen learning gaps or difficulties. It can be helpful to think of lesson planning as our best guess at how learning *might* develop, based on our knowledge of the class, our subject and how it is learnt. This is an important point to bear in mind when considering the role of the written lesson plan in the lesson: your lesson plan is there to guide you, not dictate to you.

Finally, it is important to keep in mind that planning does not happen in a vacuum, it is part of a planning cycle. That cycle also involves teaching, assessment and evaluation. For me, assessment is integral to teaching *and* to lesson evaluation, and is implicit in the planning cycle, as indicated in Figure 4.1.

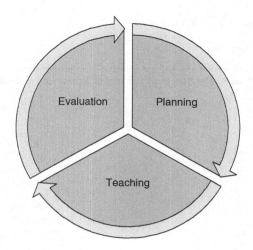

FIGURE 4.1 The planning cycle

Lesson evaluation

Increasingly, as you start planning and teaching whole lessons for different classes, lesson evaluation is vital for informing your planning for any given class. And evaluation needs to be informed by your assessment of what pupils achieved in the lesson and their strengths and weaknesses as language learners. When assessment informs planning, it means that the next cycle of planning and teaching for that class can be more focused and tailored to the needs of the pupils you are teaching.

At the heart of lesson evaluation is ascertaining to what extent pupils learnt what you set out to teach them and how you know this. Sometimes you may need to answer this after you have marked pupils' work; but if you have built continuous assessment opportunities into your lesson planning, you should have at least some idea by the end of the lesson. The more information you can collect about pupils' learning during or after the lesson, the better planned your lessons can be.

> The most important single factor influencing learning is what the learner already knows. Ascertain this and teach him accordingly.
>
> (Ausubel, 1968, p*vi*)

Lesson evaluation can take different forms. If time is tight, it might simply be a sentence or two written on the end of your lesson plan, or it might take the form of annotating the lesson plan during or after the lesson. In some cases, you might be given a generic lesson evaluation template to complete, such as the examples shown in Table 4.1.

It is important that lesson evaluation is understood as part of the lesson planning cycle. Lesson evaluation is also essential to improving your own practice and it is worth investing time to develop this skill as a beginning teacher from the outset. We will consider this point further in Chapter 7.

Learning intentions

Learning intentions are the lynchpin upon which other planning decisions and indeed the planning process itself depend, that's why I want to look at them here. The clearer you can be about learning intentions, the better planned your lessons will be and the greater clarity and purpose you will be able to bring to your teaching. They also provide a key focus for lesson evaluation and increasingly so as you proceed through your ITE period.

Planning for learning is the function of lesson planning. That involves thinking through what the lesson aims to achieve, how learning might develop within the lesson and why. Knowing what the lesson aims to achieve lends a

TABLE 4.1 Two examples of generic lesson evaluation templates

Template one

What progress did pupils make in the lesson? (refer back to your aims & objectives for the lesson)

How do you know?

What were the factors affecting progress?

What will you do next time?

Template two

How effective do you feel your planning and teaching of the lesson were?

To what extent do you think the pupils understood and met the LOs for the lesson? (you may need to answer this after marking their work)

What might you do differently next time you teach this class or teach a similar lesson?

sense of direction and purpose to the planning process, and to the teaching of the lesson itself. Without this sense of direction it is difficult to start mapping out what lesson content will be needed, what we will be asking pupils to do and what the teacher will do to foster the learning that is to be achieved.

A clear sense of direction and pedagogic purpose, knowing why you are asking pupils to do the things you ask them to do, helps you to respond flexibly and appropriately to what happens in the lesson. For example, if pupils surprise you by knowing more than you had anticipated, then you might choose to skip parts of the lesson plan so that more time can be spent on more challenging activity; when pupils appear to know less than you had expected or struggle to learn as fast as you had anticipated, you might build in extra practice or you might explain a key point again.

In principle, the clearer you can be about learning intentions, not just the *what* but also the *why*, the better you will be able to plan the *how*. And yet, in practice, the formulation of learning intentions (or lesson aims and objectives) can be quite problematic especially for beginning teachers.

Formulating your lesson aims and objectives

In the early days of lesson planning, the whole idea of planning for learning and the concept of 'lesson objectives' can appear very abstract; and this can be an obstacle to lesson planning. One way round this, in the early stages, is to try and visualise what pupils will be doing by the end of the lesson or after a given period of learning; this should be something that they could not do or could not do as well at the start of the lesson. If pupils finish the lesson by completing a task they could have completed just as well at the start of the lesson, then what was the point of the lesson? For example, at the end of the Year 7 French lesson we saw in Chapter 3 (Table 3.4a), the plan is for pupils to conduct a questionnaire, using language that was presented and practised in the lesson. At the end of the Year 8 Spanish lesson (Table 3.5a), the plan is for pupils to assume different roles and take part in an interactive game, using language that was taught and practised in the lesson.

Starting at the end of the lesson, and visualising anticipated learning outcomes in this way can help beginning teachers identify the point of the lesson, and from there to formulate lesson aims and objectives. In the case of ML, this also includes anticipation of key language that we expect pupils to be using by the end of the lesson. The practice of scripting, introduced in Part II, helps beginning teachers to visualise what form that language might take.

In my experience, learning aims and objectives can sometimes be difficult to put into words at the lesson planning stage. In the early days, you might need to actually teach the lesson first and experience it before you can find the words to formulate your aims and objectives for that lesson (retrospectively). If this helps you, then I think that's fine, at least in the early days.

A word of caution

There are dangers in basing lesson aims and objectives *solely* on anticipated learning outcomes *all of the time*. This can encourage a rather reductionist view of learning and a rather superficial approach to lesson planning (John, 1991). Within the PPP model in ML, for example, there is the danger that such an approach might lead to only teaching pupils the minimum language they need in order to demonstrate progress by the end of the lesson. This would deny learners the opportunity to learn from exposure to multiple examples of the language they are learning, one of the most fundamental conditions for successful language learning. In other words, it would put a cap on the learning that is possible in the lesson. Another possible danger is that the teacher focuses only on learning outcomes that are demonstrable or measurable within the scope of one lesson. Again, there are dangers in viewing lesson planning and language learning in such terms.

I think it is also important to bear in mind that progress in ML can be rather a slow burner. Progress in the different language skills needs weeks or months to develop and manifest itself; and understanding of grammatical concepts *develops* rather than being achieved or reached by a set time. Consider, for example, how many lessons it might take for a class to spontaneously use the language needed to agree or disagree with what they hear or read; consider how long it took you to understand the concept of gender in French, German or Spanish.

Due to the nature of our subject, there are bound to be some ML lessons which cannot be planned in terms of neat learning objectives or intentions that are achievable by the end of a 60 minute lesson. Rather there will inevitably be some ML lessons, or bits of lessons, which are planned as steps in a longer-term progression of learning. Their aim is to enable all pupils to make some progress towards a longer- term learning goal. We will consider this further in Part III, where we will also consider longer-term planning.

Writing lesson plans

The lesson planning process usually results in written plans, at least for beginning teachers. There are important reasons why beginning teachers are expected to write lesson plans and these are summarised in Figure 4.2.

Such arguments underline the importance of written lesson plans for successful teaching during the early stages of the ITE period and for the continuing professional development of beginning teachers. It is also worth noting that lesson plans are not only written for yourself, the beginning teacher, they will also be read by tutors and mentors.

What to include in a lesson plan and how to present it

Universities and other training providers normally provide guidance on what information they expect to see included in a lesson plan. It is also usual to be given guidance on how to present lesson plans, and in some cases you will be given a particular template to use for this purpose.

However, in other cases the format of lesson plans is either left up to the beginning teacher or it can be negotiated. If you find yourself in either of these situations, you might want to try a few different formats until you find or adapt one that suits you. My own view is that the lesson plan should first and foremost be there to help the teacher. This is neatly summed up by educational consultant Mike Gershon: 'A good lesson plan should be a guide that enables a teacher to get to grips with what they are trying to achieve and why' (2013, p35). Many beginning teachers like to refer to their lesson plans when getting ready for lessons and in the lesson itself, to remind themselves of what they are planning to do and why. You might want to bear these points in mind when deciding what information to include and how to present it. In my experience, beginning teachers tend to tweak the template they use for lesson planning over the course of the PGCE year; extra headings are sometimes added or some are replaced. It is normal for your thinking and planning to change in the course of the ITE period and not everyone will think in the same way. I have included two examples of lesson plan templates, that have been useful to different beginning ML teachers I have worked with over the years (see Tables 4.2 and 4.3). These show two different layouts; please note these are intended purely as examples. I hope that the templates in Tables 4.2 and 4.3 might be useful to any readers who are in need of a template, and that they can be adapted as appropriate. For example, you might

- Writing focuses the mind and helps to clarify your thinking without undue haste.
- Writing helps you to see potential problems and to prepare solutions in advance.
- Writing is a chance to check any Subject Knowledge implications, such as spellings.
- A written plan gives you confidence when you go into the classroom.
- A written plan can act as a prompt in the classroom, helps you remember.
- A clearly written plan can be a lifeline in the classroom, especially under stress.
- A lesson plan provides a basis for lesson review/ evaluation after the lesson.
- A good plan stands the test of time and can be used again in subsequent years.
- Written plans enable you to achieve and maintain continuity, when teaching a series of classes and lessons.
- A written plan provides a record to refer back to; a collection of those provides a record of sustained teaching.
- Over time, written plans are indicative of your progress and contribute to your evidence base for QTS.

- Mentors need to know that you've planned the lessons you are going to teach.
- Your mentor may want to discuss and approve your lesson plans prior to teaching.
- Written plans provide a basis for feedback to you on your lesson planning.
- Written plans can inform lesson observations, providing the observer with an insight into your intentions and your thinking.
- Written plans can be a focus of the de-brief conversation following lesson observation.

FIGURE 4.2 Why is it important for beginning teachers to write lesson plans?

TABLE 4.2 Lesson plan template 1

Class:	Date:
Learning objectives:	Professional development target:
Context: Links with previous lesson(s): Links with future lesson(s):	Resources needed:
Key structures and vocabulary:	

Timing	Activities and purpose of activities	Target language	Assessment

TABLE 4.3 Lesson plan template 2

Class:	Date:	Time:	Topic:	Lesson no.:
Learning objective:	Language content:		Links to prior learning:	Homework:
				Date due:
Professional development objective:				

Time	Activity	Language / Instructions	Assessment / Monitoring

it helpful to split the 'activity' column in two, so you can separate 'what the teacher says and does' from 'what pupils say and do' at any given stage in the lesson.

Outline planning

I am a strong advocate of outline planning, writing an outline or draft lesson plan before committing yourself to a more detailed written plan. Outline planning can help you to order your first thoughts into a coherent format. This is not a formal document. Rather it is a tool to support further, more detailed planning and provides a basis for feedback.

It can be helpful to have a template to support outline planning, and especially if time is tight. Tables 4.4 and 4.5a below show examples of what such a proforma might look like. Although they are organised slightly differently, essentially both are structured around these three planning questions, borrowed from Mager (1968):

> Where am I going?
>
> How will I get there?
>
> How will I know I've arrived?

In addition, Table 4.5b shows a completed lesson outline, using the second template. This is based on the Year 8 Spanish presents lesson from Chapter 3 (Table 3.9a).

Finally, the planning of individual lessons does become easier and more purposeful once you start to plan sequences of lessons. This will be looked at more closely in Part III when we consider longer-term planning. For further generic guidance on lesson planning, including the planning cycle, I would recommend Capel et al. (2016).

Summing up Part II

We have examined in considerable detail what well-planned lessons might look like in relation to just one model of teaching (PPP) and the thinking behind these lessons. We've also stepped back to look at the bigger picture of planning as part of a cycle. It is important to think not only about the detail of what you are planning but also about why you are doing it. In Part III, we add to the bigger picture as we consider planning for a wider range of outcomes and for the longer term.

TABLE 4.4 Outline lesson planning template 1

Outline Lesson for Class .... Date ....

Lesson Aims/Objectives (*what you want pupils to learn/learn how to do*)

How will you know what pupils have learnt? (*main task lesson is leading up to/diagnostic assessment opportunities along the way*)

What learning opportunities will you set up and provide? (*stages of the lesson/timings - what will pupils be doing?*)

Main language content (*key structures and vocab/what language will pupils be using/ learning?*)

Planned teacher TL use (*including instructions/explanations*)

Key questions for plenary, as appropriate.

TABLE 4.5A Outline lesson planning template 2

Outline Lesson Plan for Class .... Date ....

Learning intentions for the lesson (*what learning is to be fostered – knowledge, skills, understanding?*)

Outline of lesson broken down into stages/linked episodes + approximate timings	Linguistic objectives (*what key structures and vocab will pupils be using/ learning?*)	Intended learning outcome/s by end of the lesson (*how will you know what pupils have learnt/progress towards learning intentions?*)

Resources needed:

TABLE 4.5B Completed outline lesson plan for Year 8 Spanish

Learning intentions for the lesson (*what learning is to be fostered – knowledge, skills, understanding?*)

- To start putting together sentences which combine vocab for presents with family members
- Behaviour for learning – keeping on task

Outline of lesson broken down into stages/linked episodes + approximate timings	Linguistic objectives (*what key structures and vocab will pupils be using/ learning?*)	Intended learning outcome/s by end of the lesson (*how will you know what pupils have learnt/ progress towards learning intentions?*)
<u>Revise names of presents</u> (10mins) Match picture to word Write the missing letters to complete the words <u>Recap family members</u> (5 mins) *¿Qué número es . . . ?* Repeat if true *¿Qué compras para tu familia?* (6–8mins) Use shopping list to introduce new structure, use mime and board to write up list – keep repeating '*para mi . . . compro . . .*' Practise new structure + picture cues (8 mins) Create a chain using '*para mi familia compro . . .*' each time adding on another present <u>Writing practice</u> (13–15 mins) As a class write up together sentences created as whole group – pupils copy down. Writing Activity Sheets – just 10 minutes – stress accuracy Go through answers in class, clarify any questions or points OXO (noughts and crosses) (5+ mins) *Time at start and finish to remind about behaviour expectations + discuss/feedback at end.*	<u>Los regalos</u> *Una gorra, camiseta, caja de bombones, caja de galletas, foto Un CD, poster, llavero* <u>Mi familia</u> *Padre, madre, hermano, hermana, tío, tía, abuelo, abuela* <u>Key question + answer</u> *¿Qué compras para tu familia?* *Para mi . . . compro . . .*	Class will have 10 minutes to write at least 3 accurate sentences using '*para me . . . compro . . .*' using differentiated written support if needed. OXO game – divide class into 2 teams. Need to say full sentence to get on square, using '*para mi . . . compro . . .*'. Sentences must be grammatically correct and correspond to given cues on grid. Expect to do from memory.

Resources needed: ppt presentation; exercise books; copies of differentiated written activity sheets

References for Part II

Alison, J. and Halliwell, S. (2002) *Challenging classes: focus on pupil behaviour*. Classic Pathfinder 2. CILT: London.
Ausubel, D.P. (1968) *Educational psychology: a cognitive view*. Holt, Rinehart & Winston: New York.
Barnes, A. and Hunt, M. (2003) *Effective assessment in MFL*. CILT: London.
Capel, S., Leask, M. and Younie, S. (eds.) (2016) *Learning to teach in the secondary school*. Seventh Edition. Routledge: London.
Christie, C. (2016) Speaking spontaneously in the modern foreign languages classroom: tools for supporting successful target language conversation. *The Language Learning Journal*, 44(1), pp74–89.
Convery, A. and Coyle, D. (2000) *Differentiation and individual learners: a guide for classroom practice*. Pathfinder 37. CILT: London.
Gershon, M. (2013) Avoid a sinking feeling with perfect planning. Article. *TES professional*, 29 November 2013, pp34–35.
Gibbons, P. (2014) *Scaffolding language, scaffolding learning: teaching second language in the mainstream classroom*. Second edition. Heinemann: Portsmouth.
John, P.D. (1991) A qualitative study of British student teachers' lesson planning perspectives. *Journal of Education for Teaching*, 17(30), pp301–320.
Jones, B. and Swarbrick, A. (2004) *It makes you think! Creating engagement, offering challenges*. New Pathfinder 4. CILT: London. Available from The Barry Jones Archive at: https://www.all-languages.org.uk/student/barry-jones-archive/ [accessed November 2018].
Jones, J. and Wiliam, D. (2008) *Modern foreign languages inside the black box*. GL Assessment: London.
Kyriacou, C. (2018) *Essential teaching skills*. Fifth edition. Oxford University Press: Oxford.
Littlewood, W. (1981) *Communicative language teaching*. Cambridge University Press: Cambridge.
Mager, R.F. (1968) *Developing attitude toward learning*. Fearon Publishers: Belmont, California.
Mutton, T., Hagger, H. and Burn, K. (2011) Learning to plan, planning to learn: the developing expertise of beginning teachers. *Teachers and Teaching*, 17(4), pp399–416.
Pachler, N., Evans, M., Redondo, A. and Fisher, L. (2014) *Learning to teach foreign languages in the secondary school*. Fourth edition. Routledge: London.
Rogers, B. (2012) *You know the fair rule: strategies for making the hard job of discipline in schools easier*. Third edition. Pearson Education Ltd.: Harlow, England.
Rogers, B. (2015) *Classroom behaviour*. Fourth edition. Sage Publications Ltd.: London.
Stern, H.H. (1983) *Fundamental concepts of language teaching*. Oxford University Press: Oxford.

PART

Planning for a balanced language learning experience

Introduction to Part III

So far, lessons have been based on a simple PPP model of language teaching. Lessons have largely been planned to promote pupils' ability to produce language in relatively controlled contexts, based mainly on a behaviourist view of language learning, and with some scope for informal language acquisition through exposure to the teacher's TL output. However, relying on this model *all of the time* might result in rather a narrow understanding of language learning and a rather limited view of the ML curriculum. For example, it does not take account of explicit grammar teaching, creativity or culture.

I would argue that if all pupils are to reach their full potential for language learning in the classroom, then it is important that over time we plan lessons which allow for a variety of learning experiences and possible outcomes, using alternative pedagogical approaches. In other words, a core diet of PPP based lessons needs to be supplemented from time to time with other approaches and outcomes in order to provide pupils with a balanced language learning experience.

Part III therefore looks beyond PPP lessons to the bigger picture of ML teaching and learning. The aim is to deepen understanding of the range of different learning outcomes that are possible within our subject and also develop understanding of what is involved in planning for progression in learning within *and* across lessons.

CHAPTER 5

Different sorts of ML lessons

Introduction

Over time, ML lesson planning might focus on different sorts of learning outcomes; ones that differ from those inherent in a simple PPP model and outcomes that differ from each other. Figure 5.1 gives some examples of possible learning outcomes; these have been taken from the lesson plans of beginning teachers.

By the end of the lesson I want pupils to be able to …

- Use prepositions with the dative to describe the position of objects in a room.
- Ask and answer questions about what they like to eat, based on nine food items.
- *Pouvoir utiliser le passé compose pour parler des objets perdus*
- Act out a telephone conversation, based on the model we have been practising.
- Write a detailed and accurate paragraph about their school timetable in French.
- Know key facts about *Karneval* and how it is celebrated in Germany.
- Write sentences in Spanish about what there is and what there isn't in their town.
- Ask and answer questions about what they did in the holidays, using cue cards.
- Know how to make colours agree with nouns in Spanish and use this to talk about pets they have or would like to have.
- Develop strategies to become a more independent learner and to use those strategies to correct their own work.
- Write the first draft of a fairy story which incorporates the imperfect tense of the verbs we have been practising.
- Inquire about the weather in different parts of Germany and to learn the German for at least 6 different types of weather.
- Build extended sentences in French about what they do in their free time and when and with whom.
- Describe a city of their choice, using some key phrases that can be used in the tourism pamphlet that we're going to make at the end of this unit.
- Recognise and name different places at the train station.
- Understand the difference between the use of the preterite and imperfect tenses in Spanish.
- Listen to a recording and pick out information about directions to places in town.
- Correct a written text in German by putting in the capital letters.
- Solve a murder mystery in French, using their knowledge of the perfect tense.
- Give their opinion of two poems written by Jacques Prévert.

FIGURE 5.1 Intended learning outcomes: some examples (taken from lesson plans written by beginning teachers)

Different sorts of ML lessons

In fact, this is just a snapshot; but even from this list we can see that learning in ML includes much more than simply learning vocabulary and structures. Learning French, for example, is so much more than literally 'knowing the French for ...'. Within the scope of this book it is not possible to look at the complete range of learning outcomes that are conceivably possible within our subject. Instead, this chapter will concentrate on planning for just a few elements of the ML curriculum, drawn largely from the National Curriculum for ML. These may be taught less frequently than the standard PPP type lessons, but they are necessary to ensure a balanced 'diet' of language learning and to bring out the best in all of our linguists. The main areas are culture, grammar, creativity, literature and independent learning.

My rationale for choosing these particular elements relates to the landscape of ML education in England at the time of writing. The landscape is one that takes us from Key Stage 2, when children start to learn another language at the age of six or seven, right up to A-level at age 18 or 19. Within this context, language learning is conceived as being cumulative and progressive. There is an upwards trajectory here, with three key sets of documents that inform the longer-term planning of secondary ML teachers:

- The National Curriculum Programme of Study for languages at Key Stage 3;
- GCSE exam specifications for individual languages;
- A-level specifications for individual languages.

At the national level, each of the above has been designed to build on what has gone before and to prepare learners for the next stage in their language learning careers. The areas that I have chosen each contribute to expected progression in learning across the Key Stages to A-level. If language learning is to be cumulative and progressive, then it is important to start integrating these elements of the curriculum into our schemes of work early on, rather than bolting them on when the exam looms, or when the inspector calls, and hoping for the best!

This chapter is organised into self-contained sections. Each section has its own focus and is supported by different sources from practice, including examples of lesson plans and teaching resources. This is outlined in Table 5.1.

The value of culture

> Learning a foreign language is a liberation from insularity and provides an opening to other cultures. A high-quality languages education should foster pupils' curiosity and deepen their understanding of the world.
> (Department for Education, 2013, p1)

These are the opening words of the current Programme of Study for languages at Key Stage 3. According to the National Curriculum in England, opening up to other cultures is a crucially important part of the contribution that ML makes to the school curriculum. However, the development of intercultural understanding is not easy to assess. We should not use this as an excuse to avoid including cultural elements wherever possible in our teaching. Not everything that is worth learning is assessable and intercultural understanding may be a case in point.

TABLE 5.1 Overview of Chapter 5

Focus of the narrative	Accompanying lesson plan/ Supporting source
The value of culture	Year 9 French
	Year 6 French
The importance of grammar	Year 9 German
	Year 10 German
	Story in French
	Planning Grid for teaching the perfect tense in French
Cultivating creativity	Examples from practice
Exploiting literature	Year 8 French
Learning from authentic sources	Example of an authentic resource
Independent learning and developing metacognitive awareness	Year 10 French

> The importance of developing an awareness of and respect for others is without question.
>
> (Jones, 1995, p32)

It is important therefore that ML lessons include opportunities to foster pupils' curiosity and deepen their understanding of the world. Sometimes those opportunities need only take up a few minutes of lesson time; very often they are incidental to the main linguistic content of the lesson. And yet they can be very powerful. For example, the impact of cultural images and the value of talk about those should not be underestimated or ignored. I can illustrate this with an example from my own teaching experience. The example involves a small, bottom set Year 8 French class. I was very fond of this class because they all gave 100% effort and the group included a number of 'characters'. On this particular occasion, it was the last lesson on a Friday afternoon, we were doing the topic of Daily Routine. We had just watched together a short video film showing a typical school day in the life of a French teenage boy called Frank. The class had watched the film and picked out the times mentioned when Frank did different routine tasks. By this stage there were still about ten minutes left of our French lesson – I had underplanned! I decided to ask the class what else they had noticed in the film about Frank's daily routine. Pupils responded in English; for the most part they picked up on fairly obvious features of his everyday life, such as the fact that he didn't wear school uniform. After a bit, one of the deeper thinkers in the class, Martin, spoke. Before watching the film Martin had not realised that French people might find it difficult to speak English. This was a reference to Frank's repeated difficulty in pronouncing the 'th' sound in his English lesson. Whilst Martin spoke we listened in silence and wonderment. I think most, if not all, of us had never thought about this before. It was like a light bulb moment. And after Martin had spoken, there was a lively class discussion about whether the French really were better at learning languages than we were!

What was happening here was that the class were experiencing 'otherness'. As Barry Jones explains:

> When 'otherness' is experienced at first hand it can prompt all kinds of questions not only about 'others' but also about ourselves and whether we wish to take on or be part of that 'otherness' or not. It can point to differences and similarities which challenge or conform what we already know and feel. It very frequently questions what we believe to be true. for some, 'otherness' is worth exploring, whereas for others contact with it may bring about or even confirm a reluctance to venture into the realms of the unfamiliar and close off not only new worlds but also questions about ourselves.
>
> (Jones, 1995, p1)

I realised from this lesson that developing cultural and intercultural awareness is not only about appreciating what makes us different from others, it is also about recognising what we have in common. I realised from the insights shared in this bottom set class that the development of intercultural understanding is something that all pupils are capable of and benefit from. Finally, I also understood that experiences that change your view of the world stay with you.

This is why I have chosen to start this section by looking at two lessons which contain significant cultural content. Alongside language learning objectives, both lessons draw on different cultural images and content in order to foster pupils' curiosity and deepen their understanding of the world. It is important when including cultural content in ML lessons that we do not privilege just one country where the target language is spoken. The lessons which follow are French lessons. The first (Table 5.2a) focuses on aspects of culture and society in Morocco and Switzerland; the second (Table 5.3a) introduces French speaking artists from France and Belgium. The second lesson also introduces some of the ideas associated with CLIL (Content and Language Integrated Learning) which I will return to separately.

TABLE 5.2A Year 9 French lesson plan: '*Tu préférerais visiter le Maroc ou la Suisse?*'

Year 9 French class. This was lesson 6 in a unit of work '*Ma Région*', covering places in town, *il y a. . . il n'y a pas de. . .*, adjectives to describe places, advantages and disadvantages of where you live. In the last lesson pupils were introduced to *on peut/on pourrait* with key verbs linked to tourist activities. They are familiar with peer assessment and Venn diagrams; and are used to collaborative learning.

LO: To be able to talk about what you can or could do in two different francophone countries

Ongoing LO: To be able to express opinions in French

Key structures	New vocabulary
Tu préférerais visiter le Maroc ou la Suisse?	*Déguster du thé à la menthe/les spécialités culinaires*
Je préfère . . . parce que	*Se promener dans le désert/dans les montagnes*
On peut/On pourrait + infinitive + complement	*Jouer au casino/au football sur la plage*
Recycled opinion phrases: *je pense que . . . je crois que . . . à mon avis . . .*	

1. Reactivation of previous learning – *C'est quelle ville? Pourquoi?*

    Music in background as class arrive and settle. Brief description of Paris already on board. Pupils write on mini-boards which place they think this is and why. Encourage pupils to use *je pense que* etc. *Quels sont les mots clés?* Take multiple answers (no hands).

2. Big Question and register – *Tu préférerais visiter le Maroc ou la Suisse?*

    Whole class repeat question. Use pupil interpreter to translate question. Pupils write an answer to the Big Question on post-it – to be reviewed at the end of lesson. Ask some pupils the question.

3. Preparation for video activity

    Pictures of Morocco and Switzerland displayed on board. For each picture ask *C'est la Suisse ou le Maroc?* No hands. Encourage pupils to use *je pense que c'est . . .* etc.

    Venn diagram in pairs – *C'est le Maroc? La Suisse? Ou les deux?*

    Sentences to classify, most of which use *on peut* or *il y a/il n'y a pas de . . .* Timed with Moroccan music. Extension – add more sentences using *on peut . . .* Whole class feedback taken.

4. Video activity

    Pupils watch short video clips promoting Morocco and Switzerland as holiday destinations. Write down what you can do in each country. Example provided on sheet using *On peut . . . .* Two levels of difficulty, pupils choose. Before first viewing one minute to read through sheets and try to predict which verbs are needed. Before second viewing compare answers with partner. Whole class feedback – no hands. Answers then flashed up.

    Finally ask *Tu as préféré la publicité pour le Maroc ou pour la Suisse? Pourquoi?*

5. Writing task – improving answer to the Big Question + Post-it notes

    Show model answer to the Big Question. Read together. Elicit success criteria, write up on board. Pupils have a few minutes to improve the answers they wrote at start of lesson. Extension – write a second note about why you prefer not to visit the other country.

6. Peer assessment

    Pupils swap post-it notes with a partner and peer assess using the success criteria on board. Check all have put names on their own work. Collect in.

7. Homework (HW)

    Design a promotional poster for a francophone country to attract visitors. (Previous HW was a webquest to find information about a francophone country.) Hand out HW task sheet.

Copyright material from Cheryl Mackay (2019), *Learning to Plan Modern Languages Lessons*, Routledge

TABLE 5.2B Commentary on Year 9 French lesson: '*Tu préférerais visiter le Maroc ou la Suisse?*'

This lesson was planned by a beginning teacher, a few weeks into her second (long) teaching placement. It is a well-structured, ambitious plan; the thinking behind it shows a high level of sophistication, especially for a beginning teacher.

The first point to note is that the lesson was planned with two learning goals in mind: one is specific to that particular lesson, the other is an ongoing longer-term goal. I will return to the idea of 'longer-term goals' later in Section 2.

The linguistic content of the lesson is difficult to separate from the cultural context of Francophonie. It would be possible for pupils to learn how to use *on peut* + infinitive + complement without any reference to other countries but the cultural input has been planned to add an extra layer of learning and provide links to the wider world. The authentic pictures and video clips, including extracts of Moroccan music, bring alive the content of the lesson. Pupils are not only learning forms of the French language and how to use them, through the medium of French they are also learning about the wider world and expressing their opinions about what they see and hear.

All of the authentic resources used are readily available on the internet; incidentally the promotional videos had no speaking, just music and film. However, it is not the resources themselves that make most difference to learning, but how the teacher has planned to use them. Of particular note on the plan is how pupils are prepared for the video activity. By the time they come to view the video they have already started to form some idea about what they can expect to hear and see, and they are equipped with the language needed to be able to express this.

It is important to note that the integration of cultural elements has not been planned at the expense of linguistic progression or progress in language learning. Within the lesson, there is still evidence of a suitably scaffolded PPP sequence leading to pupils producing sentences that they were not able to produce at the start of the lesson (point 2 – point 5). This progression is based on language learnt in this and the previous lesson. For example, it is worth noting that *on peut/on pourrait* were introduced in the previous lesson. The Venn diagram activity helps to consolidate those structures from last lesson and at the same time provides multiple examples of their use with a wider range of vocabulary, some of which is new. Pupils are learning the language by using it. In addition, the extension tasks that have been planned to challenge high achievers relate directly to the main LO for the lesson and call for further language manipulation.

<u>Follow-up Reflective Task/Points to discuss</u>

As part of the planning for this lesson, a model answer to the Big Question was prepared to share with pupils, at point 5. If you were teaching this lesson, what would or could that model answer look like? Try and identify three success criteria that you would have. For example, you might want to consider length, particular structures to use, what sort of information to include. Then draft a possible answer to discuss with someone else who has done the same task.

If you are teaching German or Spanish alternative Big Questions might be:

Möchtest du lieber die Schweiz oder Österreich besuchen?   **¿*Preferirías visitar Perú o Costa Rica?***

Copyright material from Cheryl Mackay (2019), *Learning to Plan Modern Languages Lessons*, Routledge

TABLE 5.3A Year 6 French CLIL lesson plan: 'French speaking painters'

This was a one-off lesson taught to a Year 6 mixed ability French class in a middle school. The class have been learning French for two years, two lessons a week. Their French teacher is a linguist; she has a PGCE in teaching French. They have recently been learning the colours + agreements.

Linguistic LO: To be able to use simple French to talk about paintings

Content LO: To be able to recognise the painting styles of a range of four French speaking painters

Key language	Key names
Il y a + un/ une/ des . . .	Henri Rousseau, Georges Seurat,
Colours + agreements	René Magritte, Paul Cézanne,
Je préfère/j'aime/je n'aime pas le tableau de . . .	
Car c'est bizzare, fantastique, triste, intéressant, mulitcolore, super.	
Car il y a beaucoup de couleurs, des animaux, des fruit, des personnes.	

1 Bell-task – ppt slide + four different paintings

   Discuss with person next to you – what might today's lesson be about? And say why.

2 Starter – ppt slide + names of four painters

   Tell your partner how you would say these names in French. Take feedback. Choral repetition, revise sound-spelling links (**H**enri, George**s** etc). Who do you think these people are?

3 Revision of colours

   Tell your partner how many colours you remember. Competition – which pair can name the most colours in French in one minute. Ping-pong + colours. Model first with three examples.

   C'est quelle couleur? + PPt slide, pupils say each colour as revealed, choral repetition of each.

4 Focus on one painting (Henri Rousseau – man on tiger) – up on ppt

   Competition – tell your partner in French all the things you can see in this painting. Write them down. Show example (*il y a un tigre orange*) – any words possible as long as pupils can justify their choice. Pupils feedback ideas – write up on board in sentences.

5 Phrase matrix – in groups of 4 match up phrases to paintings on A3 handout

   Pupil handout has four paintings from start of lesson, each with name of painter. Phrases are on strips of card, read phrase and decide where to place it on matrix. Do example to model. *Il y a un tigre orange* is placed on part of matrix for Henri Rousseau. Most phrases can be accessed via colour vocab only. Check answers – read out phrase and ask pupils to say name of painter. Sum up each painter's key features. *Alors, dans les tableaux de Henri Rousseau il y a des animaux etc.*

6 Opinions of paintings *Quel tableau préfères-tu?* + model on ppt

   Model pronunciation of Q+ possible answers. Then do example. Pupils follow model and tell partner which painting they like best and why. Feedback to rest of class – time dependent.

7 Create your own picture in the style of . . .

   Show one I did earlier. *Mon tableau est dans le style de René Magritte. Il y a des bananes. C'est un peu bizzare.* Stress importance of key features (*il y a beaucoup de couleurs, des animaux, des fruits, des personnes*), not brilliant colouring at this stage. Pupils draw their interpretation of one artist's style. *Montrez les tableaux.* Pupils use ppt as model to give opinion of peers' work.

8 Plenary – Elicit name of painter + key features of his style *Qui est le peintre et pourquoi?* – ppt

   Each slide has five paintings by one painter. Pupils select name of painter from three options.

9 Final Reflections – what do you think today's objectives were? What have you learnt?

   Tell your partner, 30 seconds. Receive feedback. Provide feedback to class.

Copyright material from Cheryl Mackay (2019), *Learning to Plan Modern Languages Lessons*, Routledge

TABLE 5.3B Commentary on Year 6 French CLIL lesson

This lesson was collaboratively planned and taught by a small group of beginning teachers, as a one-off CLIL lesson. None of them had taught this class or this age group before. The lesson plan illustrates some of the features of a typical CLIL lesson, as understood by these beginning teachers, and some of the key planning decisions made. The first point to note is that the lesson was planned with two learning goals in mind: one is French subject specific, learning French, the other relates to the content of the lesson, learning about famous French speaking artists.

In terms of French, there are three points I would make. First of all correct pronunciation of the names of painters is prioritised and exploited as an opportunity to revise sound-spelling links, especially knowledge of silent letters in French. Secondly, a new structure [*il y a . . .*] is introduced in context, and pupils learn it by using it to talk about what they can see in the paintings. Before collecting ideas as a class, pupils have the opportunity to share ideas with a partner. Even just a few seconds thinking time like this can help to generate even more and even better ideas so that everyone can contribute to the whole class feedback (point 4). Repeating what pupils have said and writing their ideas up on the board in sentences implicitly adds to their French learning and gives an important message to pupils that their ideas are valued. The focus here is very much of what pupils want to say, rather than how they are saying it. In the actual lesson, pupils responded very well to this task – there was lots of animated talk and the teacher accepted all answers. Here are some of the ideas that pupils came up with: *orange, un chapeau noir, la tête blanche, les fleurs multi-colores, les plantes vertes, il y a un lion, il fait beau, il joue de la guitarre.*

The third French point to note is that PowerPoint is used to provide a talking frame, or model, to scaffold some of the pupil-pupil talk, see points 6 and 7. Again, this helps pupils to focus their attention on what they want to say to each other rather than trying to remember the French for how to say it.

In terms of the art content of the lesson, learning was greatly helped by the preparation of some very clear, coloured resources; images of the paintings were downloaded from the internet and used on ppt slides, and on A3 sized sheets for the group task at point 5.

This lesson plan shows thorough planning and preparation, which help to maintain a good pace in the lesson and makes it more likely that pupils leave the lesson with a sense of achievement.

Postscript. When the class teacher took the class back again she decided to let pupils have more time to complete the drawings they had drafted in this lesson. The influence of the painters they had briefly looked at in this lesson was very definitely there in some of their work; a sample of which was reproduced in the school's termly newsletter together with comments from the 'artists' themselves. The lesson had clearly made an impact on pupils' knowledge and understanding of art.

<u>Follow-up Reflective Task/Points to discuss</u>

This was a one-off CLIL lesson. How might you develop the same theme across a series of three lessons with the same class? What potential can you see for developing both the art and the linguistic content across those lessons?

How might you develop this as a one-off CLIL lesson for a KS3 or KS4 class? What changes might you need to make? Discuss your ideas with others.

Copyright material from Cheryl Mackay (2019), *Learning to Plan Modern Languages Lessons*, Routledge

These two lesson plans show different ways of planning to integrate cultural elements into ML teaching and learning. The first lesson is planned around one Big Question which pulls together the main linguistic and cultural content of the lesson. The second lesson is planned with both cultural and linguistic LOs in mind in accordance with a CLIL approach.

In my experience, to divorce language teaching lower down the school from any reference to or any discussion of the cultures where that language is spoken is to miss a trick. And especially in view of the increased focus at A-level on the culture and society of the countries where the language is spoken. In the final exam, A-level linguists are assessed on their ability to:

> Show knowledge and understanding of, and respond critically and analytically to, different aspects of the culture and society of countries/communities where the language is spoken.
>
> (Ofqual, 2017, p14)

This is one of the assessment objectives at A-level and counts for 20% of the final grade.

Quite apart from that, for some pupils it is the combination of linguistic input with cultural input rather than the purely linguistic aspects that holds most interest and that can be deeply motivating. It is not by chance that Dörnyei and Csizér include 'Familiarize learners with the target language culture' (1998, p218) as one of their ten commandments for motivating language learners. I know from my own school experience that what motivated me to continue with Latin was more to do with a curiosity to find out more about the Romans and the Roman way of life than any particular love of Latin as a language. From my teaching experience, I have known pupils who opted to continue with German to AS or A-level precisely because they wanted to find out more about the Germans and to learn first-hand about the Berlin Wall. To omit cultural elements from our lesson planning would be to impoverish the next generation, deprive them of learning experiences that might change their view of the world and their understanding of what it means to be human. That said, in terms of language learning, we do need to be clear that a focus on culture and society should not be instead of or at the expense of linguistic input; rather, the trick is to develop cultural awareness and linguistic competence simultaneously.

For more on teaching and learning culture please see Pachler et al. (2014); their conceptual frame for sequencing culture-related activities is of particular relevance here.

A word about planning for CLIL

This is how CLIL is defined in the National Guidelines:

> Content and Language Integrated Learning describes a pedagogic approach in which language and subject area content are learnt in combination. The generic term CLIL describes any learning activity where language is used as a tool to develop new learning from a subject area or theme.
>
> Within the CLIL classroom, language and subject area content have complementary value. Learners process and use language to acquire new knowledge and skills and as they do so they make progress in both language and subject area content.
>
> (Coyle et al., 2009, p6)

For me, CLIL can be a useful vehicle for more fully integrating cultural elements into ML lessons. It is, however, not limited to the teaching of 'culture'; in principle any subject content (e.g. history, geography, science) can be taught through a CLIL approach. For further discussion of CLIL, including implications for planning, please see Coyle et al. (2010). I would also recommend Bower (2017) for further discussion of the motivational value of CLIL and insights into pupils' perceptions of CLIL in state secondary schools in England.

The importance of grammar

A little grammar teaching, appropriately planned, can go a long way. Imagine if you will that planning for language learning is like baking a cake, not just any cake but a beautiful fruit cake filled with exotic spices and fruits. In my opinion, the single most important ingredient to go into that cake mix is the raising agent, or baking powder. You don't need a lot of it: add too much and all the fruit will sink to the bottom; don't add enough and the cake won't rise. The trick is to get just the right amount and so it is with grammar teaching. Sometimes the smallest ingredient makes the biggest difference.

To be clear, what we are looking at here are lessons which illustrate an explicit approach to the teaching and learning of specific grammar points. The main learning objective in each case is grammar related. This is different from some of the other lesson plans included in this book, where the main learning objective is couched in terms of communicative ability or skills and which rely on a more implicit approach to grammar teaching and learning.

The role of grammar is central to any discussion of ML teaching and learning. Developing control of the language system to convey meaning with an ever increasing range of vocabulary and in an ever increasing range of situations and contexts is central to the aims of the Programmes of Study and all ML examination specifications at all levels. *How* that control might best be achieved is another matter. This is where viewpoints can fundamentally differ. Macaro discusses three main approaches that might be used to develop 'the patterns in the heads of our learners' (2014, p111). He refers to these as follows:

1 natural interaction
2 implicit form-focused exposure and practice
3 explicit teaching of grammar rules

(Macaro, 2014, pp111–115).

Essentially, some would argue that developing control of the language happens unconsciously; others would assert the very opposite; and yet another group still takes the view that both implicit and explicit learning processes are possible in the ML classroom. It is well beyond the scope of this book to go into the different theoretical positions relating to the teaching of grammar. Nevertheless, understanding the role of grammar within communicative language teaching is a fascinating subject and I do recommend to beginning teachers to embrace this as an intellectual challenge. Informing and developing your own views on how to deal with grammar is part of becoming a languages teacher; it goes to the very heart of the view of language learning that informs your practice and will have a huge impact on your planning. A good starting place for starting to get your head around some of the theoretical issues is Macaro (2014).

What I would like to examine here are some related points over which there is perhaps rather less controversy. Firstly, scholars and experts tend to agree that it is possible for learners to consciously learn rules of grammar; and most of them accept that knowledge of rules of grammar can be helpful to learners in non-spontaneous communication. In the short term, for example, learners can use their grammatical knowledge to monitor the accuracy of their written work and spoken output (especially controlled, prepared acts of speaking), as well as to deduce meanings such as the meanings of unknown words in texts they are reading. However, it can take a much longer time before consciously learnt grammar points become deeply internalised so that they are available for spontaneous communication or less controlled speaking and writing. So, even if it appears that pupils have 'got it', much recycling and practising of particular grammar points will almost certainly be needed before pupils are able to apply their understanding in order to use the language 'purposefully, appropriately, creatively and accurately' (Johnstone, 1994, p9).

The second point is that learners are likely to benefit most if we teach grammar that helps them to make the language their own, and use it to grasp or express meanings that matter personally to them (Hawkins, 1999; Dearing and King, 2007). This is an important point for motivation; learners are likely to be more inclined to learn the grammar if they can see a purpose for using it. It is also an important point for ensuring that pupils make progress in their language learning. Some grammar rules or patterns are potentially more useful than others. Verbs, for example, make a huge difference to the meaning of what we say or write; learning how to conjugate verbs and use them to convey different time frames or tenses can make a significant difference to what pupils are able to use the language to do. This applies both to both comprehension and production skills. More specifically, some frequently used verbs have a high communicative value, in that they can be used to generate multiple meanings and can be used in a range of different situations and contexts. In French, for example, this might include the verbs '*aller*', '*être*' and '*avoir*'; not only are these frequently used verbs in their own right, they also function as auxiliary verbs when forming future and past tenses. These are examples of useful grammar; knowing the grammar of auxiliary verbs allows learners to successfully manipulate the language for their own purposes.

In contrast, other grammatical features that pupils use may be best learnt as 'an unanalysed whole' or 'prefabricated chunk' (Mitchell and Myles, 1998, p12). In French, for example, this might apply to the construction '*il me faut . . .*' which can be used by both teacher and pupils within the context of everyday interactions in the classroom. The teacher might use the construction to let the class know she needs volunteers (e.g. *il me faut un volontaire*); pupils might use it in order to let others know that they don't have or need a particular item (e.g. *il me faut du papier*). The point is that pupils can learn this construction as a sort of formula without, at least in the short term, needing any explicit teaching about the underlying grammar. The SLA literature indicates that a balance of both these approaches is appropriate. For example, Ellis (2005) suggests that curriculum plans should cater for the development of both formulaic expressions (such as *il me faut* ... above) and rule-based knowledge (e.g. forming the perfect tense in French).

To sum up, when planning for grammar teaching, it is useful to prioritise high frequency patterns with high generative value, unless you have a special reason for doing otherwise. Even more important is that alongside grammar teaching, we also plan opportunities for pupils to manipulate and use their grammatical knowledge to generate language of their own. We will consider this last point further in the section on creativity.

There are important implications here for long-term planning. How do schools decide what grammar to teach explicitly? And what grammar to teach implicitly? To what extent are pupils taught unanalysed chunks? These are very good questions for beginning teachers to ask of departments they are placed in. The responses will give you an insight into how the departments view the place or role of grammar within ML teaching and learning.

Against this background, the following lesson plan introduces pupils to a distinctive feature of the German language; namely word order in subordinate clauses, in this case after '*weil*' (meaning 'because'). This is an example of a grammatical rule that may take many, many years to convert into spontaneous and accurate productive use, even with repeated exposure and opportunities for practice. In the short term, however, knowledge of word order and where to look for the verb in clauses beginning with '*weil*' will help with reading comprehension, as well as with the ability to write compound sentences in German which are grammatically correct.

TABLE 5.4A Year 9 German lesson plan: introducing word order with '*weil*'

Year 9 mixed ability German class in a high achieving school. The class had been learning German since the start of the school year, one lesson a week, as a second language. The previous lesson had covered likes and dislikes, within the context of hobbies, and giving reasons with '*denn*'. The class are already familiar with the full present tense paradigm of regular verbs in German.

LO: To know what '*weil*' means and how to use it in a sentence to give reasons for what we like or don't like doing

Key language from previous lesson	NEW
Ich höre gern Musik denn ich finde das entspannend.	*Ich höre gern Musik, weil ich das entspannend finde.*
Ich spiele nicht gern Tennis denn ich bin nicht sportlich.	*Ich spiele nicht gern Tennis, weil ich nicht sportlich bin.*

1 LO

   Unsere Lernziele für diese Stunde: Was machst du gern? Warum? Explain in German then check comprehension through translation.

2 Starter: vocabulary revision/ introduction of some new items

   Match German with English – 8x reasons for liking/disliking activities; then create German sentences using '*denn*' based on picture cues with reasons just seen. Extension – make up more sentences of your own. [5 mins allowed]

   Check + Smartboard – nominate pupils to read out German

3 Listening activity

   (i) Listen and note keywords related to hobbies, then compare notes with partner

   (ii) Listen again and complete table – what activity does each person like doing and the reason

   Play 2x pausing after each segment

   Check + Smartboard

4 Focus on '*weil*' + transcript

   Listen and follow, underline the sentences which give reasons. In pairs, 30 seconds to discuss which word is used instead of '*denn*' and if they notice anything strange about these sentences.

   Display key sentences from the transcript on Smartboard and ask pupils to feedback on what they noticed. Encourage to think about the position of the verb + use of comma.

5 Explanation of '*weil*' – the vile monster!

   Display a series of slides explaining the rule, using monster analogy. Show some examples, pupils predict what will happen to the sentence – read out complete sentence. Check correct pronunciation of '*weil*'.

6 Human Dominoes – whole class practise word order with '*weil*'

   Hand mini whiteboards with one word written on to several pupils = two sentences. Nominate one pupil to play the '*weil*' monster and one to be the comma. Pupils get themselves into the correct order at the front to form two sentences, with help from those still seated. Class reads out the two sentences. T shouts out '*Passt auf! Monster und Komma kommen!*' Pupils who are the monster and comma arrive. The verb gets a fright and runs to the end of the sentence. Meanwhile quick changes to mini-boards – full stop becomes comma and capital at start of second clause becomes lower case. Class reads out the new sentence. Repeat same activity 2–3 times more with other pupils and using different reasons.

7 Individual writing practice using '*weil*' – worksheet

   Pupils combine short sentences using '*weil*', then compare with partner. Some sentences using '*wir*' and '*sie*' are provided as an extension. [task timed for 4 mins]

   Answers checked collectively on Smartboard.

8 Homework – further consolidation

   Sentences with '*weil*' to translate into English + sentences to translate into German using '*weil*'.

   Extension – *Warum lieben wir Deutsch?* Pupils suggest as many answers as possible using '*weil*'.

Copyright material from Cheryl Mackay (2019), *Learning to Plan Modern Languages Lessons*, Routledge

TABLE 5.4B Commentary on Year 9 German lesson: introducing word order with '*weil*'

This lesson was planned and taught by a beginning teacher on her first teaching placement. Following the departmental scheme of work, she was asked to introduce and teach '*weil*', using familiar vocabulary within the context of hobbies. There are a number of reasons why this was a well-planned and prepared grammar lesson. The first of these is that through her planning this teacher demonstrates a very secure understanding of this particular grammar point.

It should be pointed out that the listening material used in the lesson had been written by the teacher herself and recorded by the school's German language assistant, with this particular lesson in mind. In the short text, a German girl introduces herself and her family with information about what hobbies they all do and reasons for doing those. The text includes six instances of the new grammatical pattern ('*weil*' + changed word order). The thinking behind this was to increase pupil exposure to the new grammatical pattern in use, through listening and reading the transcript.

There is a very clear structure, showing how the teacher plans to make the implicit explicit. It is worth looking in detail at this process and the planned sequence of activities (points 4, 5 and 6).

The process starts with pupils looking at the transcript from the listening exercise and noticing the pattern for themselves. Significantly, the teacher tells the class where to look (the sentences which give reasons) but not what to see. Comparing notes briefly with a partner is an opportunity to involve everyone in talk about the language; and displaying key sentences on the Smartboard, when pupils feedback, confirms for everyone what the grammatical pattern looks like.

The new grammar point is made more explicit at points 5 and 6. For example, the analogy made with a vile monster brings the abstract to life in a memorable way; and the use of PowerPoint technology provides a very visual demonstration of changes to word order when '*weil*' is used. Similarly, human dominoes and the idea of moving words around reaffirms the message that words are not static. Verbs don't always come after the subject; German word order is different from English.

At each step along the way, learners are involved in reading out complete sentences: hearing and seeing the new word order helps to reinforce the pattern and enables pupils to take in the new grammar as chunks of language. These steps help prepare learners for the written exercise at point 7. By this stage, pupils have been exposed primarily to instances of '*weil*' with verbs in the first and third person singular; extension tasks bring in other parts of the verb (points 7 and 8) and scope for more independent language production, using the new grammar point.

Follow-up Reflective Task/Points to discuss

Can you think of other examples in French, German or Spanish where the idea of human dominoes or moving words around could be used or exploited?

In this lesson 'weil' is introduced as a synonym of denn. Can you think of other grammar points that might be introduced in a similar way? Perhaps as another, more sophisticated way of saying something that learners are already familiar with? This lesson uses the analogy of a monster to explain how word order changes after 'weil'. Can you think of other analogies that could be used to explain other grammatical concepts? In what ways can devices such as these support learners in their grammar learning?

Copyright material from Cheryl Mackay (2019), *Learning to Plan Modern Languages Lessons*, Routledge

Explicit grammar teaching, or an explicit focus on form, is one way of capitalising on learners' relative cognitive maturity, in particular their ability to understand and talk about how language works. In my opinion, that process includes conversations about why it is useful to have some knowledge of the underlying rules; and the expectation that over time, learners become increasingly accurate in their language use. Inevitably conversations about grammar and accuracy lead to debates about error correction.

Error correction and implications for planning

Beginning teachers can sometimes be overzealous in correcting grammatical errors that they hear or see! But to correct every possible error *all of the time* is not helpful. Such an approach can be detrimental to pupils' progress and harmful to their self-efficacy and self-confidence, especially in speaking the language; ultimately the fear of getting it wrong might prevent pupils from even having a go. Quite apart from that, it is also hugely misleading to suggest to learners that they need to be 100% accurate all of the time. This simply does not reflect the reality of how language is spoken and used outside of the school classroom; more importantly, to insist on 100% accuracy all of the time quite misrepresents the whole experience of learning a language successfully. Indeed, Macaro suggests that 'teachers will need to accept that learners' productions may get worse before they can get better' (2014, p115) and Littlewood regards errors as 'a completely normal phenomenon in the development of communication skills' (1981, p94).

Errors and mistakes are part of the learning process and are to be expected especially if we want to encourage learners to take risks in generating their own language. On the other hand, however, never to correct any errors at all is not helpful either. The risk with that is that misconceptions abound and pupils end up with an error strewn mishmash of language rather than developing control of the language system.

Your approach to errors is something to think through as part of your lesson planning. There are different factors to consider, but a useful starting point can be to think in terms of fluency and accuracy. Developing fluency *and* accuracy are key components of progression in second language learning: in the course of learning a language, learners should become increasingly fluent and increasingly accurate in their language use. Activities usually focus on either fluency or accuracy. Within the context of CLT, Richards and Rodgers summarise the differences between these kinds of activity, as follows:

Activities focusing on fluency

- Reflect natural use of language
- Concentrate on achieving communication through negotiation of meaning
- Require meaningful use of language
- Require the use of communication strategies
- Produce language that may not be predictable
- Seek to link language use to context.

Activities focusing on accuracy

- Reflect classroom use of language
- Concentrate on the formation of correct examples of language
- Practise language out of context
- Practise small samples of language
- Do not require meaningful communication
- Control choice of language.

(Richards and Rodgers, 2014, pp96–97)

It is very difficult for the learner to simultaneously give equal attention to both of these aspects. To avoid cognitive overload for your pupils, think through at the planning stage what you want the focus of key activities or stages in the lesson to be: developing fluency *or* developing accuracy? Be guided in this by your learning intentions for the lesson as a whole. If your main learning intention is grammatical, then I would suggest that for most of the lesson you will want pupils to be working on their accuracy, and to be concentrating on the linguistic form or forms that you want them to practise. Planning should therefore prioritise what linguistic form or forms you want pupils to notice and focus on in the lesson. And if you are expecting pupils to produce those forms in the lesson, plan how you will deal with any errors or inaccuracies that come up. Possible techniques to try are:

1   Repeating what the pupil has just said and inviting the pupil to self correct;
2   Offering the pupil two alternative versions to choose from, one of which is correct;
3   Inviting the class to correct and then returning to the pupil who self corrects;

Different sorts of ML lessons

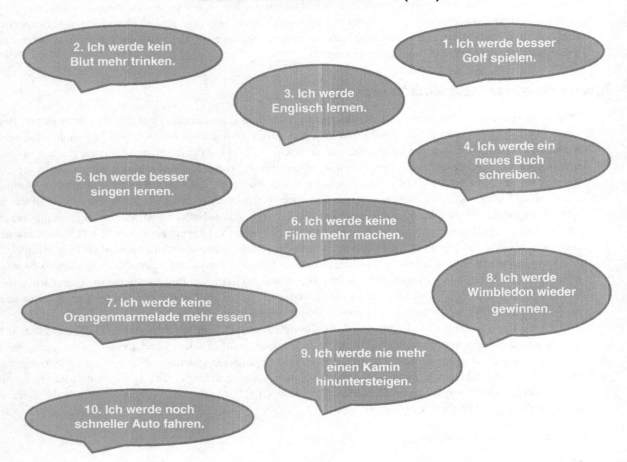

Vorsätze für das neue Jahr (20..)

1. Ich werde besser Golf spielen.
2. Ich werde kein Blut mehr trinken.
3. Ich werde Englisch lernen.
4. Ich werde ein neues Buch schreiben.
5. Ich werde besser singen lernen.
6. Ich werde keine Filme mehr machen.
7. Ich werde keine Orangenmarmelade mehr essen
8. Ich werde Wimbledon wieder gewinnen.
9. Ich werde nie mehr einen Kamin hinuntersteigen.
10. Ich werde noch schneller Auto fahren.

Wer hätte das vielleicht gesagt?

J.K.Rowling?   Paddington Bär?

Justin Bieber?   Lewis Hamilton?

Donald Trump?   Präsident Xi?

Dracula?   Meghan Markle?

Serena Williams?   der Weihnachtsmann?

FIGURE 5.2 Resource needed for Year 10 German lesson (*Vorsätze für das neue Jahr*)

4 Repeating back to the pupil what s/he has just said, but with a gap for the pupil to supply the correct form;
5 If several pupils make the same mistake, using the board to write up examples of what was said and inviting the class, in pairs, to correct.

Of course, there will be other lessons or parts of lessons where the main point is developing fluency, or where it is more important in the lesson for the pupil to talk at all than to talk correctly. That does not mean that any salient grammar errors cannot be corrected later in the lesson or in a subsequent lesson.

I would suggest that explicit grammar teaching involves a focus on developing accuracy for most of the lesson. This is an occasion when error correction is warranted; in the words of Pachler et al. 'corrective feedback is important for learning grammar' (2014, p258).

The following lesson plan (Table 5.5a) is an example of explicit grammar teaching, with built-in opportunities for corrective feedback at selected stages in the lesson. Figure 5.2 shows the main resource used in the lesson, the context is New Year's resolutions in German.

Inductive and deductive grammar teaching

So far we have looked at two grammar lessons. Both lesson plans are examples of a largely inductive approach to grammar teaching. An inductive approach begins with the teacher planning the lesson to help pupils notice and then make sense of grammatical features or patterns in the language for themselves. In the first place, this means planning for pupils to come across examples of the grammatical structure used in context and for that context to have meaning and relevance for pupils, e.g. talking about free time or New Year's resolutions. Once pupils have extracted meaning from the language they have been listening to or reading, the teacher helps them attend to the formal features of the language. This approach usually involves pupils in some form of investigative work and exploratory talk, with the teacher helping pupils to make their understanding explicit. At this stage, the teacher may also supply pupils with any relevant grammatical terminology to describe what they have been looking at, and a table or paradigm to which they can refer. Once the underlying pattern or rule has been established, it is usual for pupils to consolidate their understanding with written exercises (e.g. gap-fill, translation) or other form-focused grammar exercises. After that, pupils might have the opportunity to apply their understanding of the new grammar in a more communicative or meaning focused activity.

By contrast, a deductive approach refers to the presentation of rules before practice. Such an approach begins with the teacher or textbook telling pupils the rules; this is the starting point for pupils' learning. For example, this might take the form of a verb paradigm with the teacher or textbook explaining the underlying rule for forming and conjugating the future tense, or an explanation about word order in subordinate clauses. Thereafter, a deductive approach might involve pupils in completing form-focussed written exercises in order to practise applying the underlying rule.

Each of these approaches has its uses. A deductive approach might be most useful for A-level or university students or 'mature, well-motivated students with some knowledge of the language who are anxious to understand the more complicated aspects of the grammatical system' (Rivers et al., 1975, p245). An inductive approach is likely to be most useful with younger or less advanced language learners who have not yet developed schemata relating to grammatical concepts. Most classroom teachers tend to use a mixture of approaches and sometimes this is for practical reasons; in other words, sometimes it is simply more expedient for the teacher to tell learners what the rule is or explain the grammatical feature before learners have met it in context.

The next grammar lesson (Table 5.6A) is based on a story that can be exploited for inductive grammar teaching. It was originally written by a beginning teacher more than 20 years ago! I thought then, and still think now, that this is a wonderful idea for teaching different forms of address in French. I have adapted it slightly for the purposes of this book. I also think that stories can be a very effective tool for introducing learners to grammatical patterns in context. The beauty of this is that as linguists we can create and compose our own texts, tailored to learners' needs and the particular points of grammar that we want to teach.

TABLE 5.5A Year 10 German lesson plan: introducing the future tense

This lesson was first taught to a Year 10 German class, second set. Pupils had been learning German for one lesson a week, as a second language, in Years 8 and 9, and for three lessons a week in Year 10. They were used to lessons conducted predominantly in German and to a mixed approach of implicit and explicit grammar teaching This was their first lesson after the Christmas break.

LO: To understand the future tense formation in German (first person only)

Key Language

Ich werde . . . + infinitive [essen, fahren, gewinnen, hinuntersteigen, lernen, machen, schreiben, spielen, trinken]

1. Set the Context – *gutes neues Jahr!*

   Wish class Happy New Year. Elicit and write up on board the new date, use to introduce idea of New Year's Resolutions (*Vorsätze für das neue Jahr*). Give example/s *Also, ich werde nächstes Jahr nicht so viel essen*. Once clear, use visualiser to show matching exercise. Do first one together.

2. Reading task – matching exercise

   Pupils match resolutions to suggested names at the bottom. Who is most likely to have said what? And why? What are the keywords? *Was meinst du? Wer hätte das vielleicht gesagt? Und warum meinst du das? Was sind die Schlüsselwörter?*

3. Repetition Practice + Visualiser with list of the 10 sentences (resolutions)

   Gradually reveal, choral repetition of each. T covers up the infinitives and challenges class to supply them from memory. 30 seconds to discuss with partner then whole class questioning.

4. Noticing the pattern

   Give out copies of the 10 sentences. In pairs, pupils underline what each sentence has in common. Discussion in English. T asks class 'what do you notice?'. Elicit the pattern for future tense formation:

   (i) each sentence has '*ich werde*' (translates as 'I will' in this context)
   (ii) each sentence has an infinitive (verb form ending in '-*en*')
   (iii) in each sentence the infinitive comes at the end of the sentence.

   Does anyone know what tense this is? (future tense) We use the future to say what we intend to do e.g. New Year's Resolutions.

5. Practising the pattern – controlled practice

   Pupils have 10 future tense sentences to complete, supplying the missing words from selection given. Sentences include different future markers (*nächstes Jahr, 2025, in Zukunft*) and use language that pupils are familiar with from other contexts. Check answers are correct.

   e.g. Ich _____ 2025 Millionär _____ .

   Ich _____ nächstes Jahr nach Amerika _____ .

fahren
werde
sein

6. Practising the pattern – more independent practice

   Working individually, pupils make up and write down more NY's resolutions for famous people, using *Ich werde nächstes Jahr . . .* Encourage to use their imagination and creativity, their sentences will be used for a guessing game.

   After 10 minutes, pupils circulate reading out their sentences for others to guess. Who is it? *Wer ist das? Ich werde nächstes Jahr . . . .* 5 mins then feedback.

   T asks class what was the best idea they heard and why? *Welche ist die beste Idee? Welche Idee hat am besten gefallen? Warum?* Write e.g.s on board, peer correction if needed.

7. Plenary + Homework

   Plenary question to recap When you are reading or listening to German how will you recognise when someone is using the future tense? Check for accuracy, correct if necessary.

   Homework – write up your own understanding of this new grammar point + 5 or more sentences in German with your own New Year's resolutions. Use the future tense.

Copyright material from Cheryl Mackay (2019), *Learning to Plan Modern Languages Lessons*, Routledge

TABLE 5.5B Commentary on Year 10 German lesson: introducing the future tense

This lesson was originally planned twenty-five years ago! The original content, in terms of the examples used, may no longer be relevant to young people. However, the context of New Year's resolutions remains valid, as does the lesson structure. I would like to highlight here some particular aspects of the thinking behind this plan that have stood the test of time.

First, the plan identifies a purpose for using the future tense; we tend to use the future to express resolutions or intentions. And the start of the new year provides a context to which young people can relate. This context works particularly well because of the time of year at which the lesson takes place. It is the first lesson of a new calendar year. The opening point on the lesson plan is therefore very important. It helps to set the scene and makes it easier for pupils to deduce the idea of 'future' meaning.

The initial learning focus of the lesson is on the meaning of the resolutions presented as part of a matching exercise. This is an important point that before starting to analyse these examples of the future tense, pupils first engage with them as chunks of meaning. At point 4 the focus shifts to analysis of formal aspects of the language. The plan is for pupils to work out the new grammatical pattern or underlying rule for themselves. The teacher has not only produced sentences which demonstrate the pattern, she has also thought through exactly what she wants pupils to notice and has written those key patterns on the lesson plan. It is important that the teacher has a clear and precise understanding of the salient points she wants to elicit so that, if need be, she is prepared and ready to correct any misconceptions or fill any gaps in understanding. Planning of the grammatical content also includes the name of the new tense and a simple explanation of its use. The questions used to elicit pupil understanding are very open (e.g. 'What do you notice about the way these sentences are written?' or 'What patterns can you see in these sentences?'). When faced with such openness, it may be that some pupils go off on entirely the wrong tangent! Knowing what grammatical points you want to elicit helps the teacher to guide pupils in the subsequent discussion.

Finally, lots of opportunities to assess pupil learning and progress are built into the lesson. As mentioned above, the first learning focus is on comprehension of meaning. Once meaning has been established, however, the main focus turns to knowledge and understanding of how to form the future tense. Different opportunities to assess this and provide corrective feedback as appropriate are planned into the lesson (points 5, 6 and 7). Homework will feed back to the teacher how well pupils can articulate their understanding of the new grammar, and how accurately they can apply the grammar when writing.

<u>Follow-up Reflective Task/Points to discuss</u>

What difference do you think points 3,4 and 5 might make to the quality of German pupils produce at point 6? What difference do you think the opportunities for corrective feedback at points 5 and 6, plus the plenary question at point 7, might make to the quality of homework that pupils produce?

What other contexts might you use to provide pupils with further exposure to the future tense? What tasks might provide a communicative purpose for reading or listening to the future tense?

TABLE 5.6A Example of a story in French: 'L'Histoire d'Henri'

Les personnages

Voici Henri. Henri adore le foot. Il adore regarder le foot et il adore jouer au foot.
Voici le frère d'Henri. Il s'appelle Fred.
Voici la sœur d'Henri. Elle s'appelle Sophie.
Voici les copains d'Henri. Il s'appellent Bernard et Bernadette.
Voici les voisins d'Henri. Il s'appellent Christine, Christophe et Claude.
Voici le prof de maths. Il s'appelle M. Dubois.
Voici le prof de sport. Elle s'appelle Mme Dupont.

L'histoire

Henri — *Salut Fred! Tu joues au foot avec moi?*

Oui, je veux bien! — Fred

H+F — *Salut Sophie! Tu joues au foot avec nous?*

Oui, je veux bien! — Sophie

H+F+S — *Salut Bernard! Tu joues au foot avec nous?*

Oui, je veux bien! — Bernard

H+F+S+B — *Salut Bernadette! Tu joues au foot avec nous?*

Oui, je veux bien! — Bernadette

H+F+S+B+B — *Salut Christine! Salut Christophe! Salut Claude! Vous jouez au foot avec nous?*

Oui, oui, oui!!! Excellente idée!!! — Christine, Christophe, Claude

H+F+S+B+B+C+C+C — *Bonjour M. Dubois*

Bonjour à tous. — M. Dubois

H+F+S+B+B+C+C+C — *Pardon monsieur, vous jouez au foot avec nous?*

Oui je veux bien! — M. Dubois

H+F+S+B+B+C+C+C+M.Dubois — *Bonjour Mme. Dupont.*

Bonjour tout le monde. — Mme Dupont

H+F+S+B+B+C+C+C+M.Dubois — *Pardon madame, vous jouez au foot avec nous?*

Oui je veux bien! — Mme Dupont

H+F+S+B+B+C+C+C+M.Dubois+Mme.Dupont — *Excellent! On joue au foot!*

> Possible adaptations
> - Use names (and pictures) of famous people
> - Use fewer names
> - Change the gender balance
> - Focus only on singular forms (omit the plural example)
> - Focus only on informal forms (omit the formal examples)

TABLE 5.6B Commentary and planning task relating to the story: 'L'Histoire d'Henri'

The idea behind the story was to demonstrate how people address themselves differently in French. The grammar point relates to the conjugation of the present tense of regular –er verbs, especially the 'tu' and 'vous' forms of the verb. From a pedagogical point of view, the repetition of these key structures within the context of the story is a particular strength.

What we have here (Table 5.6A) is the linguistic content of the story: a list of the characters and the dialogue which makes up the story. I have also added some possible ways of adapting the input depending on your teaching context. The original idea was to complement the text with pictures of the characters, to show how the football team gradually increases in number. If you were planning to use this as a teaching resource it would be important to think through the practical logistics of enabling pupils to actually read the story. One possibility might be to use PowerPoint slides to introduce the characters and the text, with a copy of the text that pupils can have in the lesson as a prompt and model to follow; another option might be to involve older pupils in filming the dialogue and use this to introduce the storyline at least; or you might use flashcards to present the characters and stick them up on the board as the story unfolds.

Reflective/Discussion Task

There is no lesson plan available to go with this story! The question is how would you use this as a resource to teach the grammar point to a mixed ability Year 7 French class? Assume that pupils have covered the topic of hobbies and are already familiar with the first and second person singular of some frequently used –er verbs and how they are written. Presume that the aim of the lesson is for pupils to understand and make appropriate use of different forms of address in French, using regular '-er' verbs. Given the context of the class, I would suggest that an inductive teaching approach would be appropriate here.

Some key points to think through:

How will you help pupils to understand the story? How many times might they need to read it? Hear it? If they are reading aloud, are there any possible pronunciation difficulties to be aware of? What else will help them comprehend the French?

What is the underlying rule that you want pupils to notice? How will you help them to do that? How will you explain the rule?

What opportunities could you provide for pupils to consolidate their understanding and practise using the new grammar?

At the end of the lesson what will pupils be able to take away with them as a record of their learning?

Where in the lesson will you insist on grammatical accuracy? What will your approach be to error correction? What will be corrected and how?

Can you think of a possible follow-up task which would give pupils a communicative purpose for applying their new grammatical knowledge?

One thing for certain is that any grammar teaching needs to be planned for rather than left to chance. In my experience, the learner is not helped if grammar is introduced or taught in a haphazard way. Rather, grammatical knowledge needs to be built up systematically and that requires careful long-term planning.

Table 5.7A is an example, devised by Vee Harris, formerly PGCE tutor at Goldsmiths University of London, of how the perfect tense in French can be built up over time. The longer-term aim here is to teach the perfect tense; working backwards this has been broken down into little steps or 'experience' stages.

TABLE 5.7A Example of a planning grid for teaching the perfect tense

Year	Forms	Verbs	Topic
yr. 8	*je/tu (on?)*	*avoir: mangé/ acheté/ écouté/ regardé*	Weekend activities
yr. 8	*je/tu/on*	*avoir: acheté/ mangé + visité/ fait/ vu/bu* *être: allé/ resté*	Holidays (where/how/with whom went/ where/how long stayed/ what did)
yr. 8	*il/elle/ils/elles*	*avoir: vu/ bu + attaqué/ envoyé/ invité* *être: allé, resté + entré/ arrivé/ parti/ monté/ tombé*	TV 'soaps': what happened
yr. 9	*il/elle*	*avoir: perdu/ du/ gagné/ voyagé/ inventé* *être: allé/ parti + mort/ né*	Time line of famous people
yr. 9	*nous/vous*	negatives: *avoir/être*	Alibis
yr. 9	all forms	*avoir: déménage/ rencontré/ été/ eu* *être:né/ mort* reflexives: *se lever/se coucher/ se disputer/ s'entendre*	Important events in own life Agreable/ disagreable incidents
yr. 10	all forms	*avoir: écrasé/ exigé/ enlevé/* *être: mort/ né*	Local and national news

Table originally designed by Vee Harris, and reproduced here with her kind permission.

TABLE 5.7B Commentary and planning task relating to the planning grid

It is worth noting that the whole paradigm is built up gradually over time. There is not one single lesson or topic where pupils will be taught everything they need to know about the perfect tense. This gradual build-up creates a sort of cumulative effect; what is learnt within the topic of 'weekend activities', for example, can be built upon in the next topic.

The small steps are sequenced in a logical order. Regular forms are taught before irregular forms; affirmative before negative. First and second person singular are taught before third person singular; third person plural before first and second person plural.

At each stage, learners experience the perfect tense within the context of a topic or theme. This facilitates an inductive approach to grammar teaching. Within each topic, a relatively small number of frequently used verbs have been selected to demonstrate the perfect tense being used for different communicative purposes. In sum this helps pupils to use the grammar they are learning: the contexts are relevant to them, the language is comprehensible and the grammar is useful to them.

<u>Follow-up Reflective Task/Points to discuss</u>

Is there anything else that you notice about the different stages or about the grid as a whole?

Verbs can convey a lot of meaning in a sentence and learning to manipulate different forms of the verb as well as different tenses is a hugely important part of learning the grammar of another language. Based on the perfect tense grid above, discuss how you might break down the teaching of the perfect tense (or another tense) in a language that you teach.

A final caveat

A final caveat is needed to complete this section on grammar. Please bear in mind that the emphasis here on explicit grammar teaching does not mean to suggest that such teaching should take place *at the expense of* opportunities for learners to use the language. On the contrary, it is paramount that lessons are planned so that learners can spend as much time as possible listening to, speaking, reading or writing the target language (PDC in MFL, 2012; Ellis, 2005; NC Modern Foreign Languages Working Group, 1990).

Cultivating creativity

Let's imagine that your mentor in school gives you the opportunity to teach a one-off lesson. You can teach anything you want, provided it can be justified in terms of language learning gains. I wonder what you would choose? My choice would be creativity.

For me, creative use of language is a particular subset of the final 'p' in the PPP model, it is an example of independent language use. According to the Programme of Study for Modern Languages (2007–2013), the concept of creativity involves learners in:

- Using familiar language for new purposes and in new contexts
- Using imagination to express thoughts, ideas, experiences and feelings

(QCA, 2007, p166)

The second bullet point is particularly important here. In my opinion, it is imagination that is the root of creativity and distinguishes creativity from any other independent use of language.

According to this definition, creative language use brings important learning gains. The ability to express ideas and feelings using a limited range of language is in itself an important skill for pupils to develop, not least because it prevents them from feeling frustrated because they are restricted in what they can say or write (QCA, 2007). To this I would add that:

- Creativity provides learners with a purpose for using the language they are learning;
- Creativity helps the development of communication strategies to compensate for any gaps in knowledge of that language;
- Creativity encourages learners to explore ways of making the language their own;
- Creativity encourages risk-taking;
- Creativity opens learners' eyes (and ears) to the generative power of language;
- Creativity cultivates learners own innate creative potential;
- Creativity can be life-affirming, boosting learners' self-esteem, confidence and self-awareness.

However, my first reason for choosing creativity is rather more personal. For me, creativity is the one element of language learning that has moved me to tears, both as a teacher and as a learner myself.

As a young French teacher, I set pupils the homework task of writing their own poem in French based on Prévert's *Déjeuner du Matin*. At the end of the next lesson, one of the lads presented me with his work. It was called '*le bouton*' (the button). It followed a similar pattern to Prévert's poem with a chronology of small steps, written in the past tense, leading up to the finality of the last line. But that's where the similarity ended. His was the story of the last nuclear submarine and the sailor who pressed the button. As I read it, I was moved to tears; not because the French was flawless (which it was), nor because the content was sad (which it was), nor because he had done his homework for once (which was also true). No, the tears I shed were tears of something approaching joy. I was rejoicing in this pupil's ability to create something so beautiful and original in the French language. I think I will remember that joyous feeling forever. That was when I first really understood that whenever you tap into someone's creativity, you see a whole new side to a person's potential.

I learnt Spanish as part of a small group who met once a week in a tapas bar. On this particular occasion our teacher was very sad. He told us about a very depressing event in his life; his football team had been knocked out of the European Championship. This was sadder than anything else he could imagine! He used this context to teach us a very useful interjection to express surprise or dismay in Spanish: ¡*Caramba!* ¡*Que triste es!* (Heck! That's so sad!) and then modelled some sentences which illustrated just how sad this was. Each sentence followed the same pattern and used the same comparative construction *'Es más triste que . . . . sin . . .'* ('That's sadder than a . . . . without . . .').

Once we got the idea, the whole group repeated the interjection each time, and we took it in turns to make up new sentences, using the same pattern.

¡Caramba! ¡Que triste es! [said with feeling]

Es más triste que *una fiesta* **sin** *música.*

¡Caramba! ¡Que triste es!

Es más triste que *una piscina* **sin** *agua.*

¡Caramba! ¡Que triste es!

Es más triste que *un cuaderno* **sin** *color.*

¡Caramba! ¡Que triste es!

¡Que triste es! **Es más triste que** *. . . .* **sin** *. . . . Etc*

This was a very different language learning experience, we were playing with words and trying to outdo one another with the silliness or absurdity of the examples we created. We were literally enjoying the Spanish language and crying with laughter! But there was also serious learning going on here. The activity created a meaningful and motivating context for language use and helped to draw our attention to the language itself, in this case the use of the comparative in Spanish. This sort of interactional 'playfulness' (Hall and Walsh, 2002, p189) adds value to the language learning process.

So, in my experience, using language creatively is playful and can be a source of joy. And this matters: 'Shame on education if it seeks only to attain a given end, and brings no joy on the journey' (attributed to Goethe, source unknown). For more about creativity and benefits to the language learner, I would especially recommend the British Council edited publication 'Creativity in the English Language Classroom' (Maley and Peachey, 2015).

It is time now to discuss how creativity might manifest itself in our subject. I would like to discuss three examples taken from my own teaching experience.

Example 1: Odd One Out with English learners in China

Odd One Out is a popular activity not only in ML but also in English language teaching. I used it a few years ago in English classes of 11–14 year olds in China to get pupils talking in the TL. The activity always generated a large number of sentences. For example, three pictures of famous people were stuck up on the board: Barack Obama, Justin Bieber and Yao Ming; and these questions: Who is different and why? What do they all have in common? We also wrote up a very simple talking frame to help pupils structure their answers in English. Here is a sample of the ideas that pupils came up with:

Barack Obama is different because he . . .

- *is head of state;*
- *lives in a palace (White House);*
- *is black;*
- *is not wearing red;*
- *is not a star.*

Justin Bieber is different because he . . .

- *is still a teenager;*
- *can sing well;*
- *has light hair;*
- *is cool;*
- *is not married;*
- *has no children.*

Yao Ming is different because he . . .

- *is Chinese;*
- *speaks Chinese;*

- *plays basketball very well;*
- *is very tall;*
- *was born in Asia.*

They are all . . .

- *They are all male;*
- *They are all famous;*
- *They are all popular;*
- *They are all rich;*
- *They all live in North America now;*
- *They are all alive;*
- *They are all talented;*
- *They don't wear glasses.*

The creative part of this activity is making connections; there are endless possibilities and no wrong answers. Pupils are able to do this activity with simple structures and frequently used vocabulary; the activity provides a purpose for recycling previously learnt language. The generation of different possible answers also presents pupils with a cognitive challenge and encourages divergent thinking. And the linguistic framework scaffolds the whole process; this allows pupils to focus on their ideas, and use their imagination to come up with original ideas.

Example 2: Jokes in French

Year 9 pupils were doing the topic of 'At the Hotel' and much of the language they used to write these jokes had been learnt within that topic. The class brainstormed different possible ideas and had time in the lesson to try out some of their first drafts and get feedback from their peers. They then had to choose their best joke and write it up for homework. They were encouraged to read their work again before handing it in to check for spelling and accuracy. Some pupils felt it would help others to get their joke if they also included an illustration. The final results were mounted as a wall display '*A l'hôtel: situations amusantes*' and pupils from different classes then had the chance to read them and vote for their favourite. The Year 9 class in question then went on to write sketches for *L' Hôtel Folie* (Fawlty Towers), and were able to incorporate their jokes into that, as well as other humour. Here are some of the jokes that pupils wrote:

Garçon! Garçon! Il y a une mouche dans ma soupe!
Pas de problème. Il y a une araignée dans le pain!!!

Patron! Patron! Il y a une fille dans mon lit!
Excellent! Avez-vous place pour trois?!!!

Où est le patron? Il y a une grenouille dans ma soupe!
Et alors? C'est un restaurant français!!!

Où est le patron? Il y a un feu dans mon lit!
Et alors? Vous pouvez coucher dans la bain!!!

Garçon! Garçon! Il y a une chenille dans ma salade!
Oui, oui, madame! C'est très délicieux!!!

The creative part is looking for humour within a given setting; there are endless possibilities and no wrong answers, although some might be funnier than others. This activity is one way of recycling or using familiar language for a new purpose (making others laugh) and an opportunity to practise key structures. Displaying work for a wider audience makes this more meaningful. And the generation of different possible jokes again encourages divergent thinking.

Example 3: Lost property office sketch in German

Year 10 pupils were doing the topic of Lost Property. The topic relied heavily on transactional type language with some rather mundane, predictable dialogues that centred on these key questions: What have you lost? Where did you lose it? When was that? Working in groups of two or three, pupils were challenged to create and act out a dialogue at the lost property office, that was more interesting than the version in their textbooks but which still contained the three key questions. We had all agreed that the textbook version was *todlangweilig* (dead boring), so this was an opportunity for pupils to do something about it! Pupils had time in class to draft and act out their sketches, mostly from memory. They doubled up to form larger groups of four or five for the acting out, and then moved on to form different groups. This continued until each sketch had been performed about four or five times. Pupils and teacher said which sketches they had liked and why. The unanimous favourite was the creation of two, rather quiet, boys. Their sketch featured a bishop and a pair of black leather underpants; it involved a lot of histrionics and repetition of key phrases with the bishop speaking very quickly in hushed tones and the lost property office attendant speaking very loudly. It was hilarious. The other sketches were pretty predictable and did not vary much from the standard textbook model. Nevertheless, pupils seemed to enjoy acting out what they had written and rehearsed well what they wanted to way.

In this example, the model dialogue in the textbook provides pupils with a linguistic framework within which they can draw on language they are familiar with from other topics, e.g. describing clothes, and other classroom language, e.g. *lauter bitte* (speak up please), *sprechen Sie nicht so laut* (lower your voice), *wie bitte?* (can you say that again?). The challenge of creating an appropriate dialogue that is more interesting than the version in the textbook provides an incentive or sense of purpose.

To sum up, these examples demonstrate how pupils can use familiar language for new purposes and in new contexts and use imagination to express thoughts, ideas and feelings. They demonstrate how creativity challenges learners in different ways. The process of creativity involves thinking and it involves communicating but there is also an added factor and that is imagination. Somehow creativity synthesises all three. But perhaps even more importantly, creativity is a chance for *everyone* to shine in the ML classroom: 'linguistic creativity is not simply a property of exceptional people but an exceptional quality of all people' (Carter, 2004; as cited in Maley and Peachey, 2015, p9).

Mary Ryan (2014) provides this wonderful example of the potential impact on individual pupils:

> I used to think only posh people or very clever people wrote poetry. I never thought I could write it in French! But in our French lesson on Valentine's Day we wrote poems called '*Comme Moi sans Toi*' and mine was really good. Miss put my poem up on display.
>
> Casey, Year 9 student (Ryan, 2014, 220)

Casey's poem is reproduced in the chapter by Ryan (2014, 221).

Opportunities for creative thinking needn't take up a whole lesson; for instance, as indicated above, Odd One Out can be part of a learning sequence at the start of a lesson. Following the principle of 'a little and often', some teachers regularly use short, time constrained activities which challenge pupils to recycle familiar language in different ways; such activities cultivate creativity and help develop spontaneity and longer-term retention. Steven Fawkes, ALL Fellow and former President, argues that:

> To help them build long-term retention, learners need opportunities to use language they have learnt **in their own way** – in both Speaking and Writing – in order to gain confidence (a feeling of self-efficacy), to begin to use the language flexibly, and to feel a sense of progress in their learning of how to do things (not just in their acquisition of new linguistic items).
>
> They also need regular opportunities to remind themselves, or be reminded, of language they have already met, been taught or 'learnt' (e,g for a vocabulary test or regular assessment within a topic / module of work); the pace of our schemes of work can mean that language arises, is noted and then disappears from learners' awareness for weeks if not months. How can we expect them to retain it without an intervention?
>
> (Fawkes, 2018, personal communication)

An example of Steven's activity would be:

- The teacher puts on the screen images or individual words in the TL;
- Based on this stimulus, learners are challenged to make up as many sentences as they can within a given time-limit;
- They complete this challenge with a partner, taking it in turns to say a sentence, and they keep a tally of their progress.

> **Reflective/discussion task**
>
> *What images and/or words could you possibly use as a basis for this activity with: (a) A-level group, (b) Key Stage 4 class, or (c) Key Stage 3 class? Discuss and try out your ideas with others to identify those which seem to work best in terms of generating multiple sentences.*
>
> *How might you plan to organise this activity at the start of a ML lesson? Key questions to consider might be:*
>
> - *How could you lead up to or introduce the idea?*
> - *How many different images (or words) would you show at once?*
> - *How long would pupils have to produce as many sentences as possible?*
> - *What could you be doing during this time?*
> - *What could you do at the end of the activity?*

Planning for creativity

Creativity also lends itself well to one-off lessons. So let's imagine that you want to plan a lesson to cultivate learners' creativity. How will you plan to bring out that 'exceptional property' in all pupils? Here are some points to bear in mind.

Planning which ensures that the process of creativity is systematic and disciplined rather than random or chaotic is more likely to be successful. An important factor here is providing learners with a *linguistic framework* that they can work within. This acts as both a stimulus and as a support for creativity. Constraining the activity in this way defines the scope of the activity and allows learners to focus their attention on their ideas (as discussed by Read, 2015).

In order to support creative writing, Hadfield and Hadfield talk about *exploiting patterns* that are inherent in the written form of the language:

> Creativity, paradoxically, thrives within constraints: the adherence to rules, or following of a pattern, as in a limerick or a sonnet, both of which have tightly prescribed forms. Additionally, many poems, stories and songs gain their effect through use of repetition. This paradox can be exploited to provide opportunities for grammar practice in creative activities by the provision of tightly controlled frameworks within which to write.
>
> (Hadfield and Hadfield, 2015, p51)

Other *constraints* such as time limits or limited access to dictionaries are also helpful to the creative process. Rather like the old adage that 'necessity is the mother of invention', creativity thrives in a context of constraints. So, part of the challenge for pupils is: can you do this within a given time-limit using only the language you know, rather than if you had all the time in the world? Part of the teacher's role in the classroom is to be time keeper; it is important to be strict about time limits.

Brainstorming first as a class can help everyone start to see the potential for making links and become aware of new connections, especially if the outcomes of brainstorming are made visible to the whole class. Similarly, *pictures* can be helpful in capturing the imagination. Learners will see different things in the same picture and there are no right or wrong answers. Both of these devices can have a liberating effect on the learner and help to stimulate the creative process.

An element of *choice* is helpful. Learners feel more in control if they decide which of the given options to take. For example, a menu of different possible film genres for acting out a dialogue, or a menu of different possible audiences to write a travel brochure for. Sometimes the choice is whether to be yourself or not. Offering the option of an *alter ego* can be liberating. Also, it is hugely liberating to tell pupils that what they say or write doesn't have to be true!

Rather than thinking in terms of LO and how you will 'measure' success, try to have *broad aims* for the lesson or part of the lesson. Be guided by what you want to make it possible for learners to do. For example, to write a poem describing a scene; and think through how you might best support and challenge them to do this. This is more about an exploratory approach to teaching and learning: if I put X, Y and Z in place, what can they come up with? Can they create something original? Perhaps not original in the history of language learning, but original in the life of that learner.

Accuracy is important, in the sense that you want the work that pupils finally produce to be as accurate as they can make it. At the same time, an obsession with accuracy and correctness can kill creativity. By providing a linguistic framework and by encouraging pupils to use language they already know, you will already cut down on potential inaccuracies. Rather than planning to correct mistakes, think more in terms of expecting pupils to critically reflect on the quality of their own work before they submit or perform. Give them responsibility for the quality of their creation.

Finally, providing an *audience* acts as an incentive to bring out the best in pupils – in this case, their creative best. Possible audiences might be school assembly, other classes in your school or another school, or parents at parents' evening. Creative writing might be displayed prominently in the school, published on the school website or sent to a partner school. You might consider collaborating with colleagues teaching English to put together an anthology of poetry and creative writing in different languages; or staging a creative writing event where pupils read out work they have written or have their work read out by native speakers. Plan for an audience if you can.

> **Reflective/discussion task**
>
> Hadfield and Hadfield (2015) talk about and give examples of using 'pattern poems' to scaffold the process of poetry writing for language learners. Taylor (2000) also provides examples of French, German and Spanish poems for structure practice and creative work written by secondary school pupils. Can you think about a pattern poem you have read (a poem which is based on a repeated structure or which seems to follow a particular pattern)? If not, perhaps you could try to write one that follows a clear pattern?
>
> Discuss how you might plan a lesson or learning sequence to move from teacher control to learner choice of language, with the aim of enabling pupils to write a poem themselves, based on the same pattern. Use the 'planning for creativity' points above to help you.

Creativity and the bigger picture

Some aspects of language learning cannot be packaged neatly into lesson objectives that can be assessed or measured by the end of the lesson. If we try to define every ML lesson in this way, there is the danger that teaching and learning are reduced to that which is measurable. This makes for a diet of language learning experience which is imbalanced and unimaginative; ultimately, such a diet is limiting of human potential.

More broadly, there is the danger of excluding broader educational aims and values which transcend individual subject considerations. For more on the bigger picture of education and creativity, a good starting place is the work of Sir Ken Robinson. His talks are available on YouTube (2006 and 2014).

Exploiting literature

There is a widely held view that literature enriches the experience of studying another language. Particular learning gains include insights into other cultures, understanding specific language points or grammatical features, and development of reading skills. For further discussion, Sell (2005) provides a considered defence of the use of literature in language teaching.

From my own experience as language learner, I particularly enjoy literature that is best read aloud to be fully appreciated; for me, that is when literature fills words with meaning like no other form of linguistic expression. For instance, I still have a copy of *Abendlicht*, a short novel written by the East German author Stephan Hermlin that I bought during my last visit to the-then-German Democratic Republic. The dustcover describes the book as '*ein literarisches Ereignis*' (a literary achievement); I am not qualified to comment on that, never having read the book in its entirety. But what I can confirm is that there are three pages early on in the book that I must have read 100 times, and more often than not I have read them out loud to myself – purely for the pleasure of listening to the sound of the German language! Although written as prose, for me Hermlin's lines are pure poetry. I love the rhythm of the words, the cadence of the sentences, the imagery and the sense of timelessness that they convey. The meanings that I infer from Hermlin's writing continue to affect me today as they first did over 30 years ago. This is an example of why, for me, poetry is *the* pinnacle of linguistic achievement. To include literature in our lessons is a way of celebrating language, the ability of language to move us to tears, laughter, admiration, awe and wonder. Of course, learners and teachers probably couldn't bear the intensity of this every lesson! But every now and again, helping learners to appreciate literature written in the TL can be a real treat for all those who are present.

There are also sound pedagogic reasons for exploiting literature as an opportunity to practise reading aloud. This is not simply an exercise in pronunciation and intonation; it can also help to reinforce sound-spelling links, the association of particular phonemes with particular graphemes. The benefits of repeated reading aloud have long been recognised by scholars: 'the oftener a piece is recited by a pupil, the more firmly are the single words and especially the word combinations rooted in his memory' (Jespersen, 1944, p88). These benefits also apply to singing in the TL; song lyrics are a form of literature and singing can help with pronunciation, phonics and memorisation. In fact, there are many different sorts of literary text that we might want to use in the classroom in order to practise reading aloud. Apart from prose, poetry or song lyrics, we might also want to exploit letters or written dialogue in this way, play or film scripts are another form of literature. And of course stories lend themselves to being read aloud, not only stories written for younger children. Reading aloud can also be practised with other non-literary texts, but there does seem to be something more meaningful about using texts that were written to be heard. This is a way of encouraging learners to read with feeling, or 'natural emphasis and expression' (Jespersen, 1944, p87).

Perhaps we should not be surprised therefore that literature features as it does in the ML national curriculum. For example, at Key Stage 3 'pupils should be taught to read literary texts in the language [such as stories, songs, poems and letters], to stimulate ideas, develop creative expression and expand understanding of the language and culture' (Department for Education, 2013, p2). At A-level the study of at least one literary text is now compulsory (and assessed through a written exam in the language of study).

Planning to use literature

To start, it would be helpful to find out how and where literature or literary texts feature in the schemes of work you will be working from in school and what resources are available. Some useful questions you might ask are:

- Is literature taught in discrete lessons or is the use of literary texts integrated into different topics and themes?
- What sort of literature is used for different year groups? In what ways is literature relevant to different ages?
- In what ways are literary texts exploited? Is it always the same approach or are different approaches used?

A conversation with your mentor should help to clarify expectations and give you some insight into what it might be possible for you to achieve during your school placement. Depending on your school context, you might need to be prepared to offer to teach literature outside of normal lesson time. The advantage of this is that you can be a free agent! If you have the time and inclination, this could be an opportunity to run an informal lunchtime ciné-club, read extracts of Harry Potter in German, learn some South American songs, etc.

In terms of lesson planning, start at the end and decide what you want learners to gain from this experience of using literature. It might help to try and visualise what you expect learners to be doing with the text, and how you expect them to respond to what they read. Here are some general rules of thumb to bear in mind when planning to use written text, including literature.

Focus first on the meaning of the text. Even if you are planning to use the text later for grammatical purposes, start by making the text comprehensible to learners. Consider what you can do to help get the meaning over. Possible strategies might be:

- Use pictures, photographs or film to give clues to the meaning of the text;
- Read the text aloud with expression and feeling;
- Read just part of the text to start with and gradually build it up;
- Read an abridged version first or a summary before looking at the full version;
- Read an adapted or simplified version of the original;
- Before reading, explain any cultural references that might interfere with comprehension e.g. names of places or people, culturally specific items of food or drink, events or celebrations.

When planning, please don't feel you *always* have to exploit texts for their grammatical or language content. It is perfectly fine to concentrate only on meaning sometimes! If you are lucky enough to find a text that speaks to your learners, think about how you might exploit it for speaking or writing purposes.

Equally, please don't feel that learners *always* need to translate every word of what they read into English. Sometimes you might want to progress from the gist to a more detailed understanding of the text. However, other times an understanding of the main ideas may be all that is needed. It is important for learners to know that you don't always need to understand every single word of what you read (Mitchell and Swarbrick, 1994; Nutall, 2005).

Finally, do not assume that learners are aware of skills and strategies that they can use to help them understand what they read. We return to this point below in the section about independent learning.

The lesson which follows is an example of how some of these rules of thumb might translate into a lesson plan.

TABLE 5.8A Year 8 French lesson plan: '*Déjeuner du Matin*'

This was a one-off lesson with a Year 8 French class; about half of the class were absent due to a school trip. Pupils were seated in groups, allocated by the teacher to facilitate peer learning. The LO for the lesson is couched in quite general terms, the teacher mainly wanted to see how pupils would respond to a lesson based on a French poem. Pupils had learnt breakfast foods in an earlier unit of work but had not yet looked at the past tense.

LO: To be able to understand the meaning of a French poem

Key skills to help deduce meaning:

From pictures (video) that accompany the poem, making links between the two

Highlight words/bits of the poem that you understand

Work out other words from the context – what do the words around it mean?

Recognition of different personal pronouns

---

1. Hook to get pupils interested – '*Quand la verité n'est pas libre, la liberté n'est pas vraie*'.

    Quotation from Prévert + his photo up on board with task as pupils arrive. In pairs translate into English. What does this really mean?

2. Introduction to the lesson

    Invite pupils to speculate on what doing today. What poets do you know? What French poets or writers have you heard of? Remind class of behaviour before showing the video.

3. Presentation of poem with video performance (two actors acting out the poem as it is recited)

    Le poème s'appelle 'Déjeuner du Matin' – write on board. Write next to it '*le petit déjeuner*'. *Qu'est-ce que c'est?* Use mimes + key phrases to explain, elicit translation. *Moi le matin je mange des Cornflakes et je bois du thé, c'est ça mon déjeuner du matin etc.*

    Watch the video, listen to the poem, what do you notice? What do you think the poem is about and why? Listen to ideas, get the gist [sadness, he's leaving, not talking].

    Give out text of poem. Read out and pupils follow. Two minutes thinking time, underline the words/ bits you know. Share with partner. Listen to ideas together.

    Read poem together, guided reading after me. Check pronunciation (*parler, regarder*)

    Pupils watch video again with text in front of them – encourage to read aloud with the narrator.

4. Find the French for phrases in the poem

    In pairs, read the poem again to find the phrases/vocab listed in English on Smartboard.

    Use poem on Smartboard to show answers. Extension: Look at the French. How many people are in the poem? Is it all about him, is there another person in the poem? How do you know? What are the French clues? What tense is this poem written in?

5. Reconstruct the poem

    With a partner, pupils put lines back in order. Listen to video again to check answers. Is there anything from the poem that you don't understand?

6. Check comprehension of poem – reading out and acting out in twos/ threes

    Allocate roles – one person is woman (and narrator), one person is the man. Circulate – listen in.

7. Plenary and Final Reflections

    Est-ce que vous aimez le poème? Pourquoi?

    What skills did you use today to help you understand what the poem is about? Can you give an example of what you found out and what helped you?

Copyright material from Cheryl Mackay (2019), *Learning to Plan Modern Languages Lessons*, Routledge

TABLE 5.8B Commentary on Year 8 French lesson: '*Déjeuner du Matin*'

This lesson was planned by a beginning teacher, a few weeks into her second (long) teaching placement. The lesson plan shows how you might exploit a piece of authentic French literature in the classroom. The teacher also planned to use an authentic French video resource in the lesson; this video was downloadable from YouTube.

The rationale behind the plan is to help pupils work out for themselves what the poem is about. In the first instance, the video makes the gist meaning of the poem accessible; some pupils may start to hypothesise about the meaning based on what they can see and without much awareness of the poem that is being recited, others may already be making links between the two. Following this, engagement with the written version of the poem scaffolds progression to a more detailed understanding. In her planning the teacher pre-empted some of the skills or strategies that pupils might use to help them deduce meaning and the lesson is structured to progressively introduce those (points 3, 4 and 5). At point 6 pupils work in pairs to demonstrate what they have understood; this is an opportunity for the teacher to circulate and pick up on any difficulties.

Within the lesson, there is progression from guided reading of the poem to reading it aloud more independently. An important part of this is modelling for pupils the correct pronunciation, especially of words that rhyme, and checking pupil pronunciation. This poem was written to be heard, getting the pronunciation correct will increase pupils' appreciation of this as a piece of literature. This has been planned for and one of the advantages of the video is that pupils can be exposed to multiple readings of the poem.

Finally, the teacher has thought through some of the key ideas that she wants to elicit from pupils, and written those on the lesson plan. For example, at point 3 the plan is to elicit ideas of 'sadness', 'he's leaving' and 'not talking'. This is good lesson preparation; it means that the teacher is prepared to guide pupils if they go off on a tangent. Also, once the key ideas have been covered she can move onto the next part of the lesson without losing the focus of the lesson.

As an aside, this lesson plan also highlights the initiative of a beginning teacher in making the most of opportunities. Knowing that the class would be depleted on this occasion, she used this as an opportunity to follow her intuition and try something different. She had never taught a lesson like this before; nor was there any provision for this within the scheme of work. It is worth noting that this would not have been possible without the support and backing of her mentor.

Follow-up Reflective Task/Points to discuss

Pupils first listened to the poem with the video before they look at the written version. What difference do you think this makes to learning?

This was a one-off lesson. If you had two lessons to plan for, or one lesson and a follow-up homework, how else might you plan to exploit the poem? The lesson was planned in the knowledge that only half of the class would be present. If the class had been full, let's say 30 pupils, how might this have impacted on planning? If you were teaching this lesson to a full class is there anything you would plan to do differently or add to this plan and why?

Copyright material from Cheryl Mackay (2019), *Learning to Plan Modern Languages Lessons*, Routledge

I would recommend that if you are not feeling confident about reading aloud yourself in the classroom, you seek out help from your school's drama department. When it comes to passion and enthusiasm, drama teachers are second only to ML teachers! Over the years, Newcastle University ML PGCE students benefitted greatly from voice coaching provided by drama specialists. For example, I was amazed at the difference this made to the 'natural emphasis and expression' they were able to bring to reading out poems and short stories on the theme of Christmas.

For further ideas for exploiting poetry, please see *Using Poetry in the French Classroom*, by An Gulinck (2015), it is free to download. The ALL Literature Project is also a fabulous online resource (Wiki) dedicated to ideas for literature teaching and learning in ML at all Key Stages. The wiki offers the following advice on planning lessons based on literary texts:

> Always consider what the students are actually expected to do with the text as you are planning the lesson. This will help you sequence the steps into it with appropriate support and/or challenge.
>
> - Are you asking them to understand the whole text? (Implications for pre-teaching)
> - Or are you asking them to enjoy the text? (Implications for the mood of the lesson segment)
> - Are you asking them to translate (a section of the) text? Or complete a gapped translation? (Implications for the attention to detail you ask for)
> - Or are you asking them to review the text? (Implications for preparing the language of opinion and description)
> - Are you asking them to manipulate the text? E.g. through redrafting, creative writing or speaking. (Implications for managing the idea-generating stage, attitudes to error, expectations, publication etc.)
> - Are you asking them to recite, perform, enact the text? (Implications for a focus on speaking skills, phonics, intonation, etc. in the rehearsal phase.)

(http://all-literature.wikidot.com/advice)

Learning from authentic sources

The last lesson is an example of how authentic sources might be used in the classroom. Authentic sources such as literature, news items, brochures, video clips, magazines and blogs create links between the ML curriculum and the outside world and this makes for more meaningful learning, as discussed by Newmann and Wehlage (1993). Added to which, one of the four aims of the national curriculum for languages is to ensure that all pupils 'understand and respond to spoken and written language from a variety of authentic sources' (Department for Education, 2013, p1).

The availability of authentic sources on the internet is a godsend to ML teachers. With little effort it is possible to download a wide range of original materials; short news items, for example, are readily available and can be imported into Word documents. After that, it is then worth deciding to what extent the text needs to be adapted for the pedagogic purpose you have in mind. For example, it might be helpful to modify or even rewrite key sections, and to add pictures that give clues to what the text is about.

The ability to adapt or modify authentic sources for your own pedagogic purposes is a very useful teaching skill and an important part of your lesson preparation as ML teacher. Learning to reframe your subject knowledge in this way is part of learning to teach your subject. Quite apart from which, it is also an excellent language exercise, especially in your second or third language. Many of the strategies used to adapt authentic written sources overlap with TL output modification strategies mentioned earlier (Figure 1.4). The aim of both is to make input sufficiently comprehensible for learners so that they can derive meaning from what they are reading or hearing, but at the same time to ensure that the sources are sufficiently challenging so that learners are required to make an effort in order to arrive at the intended meaning. I find that if you are in the habit of modifying the TL you use in your teaching, then adapting authentic texts is relatively straightforward.

Apart from the language of the text, it is worth bearing in mind also that the content or subject matter of the text itself can also affect how difficult it is to read. If we want to build up learners' confidence and fluency in reading in another language, then it is best to avoid texts where the language is *too* difficult and the content *too* far removed from the knowledge and experience of the learner (Turner, 1998).

Sometimes we might want to use authentic sources to introduce learners to particular grammatical patterns that we want them to be aware of. In this case, it is well worth adapting the original text to fit your teaching focus. For example, literary texts (especially fairy stories) provide an excellent context for introducing the past historic in French, the *Imperfekt* in German, or comparing the preterite and imperfect in Spanish. Fairy stories are helpful because pupils tend to be familiar with particular storylines or at least with the conventions of a fairy story. Even so, you might still need to adapt the original to include frequently used verbs, simpler syntax or more familiar vocabulary. A useful exercise for more advanced learners is to compare the adapted, simplified version with the original.

Different sorts of ML lessons

TABLE 5.9 Example of an authentic resource to discuss: '*Notizen auf dem Küchentisch*'

Bin bei Petra. Repariere ihr Rad.
Bin zum Mittag wieder da.
Lieber Kartoffelsalat zum Mittag,
hasse Spinat!!!   Peter

[At Petra's. Fixing her bike. Back for lunch. Prefer potato salad for lunch, I hate spinach!!!]

Muss um 15.30 zum Zahnarzt.
Bitte erledigen:
1) Käse, Milch kaufen
2) Spielzeug aus Wohnzi. räumen
3) Kaugummi von Tischkante entfernen!
   Mama

[Have to go to dentist at 3.30pm. Please sort out:
1. Buy cheese and milk
2. Clear toys from living room
3. Remove chewing gum from corner of table!]

10.00 – Anruf Heiko wegen Fußballspiel- heute in grün?
Warum ist der Junge nicht in der Schule?? Gehe jetzt auf Markt.
Bitte Kartoffeln schälen.
   Mama

[10.00 am. Call from Heiko about football match – is it green today? Why is that boy not at school?? I'm off to market now. Please peel potatoes.]

Bin beim Tierarzt. Foxi hat Flöhe!!!
Komme gegen 5.00 zurück. Bitte Tisch decken, danke.   Mama

[At the vet's. Foxi's got fleas!!! Back about 5 o'clock. Please set the table, thanks.]

Bin bei Co-op. Bringe Milch + Zeitung mit. Geschirr vom Mittag abwaschen + Wohnzimmer aufräumen- Tante Elsa kommt um 18.00!!!   Papa

[At the Co-op. Will get milk and the paper. Wash the dishes from lunch and tidy up the living room- Aunt Elsa is coming at 6pm!!!]

Anruf von Papa 17.00 – kommt nicht zum Abendbrot → Tagung. Gehe zu Uschi, üben für Mathearbeit. Bin um 22.00 zurück.
   Susi

[Call from Dad at 5pm – not home for supper → meeting. I'm going to Uschi's to practise for maths test. Back at 10pm.]

Ca. 16.00 Hole Kuchen. Bin in 20 Minuten zurück. Setzt schon Wasser für Kaffee auf!
   Klaus

[About 4pm. Nipped out for cake. Back in 20 minutes. Get water on for the coffee!]

Reflective/ discussion task

How could you plan to exploit this resource to support language learning (in German or another language)? Consider KS3, KS4 and KS5 learners.

What other contexts can you think of when people might leave notes or short messages for one another? What areas of vocabulary or language structures could be re-cycled?

Possibly even more valuable than the internet is a good foreign language assistant. If you are fortunate enough to have foreign language assistants in your school, then please use them! An excellent way to employ an assistant is in the production of authentic teaching resources. We have already seen how a recording made by the German assistant was used in a German grammar lesson to introduce '*weil*' clauses, and in another lesson to introduce a typical German timetable. These are examples of scripted recordings, designed to model the use of particular language points in context and to introduce cultural elements. You can also record the assistant talking in simple, unscripted language with a view to developing pupils' listening skills. The trick here is to recycle familiar language and build in lots of repetition. This approach lends itself well to descriptive narrative accounts; suitable topics might be a recent holiday, arriving in England, a witness account of a road accident, etc. If you don't have an assistant in your school, you might want to use your contacts who live in a TL speaking country. There will be more on this point in 'Next Steps', where Josh talks about how he uses short video clips of family and friends in France.

Assistants can also be an excellent source of authentic reading material. Table 5.9 shows an example written by former German assistant, Marianne Claussen. The context here is notes left on the kitchen table, recycling language that pupils are familiar with from different contexts. The original version was handwritten and this is something I would recommend for added authenticity.

Independent learning

This final section will consider an alternative way of planning lessons, in order to foster independent learning. By independent learning I mean pupils working and learning independently of the teacher, perhaps in pairs or groups or perhaps on their own. The sort of lesson I am envisaging here is one where pupils are working independently of the teacher for a good amount of the lesson. This implies a shift from a teacher-led to a more learner-centred approach.

Independent learning is not a simple matter of letting pupils get on with it! It is not enough to provide opportunities for pupils to learn independently. The crucial point is that pupils need the tools or strategies to be able to exploit those opportunities (Grenfell and Harris, 2014, p189). If learners have some ideas about how to approach the tasks that they work on independently of the teacher, then they are more likely to complete these tasks effectively and learn from them. So, for me, an integral part of fostering independent learning is thinking through what skills or strategies pupils might need in order to successfully complete the tasks that we set them, including how best to equip pupils with those skills and strategies as appropriate.

What drives the planning for independent learning is *how* pupils are learning, rather than *what* they are learning. This emphasis on the processes of learning is rather different from other lessons we have looked at so far, with their focus on intended outcomes or the product of learning.

At the end of the lesson I am envisaging here there is a whole class plenary, or debrief, which is led by the teacher and where pupils are helped to reflect on their learning and evaluate the processes, skills and strategies they used to help them learn in the lesson. Providing time and opportunity for pupils to reflect on and talk about their learning in this way helps to develop their metacognitive awareness. Williams and Burden (1997, p165) advocate periodic metacognitive reflection on the processes used in carrying out tasks, as well as reflection on the feelings and emotions involved. The benefits to pupils of reflecting on their learning are summarised below:

> Experience suggests that where pupils have had no chance to reflect on their learning and thought processes, their accounts of learning outcomes are dominated by describing lesson content. Where teachers have made learning more explicit, used collaborative groups and conducted whole class plenaries which focus on processes, the pupils' accounts of learning outcome are broader and include greater awareness of how learning has been achieved.
>
> (Department for Education and Skills, 2001, p86)

The lesson plan that follows illustrates what fostering independent learning might look like. In this case, the focus is on developing independent reading skills. The lesson plan includes these fundamental features, as outlined above:

- The lesson is largely learner-centred;
- It has been structured to lead to a metacognitive plenary;
- Learning is focused on the process of independent reading.

TABLE 5.10A Year 10 French lesson plan: independent reading skills in French

This lesson was planned for a Year 10 French class, third set. It was a smallish class, of about 20 pupils and they sat in groups of 4 for French. There were a number of 'reluctant learners' in the class and this was the lesson after PE, so pupils tended to arrive in dribs and drabs. They had done some work on reading skills in the previous lesson.

LO: To continue to work on reading skills and think about ways you can work on your own to improve your understanding of French

---

Reading Skills from previous lesson – skimming for gist

Look for keywords – names, places, nouns; and numbers – dates, prices, times

Reading Skills for this lesson – reading for deeper understanding

1. Highlight what you do know. 2. Underline words you could guess from the context.

3. Use dictionary to look up 3 words that you didn't understand at all.

---

1 Match headlines to stories

Sets of headlines and articles numbered and lettered. Work on desks when pupils arrive, instructions up on Smartboard. Early finishers can write down how they worked out each one. Discussion afterwards of outcome (which headline matches which story and why?) AND method used. Did anyone look for keywords? Did anything else help? Circulate to check all on task.

2 State LO for today – have brief discussion

Building on what we learnt last lesson – reading for deeper understanding. Authentic sources. Run through organisation of lesson, make link to building resilience – why important.

3 Choose an article to look at in more depth [5 mins max]

Pupils each pick an article and spend a couple of minutes reading it to take in as much detail as they can. Explain that will need to summarise the article in French for others. Ask pupils to ensure that only those next to them can see which article they have chosen. Circulate to check all understand what to do.

4 Modelling – how to read a complicated text you haven't seen before

Show sample article on Smartboard. Elicit from class, what words they already know – highlight those mentioned. What new words can you work out from the context? Can you explain how you worked out what they mean? What 3 words would you look up in the dictionary? Why? Are you sure those would help you write a summary of the story?

5 Independent reading for meaning

Pupils work independently with the article they have chosen. Instructions on Smartboard.

(i)Highlight all the words you definitely know already. (ii) Underline words you could guess from the context. (iii) Look up three words that you didn't understand at all. [10 mins] Circulate to check all understand what to do.

6 Prepare and share summary of article in TL

Pupils work alone and spend 5 minutes preparing how they would summarise the key details of the article in French. Can write down key points to read out. Then in 4s they all read what they have come up with and see if others can work it out. Circulate and help only if necessary, listen to pupils' summaries.

7 Plenary discussion – based on questions in English (ppt)   [10 mins]

Pupils have 2 mins to discuss the questions in pairs and agree on 1 point for each to share. Explain your answers to opposite pair in your group of 4. In main discussion I will ask pupils to answer on behalf of opposite pair.

8 Pack away and wait quietly for bell

Instructions for next lesson. Dismiss in TL.

Copyright material from Cheryl Mackay (2019), *Learning to Plan Modern Languages Lessons*, Routledge

TABLE 5.10B Commentary on Year 10 French lesson: independent reading skills

This lesson was planned and taught by a beginning teacher on her second teaching placement. This was not an easy class to manage. In planning the lesson the teacher was focused on helping pupils to learn independently but this was not her only reason for deliberately planning a less teacher-led lesson. She also wanted to see how this change of approach would impact on behaviour and engagement and what she could learn from this for her own professional development.

It is significant that despite the emphasis on independent learning, the teacher still has a pivotal role to play in shaping the learning experiences presented to pupils in this lesson. First of all, it is worth noting that the lesson starts with a revision of reading skills practised in the previous lesson. The teacher plans to use questioning to focus pupil attention on how they are learning (the skills they are using) and to get them to articulate those skills. This explicit recap is planned to help all pupils recall the learning from the previous lesson. And it is a first step towards preparing pupils to read independently of the teacher, later in the lesson.

At point 4, the role of the teacher in modelling relevant reading skills and strategies is significant. The thinking behind this is to help learners see for themselves how they could break down a French text and realise how much they know or can work out for themselves. The plan here is to use questions to try and elicit as much as possible from pupils, rather than the teacher telling them; to actively involve pupils in the process of working out what the text means; and to get pupils to think through for themselves how to make strategic use of the dictionary.

Another key role of the teacher is leading the plenary discussion at the end of the lesson. Ten minutes of lesson time have been earmarked for this and the time has been clearly organised. The thinking behind this is to make the plenary focused and to encourage all pupils to contribute and articulate their thinking, even if it is only to each other. Questions are displayed on a prepared ppt slide.

Finally, a word about timing. It is not always easy to anticipate how long specific stages in lessons such as this will take. In particular, you may well find that the interactive modelling part (point 4) takes longer than anticipated. If this happens, then it would be better to shorten or omit point 6 rather than to rush or omit the metacognitive plenary. The plenary is an opportunity for learners to reflect on *how* they are learning and this reflection is central to the learning process. This is an example of how pre-lesson planning decisions might need to be revised in the course of the lesson itself.

Follow-up Reflective Task/Points to discuss

I have deliberately omitted from the lesson plan key questions that were asked in the plenary. If you were teaching this lesson, what key questions would you want the class to discuss at the end of the lesson? And why? What would you want to know or find out from the discussion? And why?

What sort of content do you think typical 14–15 year olds would be interested to read about in this lesson? What sort of news stories might be relevant to typical 11–12 year olds or to 16–18 year olds?

Are there parts of a lesson like this where it might be more helpful to learning to use English rather than the TL?

Copyright material from Cheryl Mackay (2019), *Learning to Plan Modern Languages Lessons*, Routledge

Different sorts of ML lessons

In their review of independent learning, Meyer et al. (2008) stress the key role of teachers in assisting pupils to become independent learners. One way of thinking about this is in terms of the teacher mediating pupils' transition to becoming more independent learners. In the lesson above (Table 5.10A), for example, the teacher mediates pupils' learning by helping them to see what they already know, modelling mental strategies and processes for them to use, and using questions during the plenary to develop pupils' metacognitive awareness. The principle of mediation, or mediated learning experiences, has its roots in psychology and is much broader than the context of language learning. Nevertheless, it is a useful theoretical construct when talking about independent learning. For more about mediation and how it relates to language classrooms, please see Williams and Burden (1997).

Planning for independent learning

I believe that independent learning starts with the teacher. I would like to highlight next some important implications for lesson planning. These ideas are drawn from Meyer et al. (2008) and my own experience.

Plan to create an 'enabling environment' (Meyer et al., 2008, p1)

- Consider how the physical layout of the classroom may impact on learning. For example, if you want pupils to work in groups or talk in groups, then it will be helpful if they are able to see each other. Time spent re-organising furniture to make this possible is time well spent.
- Consider how best to group pupils in order to create an enabling environment. For example, some teachers let pupils choose their own groups because they find that pupils are more confident with friends, especially if they are expected to talk to each other in the TL. There might be other factors to consider: some teachers favour mixed ability groupings to support differentiation; there might be some pupils who cannot be trusted to work together etc. Time spent thinking through the seating plan is time well spent. If this involves a change to usual seating arrangements, consider how you might most efficiently inform pupils of where to sit; for example, some schools have name cards which they put out on tables, whilst some teachers produce a seating plan which is shown on the board at the start of the lesson.

Plan the lead up to the independent learning task

- Think through what skills and strategies will help pupils to learn independently. Consider ways of eliciting those from pupils, rather than assuming that you will need to tell them how to approach the tasks you have set. Identify any particular strategies that you want everyone to be aware of and how you might model those for the class. When you model particular strategies, consider using a 'think aloud' approach; in other words, give pupils a running commentary on what you are doing so they can understand the thinking behind your actions. Modelling, particularly of mental processes, can play a significant role in helping pupils to learn independently.

Plan how you will manage the independent learning part of the lesson

- Consider what you will be doing at those stages in the lesson when pupils are working independently. Pupils should not be dependent on you, the teacher, as a resource but that doesn't mean that you just leave them to it. There are ways you might help without interrupting the flow of pupil-pupil interactions. For example, you might decide to quietly write up a list of tips on the board for pupils to refer to. Or, if a pupil asks you a language-specific question, you might try to provide hints and clues to help the pupil work out the answer for themselves rather than telling them the answer (e.g. *What do you think? Is there anything that gives you a clue? Look again at the first sentence*).
- When pupils are working independently, consider how you might use that time as a learning opportunity for yourself. It might be an opportunity to develop your own understanding of how well pupils are learning, or to collect information that you can feedback to the class at the end of the lesson. For example, you might want to listen in to a sample of pupil-pupil interactions and make a note of good examples of independent language use that you hear or see.

Plan the questions for the debrief

Debriefing distils the essence of what pupils take away with them from the lesson. Through questioning you want to help pupils to reflect on their learning and their role in that process. The interaction between teacher and individual pupils that takes place at this stage is not just filling in time at the end of the lesson, it is purposeful with the teacher using questions to elicit further thought (Quigley and Stringer, 2018). So, this part of the lesson requires careful planning.

- Plan plenty of time for the debrief until you become familiar with what is involved. I would suggest at least 10 minutes to start with, so that you can build in plenty of thinking time for pupils.
- Plan your questions carefully and write them onto your lesson plan. As a rule of thumb 4–5 key questions is probably ample. Here are some starter questions that can work well:
    - ☐ How did you get on? Did you enjoy the task?
    - ☐ How did you do it? What helped you?
    - ☐ Did you have any difficulties? What did you do to help you get over those difficulties?
    - ☐ Would you do anything differently next time?

This can be the most challenging part of the lesson for teachers who are new to metacognitive approaches. My advice would be to observe good practitioners who can model for you what is involved in managing a metacognitive debrief, this might be in ML or in another subject. For further practical advice on getting the debriefing right, see Lin and Mackay (2004).

And finally . . .

- Based on your prior knowledge of the class, ask yourself if there anything else you could do that might make a difference to the success of the lesson.

For further relevant advice on planning for independent learning and developing metacognitive awareness in ML, I recommend looking into language learning strategies (strategy instruction) and teaching thinking skills. You might see explicit strategy instruction or thinking skills lessons in school or you might read about them. See, for example, *Learning Strategies in the Language Classroom: Issues and Implementation* (Chamot and Harris, forthcoming) and *Thinking Through Modern Foreign Languages* (Lin and Mackay, 2004).

Why bother with independent learning?

We live in a world where future language needs are increasingly difficult to predict. And there is an argument that learning how to learn another language is going to be more useful to future generations than knowledge of any one particular language. Fostering independent learning, so that pupils leave school confident in their own abilities to learn independently, helps to prepare pupils for future success as language learners and users, and builds a strong platform for learning further languages.

Setting up classrooms to foster independent learning, including metacognition, is also seen as part of a bigger goal: promoting learner autonomy. Ultimately, learner autonomy is about learners taking control of their own learning, equipped with the appropriate skills and strategies to learn a language in a self-directed way (Williams and Burden, 1997, p147). Terry Lamb is a national authority on learner autonomy in ML. In his view, 'someone who is both able and (at least some of the time) willing to learn independently could be called an autonomous learner' (Lamb, 2009, p23). Much has been written about the concept of learner autonomy in language learning and particularly its impact on motivation; Williams and Burden (1997) provide a good introduction.

So the focus on *how* we are learning and discussion of what is helping us to learn can make a big difference to longer-term progress and to learner autonomy. However, I have another particular reason for choosing to include this focus in the book. Lessons, such as the one presented above (Table 5.10A), which are planned to include a metacognitive plenary can be immensely helpful to the teacher, especially the beginning teacher. Listening to pupils reflect on how they are learning and their role in that process will give you valuable insights into how pupils see the world and useful starting points for future lesson planning. In short, this will help you get to know your pupils as learners. This is particularly pertinent in ML, a subject where the relationships that are formed can sometimes feel rather artificial compared to pupil-teacher relationships in subjects which are taught through the medium of the mother tongue. Feedback from student teachers, over many years, suggests that lessons that lead to a metacognitive plenary in English can feel more authentic; teachers feel they are interacting with pupils in a more meaningful way than is often the case in a typical ML lesson.

Teachers who contributed to the MFL Network for Thinking Skills at Newcastle University noticed that teaching thinking skills made lessons more motivating and interesting, not only for pupils but also for the teacher. Apart from higher levels of pupil motivation, teachers also noticed an increase in pupils' self-confidence; and teachers started to see themselves more as equal participants in the learning process (Lin and Mackay, 2004, pp194–195). Based on these outcomes alone, I would encourage beginning teachers to be proactive in seeking out opportunities to experiment with lessons which are designed to foster independent learning and develop metacognitive awareness. Fundamentally the learning experiences you plan in such lessons are giving a clear message to pupils that you expect them to be able to learn. And that can be a very powerful message.

Finally, such lessons add variety to the language learning diet; and variety, so we are told, is the spice of life! However, too much emphasis on thinking and talking about learning could lead to a disconnection from the actual process of learning a language. In other words, 'the final aim is not to be constantly thinking about our learning, but to move towards a situation where the use of appropriate strategies becomes unconscious, where the skills of learning become intuitive' (Williams and Burden, 1997, p155).

Summing up Chapter 5

We have looked here at planning for a wider range of possible learning in ML, including cultural knowledge, appreciation of literature, explicit knowledge of grammar, creative use of language, independent reading skills and metacognitive awareness – and we have considered related pedagogical approaches. Whilst some of these elements contribute directly to language learning, others contribute indirectly by having a large impact on motivation. The key point is that *together* they help to create the conditions needed for successful language learning. With all of these it is a case of 'less is more'; rather than replacing the simple PPP model, they add to it and complement it.

CHAPTER

Longer-term planning

Introduction

Longer-term planning is a huge remit. The aim of this chapter therefore is to *start* to consider what is involved in longer-term planning in ML. We will consider planning for learning across a sequence of lessons. Three key concepts will be introduced: progression, coherence and balance; together with a simple template that can be used for writing up medium-term teaching plans.

What is longer-term planning and why does it matter?

A Framework of Core Content for initial teacher training (ITT) in England was commissioned by the Department for Education in 2016. The framework complements the Teachers' Standards by giving further clarity on effective preparation for excellent teaching. The framework includes the following advice in relation to the planning and teaching of well-structured lessons:

> **Providers should** ensure that trainees understand that all new teaching builds on prior knowledge, and use that principle to plan well-sequenced lessons and schemes of work. Trainees should understand that effective planning is not an isolated activity, but draws upon knowledge of subject, progression, assessment and skilful questioning. Providers should support trainees in their planning to demonstrate an understanding of how individual lessons fit within a lesson sequence.
>
> (Department for Education, 2016, p16)

This advice from the ITT Framework is a good starting point for a discussion of longer-term planning. It picks up on two key concepts that underpin effective longer-term planning. The first of those is the idea that new teaching builds on prior knowledge. This is rather like teaching the new within the context of the familiar, one of the principles we looked at in relation to lesson planning. When planning longer-term in ML, we should be aware, for example, of building in opportunities to recycle previously learnt vocabulary and structures and opportunities to deepen understanding of grammatical concepts that have already been introduced. The second key idea is planning sequences of lessons rather than separate unrelated lessons. Well-sequenced lessons are linked to ensure progression in pupils' learning; later lessons in the sequence will build on earlier lessons and be informed by the outcomes of earlier lessons.

To this I would add that longer-term planning is also a time to step back and consider the balance of learning opportunities that we are offering pupils. In ML, for example, we might want to ensure that over a sequence of lessons pupils are not only learning grammar or we might want to ensure a balance of listening, speaking, reading and writing skills practice.

Finally, it is worth noting that writing a longer-term plan does *not* mean writing individual lesson plans for the next half term with a given class. The sort of detail that typically goes into lesson plans is neither necessary nor advisable when planning longer term. As implied in the advice above, the only lesson you can effectively plan in detail is the next lesson in any sequence. That way you can ensure that individual lesson planning is informed by and builds on what was learnt in the previous lesson.

So, longer-term planning is an opportunity to think through the broad brushstrokes of how learning might progress over time and what that might look like for all pupils involved. The way we structure new linguistic input for our pupils is an important element of this; as is the way we factor in opportunities for recycling previous linguistic input. For many beginning teachers, planning a unit of work is their first experience of longer-term planning and we will look more closely at that now.

Units of work

I am using the term 'unit of work' in quite a loose sense here to refer to a teaching plan for a sequence of lessons on the same topic. For the purposes of this book, units of work cover five to ten lessons, or approximately three to four weeks' work. In my experience, beginning teachers tend to underestimate just how much time to allow for learning, so that what was planned as one lesson may well end up taking two or even three lessons. With that in mind, I do not recommend planning further ahead than ten lessons. Usually a unit of work has a single overarching theme to ensure continuity and coherence across lessons and a goal or end activity to work towards, which brings together much of the learning of the unit and might also provide opportunities to use previously learnt language.

In this chapter we will be looking at units of work, written by you for your own use, as a planning tool to help secure progression in learning. Some of the benefits are summarised below:

- Having a unit of work gives you a sense of purpose and direction, you have a vision of where you want to go.
- This helps with the planning of individual lessons because you can see how lessons are linked and how they fit into a sequence.
- It also helps your decision making in lessons if you know what is coming up next lesson or in the foreseeable future.
- Planning a unit of work helps develop your understanding of the bigger picture of the ML curriculum and how the pieces can fit together.
- Once you have that vision, you can communicate it to learners and help them to be proactive in taking responsibility for their progress; learners are also motivated if they know where their learning is heading.
- It can help with formative assessment and target setting, if you have an end goal or bigger picture in mind.

In short, planning sequences of lessons is a helpful thing to do, and an efficient use of your time (Wringe, 1989). Even if you are not asked to produce units of work for the classes that you teach, I would still recommend doing so. A sequence of learning is not really in your head until you have thought it through and processed the implications for yourself.

Planning a unit of work

In this section we will begin by considering some key ML specific points to consider when planning a unit of work: linguistic content, overarching aims and objectives, tasks and activities, assessment, progression and sequencing.

Preliminaries

It is best to find out first of all what schemes of work are already in place in school and that you are expected to follow. The extent of detail and prescription on those will vary considerably; in some cases you will be able to use the textbook as a guide. You should also check with your mentor how much time is expected to be spent on the topics or schemes of work you are expected to teach; also, what resources already exist that you can use. Listening or reading materials relevant to the topic can be particularly helpful as those can be very time-consuming to produce or find for yourself.

Once the preliminaries are out of the way, there is no particular order to the points which follow. Planning is a very individual thing, there is no one way to go about it. So, rather than seeing this as a linear process, consider what follows as important points that you might need to visit and revise several times until you have a coherent unit of work that makes sense to you.

Linguistic content

One of the most important points to think through is what new vocabulary and structures you are going to teach. The same principles apply here as for lesson planning. Try to avoid teaching words on their own, use structures to contextualise and give meaning to the language you are teaching. Consider also what scope there is within the unit for recycling previously learnt language.

Wherever possible, try to introduce the new within the context of the familiar; for example, there might be scope to reuse vocabulary from previous topics within the context of the new structures that you are teaching; or it might be possible for speaking or writing tasks to build on what pupils can already do. Here are some examples of what recycling might mean in practice:

- When preparing and performing interviews about school subjects, there is scope for pupils to bring in personal information questions relating to age, birthday, hobbies, etc.
- If pupils learn how to give opinions when discussing school subjects, in a subsequent topic (e.g. talking about films or books they like or dislike) there is scope to reuse and build on this by learning how to justify opinions.
- When producing a brochure with factual information about a town, there is also the possibility to include short interviews or statements from people who live in the town, perhaps drawing on prior learning to give reasons why they like or don't like living there.

Overarching aims and objectives

The overarching learning intentions for the unit of work, or sequence of lessons, might already be stated in the scheme of work you are working from. But if not, try not to have too many, this is about broad brushstrokes; you don't necessarily need to have one for each lesson, some overarching objectives or learning intentions will take more than one lesson to achieve. I would start by identifying the communicative aims and objectives for the unit: what pupils should be able to understand and communicate in the target language. This is a chance to check that aims and objectives include the development of language skills; in most cases this will mean a balance of listening, speaking, reading and writing across the unit. And a chance to cross-check that those learning intentions are compatible with the linguistic content you are teaching.

For example, a sequence of lessons on the topic of past holidays might have the following aims and objectives:

Pupils should be able to use the past tense in both spoken and written forms to:
- *Give simple information about their holidays, where they went and what they did and to express an opinion on this;*
- *Ask for and understand information about other people's holidays.*

Having identified your communicative objectives, it is then also important to identify any grammar that you want pupils to be aware of. One way to do this is to ask yourself if there are any underlying patterns you want pupils to be able to manipulate in order to meet the communicative objectives. And if you do decide to include some explicit grammar teaching, please bear in mind that you cannot teach all the possible grammar in one unit of work! A little grammar goes a long way. Be selective and prioritise any grammar that pupils will need to be able to use to help them achieve the communicative objectives for the unit. This is a very important point; it helps us to think through the educational purpose of what we are planning to teach. That purpose should not simply be 'for the test'!

So, try and identify a purpose for using the language and applying any grammar you are teaching. If there is not an obvious purpose, then perhaps you need to tweak the linguistic content, adding on a few extras so that you can plan for pupils to use the language for a purpose. For example, the inclusion of question forms might mean that pupils are not simply learning the past tense for a test, but are learning to ask and answer questions about past holidays. At the very least, there should be a task or activity at the end of the unit of work which involves pupils using the language for a purpose. We will look more closely at end of unit tasks later in this section.

Possible tasks and activities

Think through a variety of different possible tasks or activities that you might use within the unit of work to help you teach the linguistic content and achieve the aims and objectives that you have identified. To ensure variety and maximise pupil engagement, you might also want to check that you have catered for visual, auditory and kinaesthetic learning styles.

Assessment

This is about thinking through how you are going to assess how well the overarching learning intentions have been achieved. It will be important for pupils to have feedback and a sense of progress and it will be important for you to know what progress they are making as you work through the sequence of lessons. In terms of summative assessment, you might consider how you could use the task at the end of the unit of work to assess what progress has been made over the sequence of lessons. In terms of diagnostic assessment, you should also think through what opportunities you can build in for feedback along the way. You might also want to identify which of your possible tasks and activities could serve a diagnostic assessment purpose.

Longer-term planning

Overarching Learning Intentions

Pupils should be able to:

- To understand how to use some frequently used verbs in the past tense, in both affirmative and negative forms.
- To use the past tense to give simple information about past holidays, where they went and what they did and to express an opinion on this
- Ask for and understand information about other people's holidays

> Mystery guest interviews.

C'était comment?

C'était + super, génial, fantastique, intéressant, ennuyeux, nul

2

> Homework, gap-fill text about holidays in past tense.

> Cue card conversations Q+A – where did you go and what did you do?

GRAMMAR – formation of past tense
(1st and 2nd person singular)
3x parts affirmative/ 5x parts negative

1

Qu'est-ce que tu as fait pendant les vacances?

J'ai fait / Je n'ai pas fait + de la planche à voile, du ski, du vélo, une randonnée à pied, les magasins etc.

J'ai visité / Je n'ai pas visité + un château, un musée, une cathédrale, des monuments historiques etc.

J'ai joué / Je n'ai pasjoué + au tennis, au football, au ping-pong, aux cartes etc.

Je suis allé (e) / Je ne suis pas allé (e) + à la plage, à la piscine, au cinema, au concert, au marché, en ville etc

> Mini class survey – how many people went to the same place as you?

2

Tu es allé (e) où en vacances? (Es-tu allé (e) ... ?)

Je suis allé (e)/ Je ne suis pas allé (e) en + Cornouailles, Ecosse, Espagne, France, Grèce, Italie, / **au** Canada, Portugal / **aux** Etats Unis / **à** Bournemouth, Londres etc.

Je ne suis pas allé (e) en vacances. **Je suis resté (e)** à la maison.

2

End Goal

Pupils assume role of 'mystery guest' and interview each other in pairs about past holidays. Interviews are recorded and can be played for rest of class to guess identity of mystery guest.

FIGURE 6.1 Sample staircase of progression for '*les dernières vacances*'

Linguistic progression

Having identified the linguistic content for the whole unit of work, it is helpful to then think through how this language, including any grammar teaching, will build up over the sequence of lessons. This is about breaking the total content down into meaningful, manageable chunks that can be built up over a sequence of lessons in a logical progression.

One way of thinking about this, particularly with Key Stage 3 classes, is in terms of a staircase that breaks down the linguistic content of the teaching and learning sequence. Figure 6.1 shows an example of what a staircase might look like.

The first point to note is that the staircase is very much a starting point for more detailed planning. The main structures and vocabulary for the sequence of lessons are broken down into steps of progression. The first step is the step at the bottom, subsequent steps build on this in a logical progression; this means that over the sequence of lessons there is scope for plentiful practice and recycling key structures. The language of each step is contextualised with a structure and or question to ensure that pupils are not simply learning lists of words. And a short-term goal has been added to each step; this is an activity that you might use to diagnostically assess how well pupils are progressing at that stage. These activities build on each other in order to ensure progression.

Some steps on the staircase might take longer than others to complete; the number on the right hand side indicates how many lessons are planned for each respective step. One full lesson and a homework are dedicated to the formation of the past tense and these come after plentiful exposure to the grammar in use. At the end of the sequence, there is a final task (activity) which embraces most or all of the overarching learning intentions and pulls together much of the linguistic content of the unit of work.

Please bear in mind that this is just one example to show how the idea of a planning staircase works. It is worth noting that some units of work might involve spending more than one lesson on grammar or form-focused activity. For example, Figure 6.2 shows how a sequence of five lessons on the topic of fairy stories in German might be constructed for a top set Year 9 class. With thanks to Bev Hewer, Lead Practitioner at Stanground Academy in Peterborough, for sharing her planning with me.

Sequence of five lessons for a top set Year 9 German class

Lesson 1

Reading for meaning, pupils read a selection of extracts from well known fairy stories which introduce the imperfect tense in context.

Lessons 2–4

Focus on the formation of the imperfect tense with frequently used verbs both from the stories read in lesson 1 and from other familiar contexts, lots of form-focused language work including translation work, in and out of the TL, and gap-fill exercises. Along the way, learning is consolidated and extended through homework tasks which are helping to build up to the end goal.

Lesson 5

Pupils read a final longer story in the imperfect tense. Then preparation for the end of unit goal which involves extended writing in the imperfect tense. The task might be to write an alternative ending to a well known fairy story or write a fairy story in a modern setting. During this preparatory stage there is scope for pupils to work collaboratively in pairs to create their own fairy tales; this generates further discussion and practice of the imperfect and its use. Pupils' own creations are completed as homework and then re-drafted in the light of teacher feedback.

Final creations, are then mounted as a wall display with relevant pictures and other visuals. This means that final versions of stories can be read for different purposes by other pupils, from the same class and from other classes.

FIGURE 6.2 Example of a sequence of lessons

Longer-term planning

TABLE 6.1 Unit of work template

Class	Title	No. of lessons

Overarching learning intentions:

End goal: **Expectations:**

Key structures and vocabulary:

Possible teaching and learning activities:

Resources:

TABLE 6.2 Unit of work for '*les dernières vacances*'

Class	Title	No. of lessons
Year 8 mixed ability	*Les dernières vacances*	7 @ 60 mins.

Overarching learning intentions:

- To understand how to employ some frequently used verbs in the past tense, affirmative and negative.
- To use the past tense to give simple information about past holidays, where they went and what they did and to express an opinion on this.
- Ask for and understand information about other people's holidays.

End goal:	Expectations:
'Mystery guest' interviews about past holidays in pairs. Interviews are recorded and can be played for rest of class to guess identity of mystery guest.	Everyone to ask and answer holiday questions with as little prompting as possible. More able to give more detailed responses and to feed in personal information from previous topics (talking about free time, where you live).

Key structures and vocabulary (see staircase for details):

Tu es allé (e) où en vacances?	*Je suis allé (e)/ Je ne suis pas allé (e) en + Espagne, France, Italie, / au Portugal / aux Etats Unis / à Bournemouth* etc.
	Je suis resté (e) à la maison
Qu'est-ce que tu as fait pendant les vacances?	*J'ai fait / Je n'ai pas fait . . .*
	J'ai visité / Je n'ai pas visité . . .
	J'ai joué / Je n'ai pas joué . . .
	Je suis allé (e) / Je ne suis pas allé (e) . . .
C'était comment?	*C'était + super, génial, fantastique, nul* etc.

Possible teaching and learning activities:

My holidays – true/false (start the topic with this)

Spot the fib

Cue cards + picture prompts of countries/activities – build up over few lessons

20 questions – yes/no answers

Miming actions of what did/where went

Pass the Postcard/ Photo – how many different sentences can you say/write about this holiday?

Listening – others describe hols, fill in grid/use transcript to model basic interview structure

Reading blogs + photos – feed in more vocabulary (Who with? Transport? Dates?)

Washing line to show formation of perfect tense/position of *ne* and *pas* (always a pair)

Written grammar exercises from text book/gap-fill + past participles

Resources:

Cue cards, postcards, 'mystery guest' names, listening material, washing line + pegs and cards, book out textbooks – lesson 4 or 5?

Longer-term planning

The key point to note in Figure 6.2 is that both the beginning and the end of the sequence concentrates on using the language for a communicative purpose. The grammar work that takes place is focused on learning the formation of the imperfect tense and pupils will be able to apply what they have learnt within the context of the end of unit task, the purpose of which is expressed in communicative terms.

Finally, it is useful to have a template to use for writing up your medium-term plans. See Table 6.1 for a template that you might find useful, together with a worked example (Table 6.2) which is based on the planning staircase in Figure 6.1 (*Les dernières vacances*).

End of unit tasks

I want to return now to end of unit tasks. This is where the sequence of lessons is heading, so it is important to consider what form these tasks might take and some of their design features. I prefer to call these end of unit activities 'tasks' in order to distinguish them from other language teaching activities. Personally, when planning units of work, I have found it helpful to identify an end of unit task pretty early on in the planning process. In my experience, having an end goal in mind has made other aspects of medium-term planning more purposeful. In particular, this has helped me to strike a balance between high, yet realistic, expectations of all pupils, which, to me, is the essence of differentiation.

An end of unit task should have a clearly defined outcome which provides learners with a specific purpose for using the language, other than demonstrating knowledge and understanding of how the language works. Through the task, we are trying to simulate realistic, independent communication (i.e. the production stage of the PPP model). The task should also be motivating; motivation is one of the conditions for successful language learning. So it is important that the purpose of the task is relevant to pupils' interests and maturity levels. Here are some generic examples of possible end of unit tasks, together with some initial planning questions to think through.

- Produce a brochure
   What is the purpose of the brochure? Does it have to be true or can it be imaginary? Who might the brochure be aimed at? Do you have one specific audience in mind or are you going to offer learners a choice of audience? A brochure advertising a sports centre, for example, might contain different information if it is aimed at senior citizens or sports fans, families with young children or visitors from another planet.
- A video or digital production
   What is the purpose of the production? Is there a target audience? For example, it might be possible to send a film about your school to a partner school either in this country or abroad. Are learners working on this in pairs or groups? Have you checked out the technology? If recording needs to take place during lesson time, how will this be managed? Can you use the class teacher, any teaching assistants, foreign language assistants or other beginning teachers to help you?
- Live performance or oral presentation of some sort
   What is the purpose? Entertainment? Information? Have you built in rehearsal time? Have you thought through the practicalities of staging this?
- Write a story
   Is there an audience? Who will read the stories? And for what purpose? Enjoyment? Reading comprehension? Peer assessment? Have you factored in ample time for drafting and rewriting? See also 'Wall display' below.
- Produce a play or sketch
   Is this a speaking or writing task? Are pupils working in groups or individually? What is the purpose of the play or sketch? Who will watch or read what pupils have produced? In the case of acting it out, are you expecting pupils to do this from memory?
- Wall display
   What is the purpose of the display? Who will see it? How will you ensure that everyone can contribute? Is there scope for pupils to evaluate the work on display e.g. You might display what pupils have written about a 'perfect' or 'nightmare' holiday they have had (true or imaginary). This provides reading material for other pupils who might vote on which holiday sounds the most perfect and which one the biggest nightmare.
- Produce an oral or written report
   Is this going to be a factual or fictional report? Purpose? Intended audience? Have you factored in research time? Are pupils working in groups or individually?

These tasks are cumulative; they help to bring together learning from the last few lessons and are an opportunity to build on prior learning or recycle language learnt in previous units. In the interests of differentiation, it is important that end of unit tasks are sufficiently open-ended to allow for a range of different responses and outcomes, possibly including unpredictable ones; and that there is enough scope within the task to stretch and challenge the highest achieving linguists.

There are different ways of doing this, but you might want to start by focusing on the highest achievers in the group. What can you expect them to be able to produce? What sort of linguistic response can you expect from them? What structures might they use? What sort of detail might they include? I would then start to write down key structures and sample vocabulary that they might use and use this to identify any grammar that it would be useful for all pupils to know and be able to manipulate for the end task. You might then turn to the lowest achievers in the group or those who seem to have most difficult learning the language. What language could they use to complete the task successfully? You can use this line of questioning to help you establish a basic minimum of language needed to complete the task. This is the language that you need to drill and practise most intensively in lessons. This language provides a sort of safety net or backup for those pupils who might struggle to be more independent or creative in their use of language. At the same time, however, it is important to expect all pupils to take risks with the language and to stretch themselves to go beyond a minimal response. Assuming there is plenty of scope within the task to go beyond a minimal response, the important thing to remember here is to make your expectations explicit to all pupils.

Reflective/discussion task

Here are two possible versions of the same task. The context is the same for both: pupils are preparing a commentary on clothes worn in a fashion show. Consider what outcomes might result from these different ways of presenting the same task. Do you think that the way the task has been set might influence the range of outcomes and, if so, how?

- *Version one:*
  Your commentary should include names of garments, colours, descriptions and the verb 'porter'.
- *Version two:*
  You are working for the fashion house, so your commentary should make listeners want to buy these clothes items. You should try and do this through your description of the clothes, information about the price, also your own opinion of the clothes, say what you like about each item and why.

There are also potential pitfalls in planning units of work around end tasks, and it is important to be aware of those. For one thing, relying *solely* on one specific task to identify the linguistic content that you are going to teach risks ignoring other relevant content and limiting the extent of new language and structures to which learners are exposed. Similarly, to reduce the aims and objectives of the unit of work to those which can be achieved or evidenced through the end task is to ignore other possible outcomes. By all means take the end goal as your starting point in planning the unit of work but be prepared to work *outwards* from that to embrace other potential learning outcomes for the unit of work as a whole, and to capitalise on the potential for building on prior learning.

In reality, the end of unit task may take the form of a test; in my experience this is quite common. However, it doesn't have to be a test! Pupils are likely to produce better work if they are motivated to do so and a well-designed end of unit task does just that; it is also an excellent opportunity for feedback to pupils on their learning and progress over time. I would certainly recommend using end of unit tasks for assessment purposes and if the task involves oral performance of some sort, it is definitely worth recording this as evidence of learning outcomes.

This checklist sums up the main features of a well-designed end of unit task.

- ☐ Cumulative
- ☐ Builds on prior learning from the unit
- ☐ Achievable by all
- ☐ Sufficiently open ended to allow for a range of different outcomes
- ☐ Broad enough to include all abilities in the class
- ☐ Provides opportunities for recycling of previously learnt language
- ☐ Relevant purpose
- ☐ Can be used for assessment purposes

FIGURE 6.3 Planning checklist for end of unit tasks

TASK – fashion show	PURPOSE
In groups of 3, you will prepare a 30 second presentation about a set of clothes you will be given. You will be taking part in a fashion show at 2.45pm; your presentation needs to be ready by 2.40pm. Use the textbook, the vocab sheet, your exercise book and the two teachers to help you. You will be assessing each other's work using the criteria below.	Two questions that provide the context for this work are: **Can you describe clothes in Spanish, using different adjectives correctly?** **How fluently and confidently can you put over what you want to say in Spanish?**
SUCCESS CRITERIA	PROCESS
1. Your presentation must be 20-30 seconds long in Spanish. 2. It should include names of garments, colours, other adjectives, the verb 'llevar' 3. Genders and agreements of adjectives must be accurate. 4. You must have clear and correct Spanish pronunciation.	1. Assign tasks: Scribe (writer), time-keeper, facilitator (keeps people on task). You must also decide who is going to be the model and who is going to speak about the clothes (is this one person or two?) 2. Work to people's strengths- you do not have much time to complete the task. 3. Do a draft version first? Use brainstorming to collate information (initially every idea is valid). Have a sweep to check that everyone is in agreement/ has said all that they want to say? Criticise constructively? Agree on the final version? PRACTISE SEVERAL TIMES! 4. Remember to check the finished product for quality – does it meet all the success criteria?

Follow up reflective task/ points to discuss

Assuming the same topic of Fashion and Clothes, how might you adapt the idea of a fashion show for a mixed ability Year 10 class? Consider each of the headings: task, purpose of task, success criteria, process.

What might a staircase of progression leading up to this end task look like? Assume that you have about 6 lessons for the unit of work, including the end goal. Complete a staircase of progression in French, German or Spanish for a mixed ability Year 8 and for a Year 10 class. In no particular order.

- State some overarching learning intentions for the whole unit.
- Map out the key language structures and vocabulary you would teach, plus any grammar you could teach.
- Consider also what prior learning pupils might build on or recycle in this unit of work.
- How would you build a staircase of progression leading up to the end goal?
- What key activities could you build in along the way?

You might want to compare completed staircases with others who have done the same task. Or you might want to explain it to your mentor and discuss your thinking.

FIGURE 6.4 Task sheet for fashion show

To illustrate some of the key points discussed so far in this section, Figure 6.4 shows an end of unit task designed by a beginning teacher towards the end of her second teaching placement. The class in question was a lively, mixed ability Year 8 Spanish class – they were lovely kids but quite a handful to manage! The task came at the end of a sequence of lessons on the topic of Fashion and Clothes. The teacher planned this and other end of unit tasks with the help of her mentor; she designed the task sheet herself. The format of the task sheet worked well for her; it helped to clarify her thinking and it was useful for pupils and teacher to have this to refer to in the lesson.

A word about 'success criteria' and 'assessment criteria'

The task sheet in Figure 6.4 refers to 'success criteria'. My understanding is that success criteria are criteria that need to be met in order to successfully complete the task. This is rather different from 'assessment criteria' which describe *how well* the task has been completed. In principle, success criteria should be achievable by all, ensuring that everyone can be successful. However, if everyone has completed the task equally well or to exactly the same standard, then the task has not differentiated. For comprehensive guidance on this and other aspects of assessment, written for beginning teachers, please see Barnes and Hunt (2003).

Planning a sequence of lessons: planning checklist

The checklist below (Table 6.3) might be helpful when planning a short sequence of lessons, of the sort we have looked at in this chapter. It covers the main areas that need to be thought through, but there is also space for further points to be added as needed.

Used retrospectively, the checklist is a record of coverage of aspects of the Programme of Study for Languages at Key Stage 3. It is also a way of checking that across sequences of lessons learners have a balanced language learning experience, particularly in relation to language skills and grammar teaching. It will be important to ensure that across sequences of lessons learners have a good balance of listening, speaking, reading and writing tasks and that the grammar they are taught is useful and builds up to ensure progression in grammatical understanding. It is not necessary for each sequence of lessons to spend an equal amount of time on each of the four skills. For example, the topic of fairy stories might lend itself more to reading and writing rather than to speaking and listening. This is not a problem if this is balanced by other sequences of lessons which spend more time on speaking and listening. However, sequences of lessons which focus on grammar at the expense of skills development are to be avoided. At this stage, it might be worth bearing in mind this key message from recent research:

> The principal focus of pedagogy should be on developing language skills and therefore the teaching of linguistic knowledge (knowledge of grammar and vocabulary) should act in the service of skill development not as an end in itself.
>
> (PDC in MFL, 2012)

It is when we step back and take the longer-term view that this principle really becomes significant. A checklist such as the one in Table 6.3 is one way of keeping this key principle on the planning radar.

Evaluating longer-term plans and planning

Time spent evaluating longer-term planning, in this case a unit of work, is time well spent. After all, if you have taken the time to put it together, it seems silly not to take time to evaluate it. In a sense, evaluation of longer-term planning is part of the same planning cycle that you will be familiar with from lesson planning. In the same way that lesson evaluation informs the next lesson that you plan, evaluation of a unit of work informs the next unit of work that you write. Don't be surprised if you end up tweaking your unit of work before you reach the end of it! It might be necessary, for example, to add on an extra lesson or even two.

Systematic reflection and evaluation will help develop your understanding of progression in learning across lessons, this in turn will benefit your subsequent lesson planning and longer-term planning. In addition to the evaluation itself, you might also decide to amend the original unit of work or at least annotate it as a record that you can refer to next time you teach the same topic. As with lesson evaluation, the best time to do this is when it is still fresh in your mind.

Colleagues at Newcastle University have successfully used SWOT (strengths, weaknesses, opportunities and strengths) analysis as an evaluation tool with beginning teachers. In my experience, beginning teachers have found this a useful tool. It is easy to use, focuses the mind, and encourages consideration of different factors that are likely

Longer-term planning

TABLE 6.3 Checklist for planning sequences of lessons

1 Have I got a main task or learning outcome for each lesson?

2 Have I identified what new language I want pupils to learn?

3 Have I identified what language I want pupils to learn to use?

4 Have I worked out how that language will build up / build on previous language?

5 Is there scope for recycling previously learnt language?

6 Am I planning to make any grammar points explicit?

7 Have I planned how progress in learning will be assessed?

8 Have I identified a variety of different possible activities that I could use?

9 What skills have I covered? Listening? Speaking? Reading? Writing?

10 Am I planning to use any authentic sources?

11 Do I know what homework I will set and when?

12 Do I need to book any equipment, books, resources in advance?

13 Have I considered the time of day and layout of the room/s I will be teaching in?

14 If team teaching, have we agreed who will teach which lesson/s?

15

16

to or did impact on the outcomes or success of a unit of work. This might include factors that are planned into the unit of work, such as linguistic progression or use of sources and other factors that may be outside the direct control of the individual teacher such as the attitude or response of pupils, the support of a good mentor, the layout of the classroom, and the reliability of available technology.

Originally SWOT analysis was intended as a tool for evaluating the feasibility of business projects. You might want to use it in this way to review a draft version of your unit of work *before* you start teaching it; the purpose of this is to enable you to make any modifications to your planning before you start teaching. The same tool can also be used to review the unit of work *after* you have taught it; the purpose of this is to evaluate the effectiveness of your longer-term planning.

After completing the SWOT analysis, some key questions might be:

- Are there any aspects of this unit of work that I could improve at this stage? (before teaching)
- How well did pupils achieve the overarching learning intentions for this unit of work?
- Were there any other outcomes that I hadn't anticipated?
- Are there any aspects of this unit of work that I would change for the future?

Reflective and discussion task

Complete a SWOT analysis of the unit of work in Table 6.2 (Les Dernières Vacances). You might want to compare notes with others who have done the same task and discuss if there are any modifications you could make to the unit of work. Or you might want to explain your analysis to your mentor and discuss your thinking.

Summing up Chapter 6

We have looked here at planning for learning across a sequence of lessons and the value of planning in terms of medium-term units of work with end goals to work towards. Conceived in this way, learning across a sequence of lessons is cumulative, with overlap between lessons to ensure continuity and progression of learning. Developing a longer-term perspective on teaching and learning in ML goes hand-in-hand with planning for a balance of language learning experience. It is a crucial part of getting better at planning in your subject. And getting better at planning is the main theme of Part IV.

And finally . . . two recommendations

I would recommend to any beginning teacher that they plan, teach and evaluate at least one original unit of work along the lines suggested in this chapter, during the course of their ITE period (probably during the second placement). From experience, I am aware that in some teaching contexts beginning teachers may need to be proactive in negotiating the opportunity to plan their own unit of work. However, also from experience, this is a negotiation worth having; I am convinced of the considerable learning gains of doing so, especially, but not only, for beginning teachers themselves.

Planning for learning *across* units of work is not something you would normally be expected to do as a beginning teacher. But having some insight into planning beyond the medium term should further develop your understanding of key planning concepts, progression, coherence and balance, not to mention curriculum design. If you get the chance to contribute to planning at departmental level, please grab it!

References for Part III

ALL Literature Project, available at http://all-literature.wikidot.com/ (accessed March 2019)

Barnes, A. and Hunt, M. (2003) *Effective assessment in MFL*. CILT: London.

Bower, K. (2017) 'Speaking French alive': learner perspectives on their motivation in Content and Language Integrated Learning in England. *Innovation in Language Teaching and Learning*, pp1–16. DOI: 10.1080/17501229.2017.1314483.

Carter, R. (2004) *Language and creativity: the art of common talk*. Routledge: London.

Chamot, A.U. and Harris, V. (forthcoming) *Learning strategies in the language classroom: issues and implementation*. Multilingual Matters: Bristol.

Coyle, D., Holmes, B. and King, L. (2009) *Towards an integrated curriculum – CLIL national statement and guidelines*. The Languages Company: London. Also available at: https://www.languagescompany.com/wp-content/uploads/clil_national_statement_and_guidelines.pdf (accessed July 2018)

Coyle, D., Hood, P. and Marsh, D. (2010) *Content and language integrated learning*. Cambridge University Press: Cambridge.

Dearing, R. and King, L. (2007) *Languages review*. Final report. Department for Education and Skills. Available at https://www.languagescompany.com/wp-content/uploads/the-languages-review.pdf (accessed November 2018).

Department for Education (2013) *The National Curriculum in England: languages programmes of study – key stage 3*. Available at: https://www.gov.uk/government/publications/national-curriculum-in-england-languages-progammes-of-study (accessed November 2018).

— (2016) *A framework of core content for initial teacher training (ITT)*. Report commissioned by DfE. Available at: https://www.gov.uk/government/publications/initial-teacher-training-government-response-to-carter-review (accessed November 2018).

Department of Education and Skills (2001) *Teaching and learning in the foundation subjects*. Standards and Effectiveness Unit.

Dörnyei, Z. and Csizér, K. (1998) Ten commandments for motivating language learners: results of an empirical study. *Language Teaching Research*, 2(3), pp203–229.

Ellis, R. (2005) Principles of instructed language learning. *The Asian EFL Journal*, 7(3), pp9–24. Available at: https://www.asian-efl-journal.com/September_2005_EBook_editions.pdf (accessed November 2018).

Grenfell, M. and Harris, V. (2014) Learning strategies, autonomy and self-regulated learning. In P. Driscoll, E. Macaro and A. Swarbrick (eds.) *Debates in modern languages education*. Routledge: London, pp186–200.

Gulinck, A. (2015) *Using poetry in the French classroom*. Workbook. Free to download from: https://www.tes.com/teaching-resource/using-poetry-in-the-french-classroom-workbook-6255848 (accessed November 2018).

Hadfield, J. and Hadfield, C. (2015) Teaching grammar creatively. In A. Maley and N. Peachey (eds.) *Creativity in the English language classroom*. The British Council: London, pp51–63. Available at: http://englishagenda.britishcouncil.org/continuing-professional-development/cpd-teacher-trainers/creativity-english-language-classroom (accessed November 2018).

Hall, J.K. and Walsh, M. (2002) Teacher-student interaction and language learning. *Annual Review of Applied Linguistics*, 22, pp186–203.

Hawkins, E. (1999) *Listening to Lorca: a journey into language*. CILT: London.

Jespersen, O. (1944) *How to teach a foreign language*, George Allen & Unwin, Ltd.: London.

Johnstone, R. (1994) Grammar: acquisition and use. In L. King and P. Boaks (eds.) *Grammar! A conference report*. CILT: London, pp9–13.

Jones, B. (1995) *Exploring otherness: an approach to cultural awareness*. Pathfinder 24. CILT. Available from The Barry Jones Archive at: https://www.all-languages.org.uk/student/barry-jones-archive/ [accessed November 2018].

Lamb, T. (2009) Taking hold of learning: developing learner autonomy. Essay published in *Looking back – moving forward: the legacy of Brian Page*. Association for Language Learning: Leicester, pp22–26.

Lin, M. and Mackay, C. (2004) *Thinking through modern foreign languages*. Chris Kington Publishing: Cambridge.

Littlewood, W. (1981) *Communicative language teaching*. Cambridge University Press: Cambridge.

Macaro, E. (2014) Grammar. The never-ending debate. In P. Driscoll, E. Macaro and A. Swarbrick (eds.) *Debates in modern languages education*. Routledge: London, pp108–120.

Maley, A. and Peachey, N. (eds.) (2015) *Creativity in the English language classroom*. The British Council: London. Available at: http://englishagenda.britishcouncil.org/continuing-professional-development/cpd-teacher-trainers/creativity-english-language-classroom (accessed November 2018).

Meyer, B., Haywood, H., Sachdev, S. and Faraday, S. (2008) *What is independent learning and what are the benefits for students?* Research Report 051. Department for Children, Schools and Families: London. Available at: http://www.curee.co.uk/files/publication/[site-timestamp]/Whatisindependentlearningandwhatarethebenefits.pdf (accessed November 2018)

Mitchell, I. and Swarbrick, A. (1994) *Developing skills for independent reading*. Pathfinder 22. CILT: London.

Mitchell, R. and Myles, F. (1998) *Second language learning theories*. Arnold: London.

NC Modern Foreign Languages Working Group (1990) *Modern foreign languages for ages 11–16*. Final Report. Department for Education and Science.

Newmann, F.M. and Wehlage, G.G. (1993) Five standards of authentic instruction. *Educational Leadership*, 50(7), pp8–12.

Nutall, C. (2005) *Teaching reading skills in a foreign language*. Third edition. Macmillan Education: Oxford.

Ofqual (2017) *GCE subject level and requirements for modern foreign languages*. April 2017. Available at: https://assets.publishing.service.gov.uk/government/uploads/system/uploads/attachment_data/file/610131/GCE_Subject_Level_Conditions_for_MFL__April_2017_.pdf (accessed July 2018).

Pachler, N., Evans, M., Redondo, A. and Fisher, L. (2014) *Learning to teach foreign languages in the secondary school*. Fourth edition. Routledge: London.

PDC in MFL (2012) *Research for Language Teaching*. Available at: http://pdcinmfl.com (accessed November 2018).

QCA (2007) *Modern foreign languages. Programme of study for Key Stage 3 and attainment targets*. Crown copyright. Available at: http://webarchive.nationalarchives.gov.uk/20110215120931/http://curriculum.qcda.gov.uk/uploads/QCA-07-3340-p_MFL_KS3_tcm8-405.pdf (accessed October 2018).

Quigley, A. and Stringer, E. (2018) Making sense of metacognition. *Impact*, issue 3, summer 2018. Chartered College of Teaching. Available at: https://impact.chartered.college/article/quigley-stringer-making-sense-metacognition/ (accessed October 2018).

Read, C. (2015). Seven pillars of creativity in primary ELT. In A. Maley and N. Peachey (eds.) *Creativity in the English language classroom*. The British Council: London, pp29–38. Available at: http://englishagenda.britishcouncil.org/continuing-professional-development/cpd-teacher-trainers/creativity-english-language-classroom (accessed November 2018).

Richards, J.C. and Rodgers, T.S. (2014) *Approaches and methods in language teaching*. Third edition. Cambridge University Press: Cambridge.

Rivers, W.M., Dell'Orto, K.M. and Dell'Orto, V.J. (1975) *A practical guide to the teaching of German*. Oxford University Press: New York.

Ryan, M. (2014) Creative Practice in the Classroom. In P. Driscoll, E. Macaro and A. Swarbrick (eds.) *Debates in modern languages education*. Routledge: London, pp218–231.

Sell, J.P.A. (2005) Why teach literature in the foreign language classroom? *Encuentro*, 15, pp86–93. Available at: http://www.encuentrojournal.org/textos/11_Sell.pdf (accessed July 2018).

Taylor, A. (2000) *Teaching and learning grammar*. (Concept Handbooks for Language Teachers). Nelson Thornes Ltd: Cheltenham.

Turner, K. (1998) Reading: meeting the demands of the National Curriculum. *The Language Learning Journal*, 17(1), pp8–13. DOI: 10.1080/09571739885200031

Williams, M. and Burden, R.L. (1997) *Psychology for language teachers*. Cambridge University Press: Cambridge.

Wringe, C. (1989) *Effective teaching of modern languages*. Re-published as an e-book by Routledge (2013).

YouTube (2006) Do schools kill creativity? TED talk by Sir Ken Robinson. Available at https://www.ted.com/talks/ken_robinson_says_schools_kill_creativity?language=en (accessed February 2019).

— (2014) Can creativity be taught? With Sir Ken Robinson. Available at https://www.youtube.com/watch?v=vlBpDggX3iE (accessed February 2019).

PART

Getting better at planning

Learning to teach is hard. You will find yourself challenged in unimaginable ways as you take on the multiple demands of teaching young people how to speak another language, at the same time as learning to teach and learning to become a teacher. The learning curve is steep and at times may seem relentless. Simply keeping on top of the workload and ensuring that you meet all of your commitments to the best of your professional ability is in itself an immense and commendable achievement.

And yet, despite these demands and pressures, it is very important that you do make time for your own professional development and do not settle for simply surviving or functioning as a teacher. A disposition to keep learning is part of what makes you a professional.

Against this backdrop, this final part of the book steps back from planning for the learning of others, to focus on your own learning and progress.

CHAPTER 7

Developing your planning abilities during the ITE period

Over the course of your ITE period, you can expect to make progress in your planning skills *and* in your understanding of planning. Research conducted by Mutton et al. (2011) found that the student teachers they interviewed learnt more about planning than any other aspect of teaching during their PGCE year. These beginning teachers reported specific ways in which their learning about planning had contributed to the success of their teaching. For example, they reported that detailed planning helped them to better meet the needs of a range of learners and to pitch lessons more appropriately; they were also more aware that planning had to be flexible enough to take account of the classroom response of pupils.

The focus of this chapter is on the professional learning of beginning teachers and how they might be supported in the development of their planning abilities. I will be drawing largely on my own experience of working with beginning teachers and their mentors in order to highlight a few professional development opportunities that can help. These opportunities relate to the following contexts for learning:

- Feedback on planning
- Joint planning
- Extended lesson review

Feedback on planning

Feedback on outline or draft lesson plans can be particularly helpful, especially in the early days when detailed lesson planning takes up a lot of your time. Fairly early on in the planning process, before committing yourself to a final or completed lesson plan, arrange to show or discuss your initial thoughts with your mentor or the class teacher. Constructive feedback from an experienced teacher who is familiar with the class you are teaching might alert you to potential pitfalls, provide some pointers for further refinement, or points to consider before drawing up the final lesson plan.

Mentor feedback at the outline planning stage might centre on:

- Pitching the lesson appropriately for the class;
- Pointing out potential misconceptions/ difficulties e.g. pronunciation;
- Planned timings;
- Coherence and logical progression;
- Planned language content;
- Predicted teacher TL use for managing the lesson.

In my experience, feedback on completed, detailed lesson plans is most helpful if done in conjunction with a lesson observation. This means that feedback to the beginning teacher on their planning can be based on broader evidence of their planning, not just on the written plan. If the observer is provided with a detailed lesson plan, outlining perhaps a bit more of the thinking behind the plan than you would normally include, they can then give more targeted feedback on specific aspects of your planning (such as planning for assessment or differentiation) and on the ideas and the thinking behind your planning. In some cases, producing detailed lesson plans for observation purposes might mean spending more time writing the plan than you routinely would. In my view, this is a good investment of your time if it gives the observer insight into the thinking behind the lesson. This insight helps both the observer and observee to make the most of the debrief after the lesson, as a learning conversation or opportunity for professional learning. Having some insight into the thinking behind the lesson can also prevent the observer from being overly judgemental when things go wrong; even if the lesson is a disaster, credit might still be given for the quality of thinking.

Providing feedback on lesson plans is an opportunity for mentors to open up their knowledge of teaching and learning and make it available to beginning teachers. There may be aspects of a mentor's teaching skills that s/he can describe or explain for beginning teachers, so that they can consciously incorporate those into their own planning and teaching. Another option for the mentor, as well as or in place of talking about strategies or techniques, is to model for the beginning teacher what those look like in practice. In the early stages of learning to teach, for example, your mentor might demonstrate strategies for sustaining TL use, eliciting full sentence answers, setting up specific activities, or managing resources in the classroom.

Joint, or collaborative, planning is another opportunity for mentors to open up their knowledge and we will look more closely at that now.

Joint planning with your mentor

Referring to earlier work by Burn (1997), Mutton et al. advocate collaborative planning (and teaching) with experienced teachers. Through this process beginning teachers 'may gain access to the developed thinking of those teachers and thus draw on their professional knowledge and understanding' (Mutton et al., 2011, p414). From my experience I would strongly agree with this view.

Within the Secondary School Partnership at Newcastle University, PGCE students were regularly asked to review the quality of mentoring that they had received. Over many years, joint lesson planning was consistently cited by beginning teachers of ML as the single most useful mentoring strategy that they had helped them. Over the same period of time, ML subject mentors in schools also consistently rated joint planning with mentees very highly. This was particularly helpful at the start of the second teaching placement, as a way of starting to form constructive professional relationships with their mentees. Joint planning gave mentors real insights into the thinking and pedagogical understanding of their mentees and helped them to identify starting points for further development.

Joint lesson planning is an example of collaborative practice. It involves mentor and mentee sitting down together and planning a lesson together. To be clear, collaborative planning is not a matter of the mentor telling the mentee what to do or planning the lesson for the mentee. Rather this is an opportunity for dialogue which enables both the mentee and mentor to deepen understanding and gain new insights into the planning process. At Newcastle, PGCE students were expected to come to the table with some initial ideas for the lesson and usually those were the starting point for the collaboratively planned lesson which followed.

Once the lesson had been planned, there were then different models for what followed. These are labelled A–D below:

A   The beginning teacher taught the lesson and the mentor observed;
B   The beginning teacher taught the lesson, the mentor observed and then taught the same lesson (sometimes with tweaks) to a parallel class, observed by the beginning teacher;
C   The mentor taught the lesson and the beginning teacher observed;
D   The mentor taught the lesson, the beginning teacher observed and then taught the same lesson (sometimes with tweaks) to a parallel class, observed by the mentor.

I think we can see already from these different possible models that joint planning is rich in professional learning potential, for both mentee and mentor. In principle, the experience inducts beginning teaches into collaborative practice in a school context; it involves collaboration, reflective practice and focus on the primary task of planning a lesson together (James et al., 2007). In the best cases, student teachers at Newcastle felt that they were more of an equal in this process and that their ideas were valued. The experience of observing a lesson that you have helped to plan, regardless of how long you have been teaching, is always an interesting one; it is an opportunity to reflect on the relationship between planning decisions and learning outcomes, and more broadly the relationship between planning and teaching. This awareness is further heightened with the opportunity to teach the same lesson again.

Apart from these wider professional learning gains, beginning teachers have also pointed out specific benefits for the development of their planning abilities. There are five benefits I would like to highlight here. The first is that beginning teachers are able to benefit from the context-sensitive professional judgement of their mentors, based on their knowledge of individual pupils, the class and the school. It is difficult for beginning teachers to anticipate how pupils are likely to respond to given activities, to judge pupils' prior learning and to pitch lessons at an appropriate level, precisely because they have not yet acquired this knowledge. Joint planning is an opportunity to start to close this knowledge gap and start to see how teaching context influences professional judgement.

Secondly, the mentor (as an experienced lesson planner) is able to keep the planning conversation focused on what matters, notably pupils' learning. It can be all too easy for the lesson plans of beginning teachers to be focused on what they will be doing, rather than what they want pupils to learn; a good mentor will manage the joint planning process to help the mentee think through how pupils' learning might develop in the lesson.

Thirdly, beginning teachers can easily underestimate the length of time a lesson activity might take. Joint planning provides an opportunity for mentors to explain and demonstrate how they usually calculate timings and to pass on advice about managing the time in lessons.

Fourthly, there is the matter of how to put it all together into a coherent lesson plan. Joint lesson planning can support mentees in developing important planning skills of sequencing, structuring and organising lessons.

Finally, the upshot of all of these benefits is an important boost in confidence. There is an increased belief in your own abilities as a beginning teacher and a feeling of self-efficacy that comes from going into the classroom knowing that you can do this. Former PGCE students, for example, have talked about how their subject mentor gave them confidence and direction when needed and the opportunity to explore new ideas and be creative in the classroom.

In my experience, a possible drawback with joint planning can arise where mentees, for whatever reason, tend to model themselves too much on the teacher with whom they planned the lesson, rather than thinking for themselves and developing their own teaching style. Just to be clear, joint planning should not be interpreted as 'spoon feeding' (Mutton et al., 2011, p414).

Joint longer-term planning

The experience of jointly planning a sequence of lessons, or short unit of work, with your mentor brings additional benefits and learning gains for all concerned. In particular, joint longer-term planning can be instrumental in helping beginning teachers start to develop a longer-term perspective on teaching and learning in their subject. Again, conversations with your mentor are at the heart of this process. This is outlined in the guidance below which is written for beginning teachers and their mentors.

- As a beginning teacher, a useful starting point is to familiarise yourself with the organisation and content of departmental schemes of work. It would be helpful to discuss any questions you may have with your mentor. You may need to be proactive in asking your mentor to talk through how longer-term planning decisions are made, and the thinking behind existing schemes of work. This is an opportunity for mentors to share their knowledge. Progression across lessons would be a key point to talk through, as would practical strategies that are in place for assessing progress in pupils' learning.
- Departmental approaches to assessment in ML are worthy of a separate discussion. It will be important for you to be aware of potential constraints and opportunities before you embark on longer-term planning. Discussion might also include talking through with your mentor any school or departmental homework policy and strategies for dealing with missing homework.
- The value of jointly planning a sequence of lessons with your mentor cannot be stressed enough. If you have found joint lesson planning to be beneficial, then the benefits of joint longer-term planning are likely to be even more significant. When sequences of lessons are planned to lead to a culminating end task, rather than an end of unit test, joint planning also becomes a creative process. Ideally, the process is even more valuable if both mentee and mentor teach and evaluate what they had planned together, either by team teaching the same class or each teaching the same sequence to two parallel groups.
- Planning your first sequences of lessons on your own takes time. It will be helpful to be able to discuss your planning and initial thinking with your mentor or the class teacher. Their feedback at a reasonably early stage in the process can save you time and energy later on. In particular, it will be important for beginning teachers to know that plans are well-matched to the context within which pupils are working. For example, some departments may have a routine of starting lessons in a particular way in order to support spontaneous speaking in the TL, or in order to continually practise and build up knowledge of phonics in the TL. In other words, there may be potential constraints or opportunities that are not immediately obvious to beginning teachers; you will want to be aware of those when longer-term planning. Teachers who are familiar with the teaching context would be able to identify potential pitfalls and offer guidance on ways forward.
- Finally, to complete the planning cycle, you might work collaboratively with your mentor on review and evaluation of your longer-term planning. Amongst other things, it will be important to look together at the outcomes of the end of unit task and to jointly assess what those are telling you about pupils' learning and progress and links to planning.

Extended lesson review

In Chapter 4 we looked at routine lesson evaluation as part of the planning cycle; it informs your planning for pupils' learning on a lesson by lesson basis. What I want to focus on here is more detailed evaluation as part of a wider process of extended lesson review. Extended lesson review is an example of reflective practice; it calls for greater reflection than routine lesson evaluation and can promote deeper learning.

There are many different models of reflective practice, including Kolb's learning cycle, Gibbs' reflective cycle and Schön's distinction between reflection-in-action and reflection-on-action. The Cambridge International Teaching and Learning Team provide a good, clear overview of these, making the point that 'they all share the same basic aim: to get the best results from the learning, for both the teacher and students. Each model of reflection aims to unpick learning to make links between the "doing" and the "thinking"'. (Cambridge International Teaching and Learning Team, n.d.).

The Teachers' Standards (which set the minimum requirements for teachers' practice and conduct in England) promote the importance of reflecting on practice to support pupil learning and teacher development. The standards require trainee teachers to 'reflect systematically on the effectiveness of lessons and approaches to teaching' (Department for Education, 2011, p11). In my opinion, it is not by chance that this requirement is included as a component of Standard 4 'Planning and teaching well structured lessons' (Department for Education, 2011, p11).

So systematic reflection is not only important for lesson planning, planning for learning, but also for your own professional learning and development. Specifically, it helps beginning teachers to develop understanding of their subject and how it is learned, and to identify action points to develop their own practice. See also Capel et al. (2016, Chapter 5.4) for an introduction to reflective practice.

The next subsection outlines some practical suggestions for enabling systematic reflection within the context of extended lesson review. Again, this is aimed at beginning teachers and their mentors.

Practical guidance on implementing extended lesson review

For a lesson review to be worthwhile in supporting your professional learning, then it needs to go beyond simply checking that the LOs have been met. And that takes time. I would therefore recommend writing an extended lesson review, perhaps once a week or once every two weeks. You might need to set aside about 30–60 minutes to complete this review. It is important to see this in terms of making time for your own learning and to integrate this into your schedule as a beginning teacher. You are likely to find more scope for reflection and potentially to learn more if you pick a particularly good or bad lesson as the subject of your review (Hardman et al., 1994).

The review itself might be structured around a generic reflective cycle such as Gibbs (1988); or around questions to facilitate systematic reflection. Table 7.1 shows examples of question prompts that might be useful to beginning teachers of ML. Prompts are organised under the following headings: planning and preparation, teaching of the lesson, pupils' response to the lesson and looking ahead. The intention is that within these headings, teachers can choose the questions that they think are most helpful to them at any given time, rather than attempt to answer all of them at once. However, try to include each of the headings in your review.

You may find that some of the questions are difficult to answer in-depth on your own, particularly questions relating to pupils' learning. In which case, you might enlist the help of your mentor or others who observe you teach, by asking them to help you collect relevant information. If you choose to do that, then it would be helpful to discuss with your mentor before the start of the lesson the sort of information that would be most useful to you and how this might best be collected. For example, you might want to ask your mentor to listen in and monitor the progress of particular pupils when they are engaged in pair work, and to make some brief notes.

Alternatively, you might want to base a more in-depth lesson evaluation and review on a video recording of the lesson, or part of the lesson, rather than always relying on your own memory. Teachers use video as a professional development or coaching tool for different purposes; it has also been used successfully with beginning teachers, as a way of informing their practice generally (Lofthouse and Birmingham, 2010). A useful exercise is to have a copy of your lesson plan in front of you when you watch the video playback, and to compare the plan with what appears to be happening in the classroom. Video can also help us to respond to evaluation prompts (see Table 7.1) and to critically reflect on other specific questions that harness the benefits of video technology (e.g. sight, sound, pause, repeat playback). Good questions might include:

- ☐ How effectively do you think you managed to respond to learners' needs in the lesson?
- ☐ Can you pinpoint any specific difficulties that some pupils had during the lesson? (In relation to comprehension, pronunciation, confidence in speaking etc.)
- ☐ Were there any particular points in the lesson where you found yourself thinking on your feet or departing from your written plan? What occasioned this? What have you learned from this for future planning?

TABLE 7.1 Lesson evaluation prompts

Your Planning and Preparation

- How effective do you think your planning of the lesson was?
- What did you plan well?
- How hard was it to plan this lesson? What made it easy/hard to plan?
- Were your expectations high enough?
- How well did you judge prior learning? How well did you anticipate subject difficulties?
- How effectively did you plan for behaviour?
- How useful was your written lesson plan?
- How useful were the materials you prepared? Did you use all of the material? If not, why not?

Your Teaching of the Lesson

- How effective do you think your teaching of the lesson was? Were your instructions clear?
- Which activity or part of the lesson worked particularly well? And which did not work so well?
- Which activity or part of the lesson was particularly difficult or challenging for you to teach?
- Which activity or part of the lesson was rather easy for you to teach?
- Did you manage to keep all or most of the pupils engaged? What helped you to do this?
- How effectively did you deal with pupils who were not engaged or not learning?
- Did you manage to use all the TL that you had planned to use? If you spoke in L1 (English) what was the purpose? Would it be better to use the TL for this purpose? If so, how could you do this? And if not, why not?

Pupils' response to the lesson

- What impact did the lesson have on pupils and their learning? And how do you know?
- To what extent do you think pupils understood and achieved the LO for the lesson? If you can, record how progress was demonstrated by giving examples of pupil progress witnessed in the lesson (sometimes you may need to answer this after you have marked their work).
- Did any pupils not achieve the LO? Did any exceed the LO?
- Was any part of the lesson or activity too easy for pupils? Was anything too difficult for them?
- Did all pupils participate actively in the lesson? Did they all say at least something in the TL?
- Is there anything that you need to pick up on or go over again next lesson?

Looking ahead

- What could you do differently next time you teach this class or a similar lesson? And what will you do differently next time?

Learning together with your mentor

Rachel Lofthouse is Professor of Teacher Education and a leading authority on mentoring and coaching. She argues that 'creating a genuinely valuable mentoring experience is possible, and much of it comes through conversation' (Lofthouse, 2018a, p14). Research suggests that those conversations are most formative when mentors understand the need to 'stimulate' thought and reflection, to 'scaffold' discussion and 'sustain' learning conversation (Lofthouse, 2018a, p15).

I would suggest that each of the above contexts for professional learning (namely feedback on planning, joint planning and extended lesson review) provides a basis for the sort of formative conversation that Lofthouse is alluding to here. They are appropriate contexts for learning conversations between beginning teachers and their mentors. Learning with your mentor is not only about the learning of the beginning teacher, mentors also stand to benefit professionally from such experiences; in the best case scenarios, both mentor and mentee are learning together. For more on mentoring as part of professional development and learning, please see Lofthouse (2018b) for a short introduction. For further guidance on mentoring beginning teachers in ML, please see Black et al. (2017).

Summing up so far

Getting better at planning can be seen as part of a cycle. This is the learning to plan cycle, mentioned in the Introduction, and reproduced below in Figure 7.1.

What this cycle shows is that you don't get better at planning, simply by planning more of the same. Learning *to* plan is contingent upon learning *about* planning. The professional development activities we have looked at in this chapter highlight the value of constructive feedback on your planning, collaborative practice and systematic reflection. Each of these should enable you to develop and deepen your learning about planning.

So, what could go wrong?! Well, in practice beginning teachers can often feel challenged, in different ways, in the development of their planning abilities. This is an important point to address in a book such as this. The next section considers some possible planning related dilemmas faced by beginning ML teachers and provides suggestions as to how they might be addressed.

Planning related dilemmas

1. Working from the lesson plans of others, feeling that you haven't written the plan yourself.

There is a difference between literally delivering a plan that you have had no part in writing and teaching a lesson based on a plan that you have tailored to the needs of the class you are teaching. For a variety of reasons, the first is

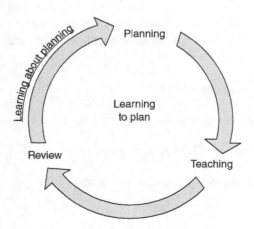

FIGURE 7.1 Learning to plan cycle

to be avoided; the second, however, can be a helpful learning experience for beginning teachers. If you are working from lesson plans written by others, the most important part of the lesson plan to consider is the intended learning outcome. Make sure that you fully understand what it is that pupils are expected to do, know or understand by the end of the lesson. Take this as your starting point and point of reference to inform any tweaks you feel you need to make to the plan. It might be that you can come up with a better final activity for pupils to demonstrate their learning, in which case you should suggest it to the class teacher. Otherwise, I would view this as an opportunity to spend more time focusing on meeting the needs of individual pupils. For example, one benefit is having the time to plan in detail your use of the TL, how you will make your output comprehensible to all pupils, your questioning strategy and how to work with different personalities of pupils.

2. Following a scheme of work which expects too much content to be covered within the time available – too content heavy.

This can be a common problem, not only for beginning teachers. Whatever you do, do not try and cover all of that content in one lesson! Too much content at the expense of process is not good for learning. In ML it is important that the principal focus of pedagogy should be on developing skills, using language rather than teaching linguistic content (grammar and vocabulary) as an end in itself (see PDC in MFL, 2012). One way round the dilemma might be to prioritise activities in lessons which actively involve pupils in practising and using language as much as possible, and to use homework for learning vocabulary or extra vocabulary. It might also be possible to exploit homework as a source of further exposure to the language in use, with lots of listening and reading exercises. If the content includes a lot of grammar, another solution might be to prioritise the teaching of grammar points which have a high communicative value and for pupils to learn the rest as unanalysed chunks. But you do then need to provide activities which enable pupils to recognise and/ or use those chunks.

3. How to become less dependent upon the written lesson plan in lessons – lesson plan as script.

The key issue here is dependence. Remember the plan should be a guide to help you rather than dictate to you. As a beginning teacher, yes, there will be times when you need to refer to your plan in the lesson, e.g. to remind you of timings or perhaps to remind you of TL instructions, particularly if you are teaching in your second language. I think this is a helpful thing to do, because it takes the strain off your memory and frees you up to attend to what is happening around you in the classroom. Attending to what is happening in the classroom is crucial and the success of the lesson will depend on how well you respond to the pupils in front of you as the lesson unfolds. If you go into the lesson with a clear sense of where you are heading and why, then this should help you become less dependent on looking at your lesson plan in the lesson. If you are brave, you can even try teaching a lesson you have planned without the lesson plan in front of you! I don't recommend doing this too often, but even if you try this just once as a beginning teacher it can help you to realise what you can achieve independently of the written plan. Of course, the caveat to this is that you do plan the lesson! I am not suggesting that you attempt to teach a lesson that you have not planned!

4. Lesson planning is taking up too much time. How do I spend less time on planning? How can I get the balance right so that I am neither spending too much time nor not enough time on planning?

I think you need to accept as a beginning teacher that lesson planning will take time, more time than it takes an experienced teacher. However, you should find that lesson planning time reduces as the ITE period goes on. The question is: how much time is too much time? If lesson planning is preventing you from getting enough sleep, then you need to talk with your mentor or tutor about this. Sometimes people spend too much time on planning because they find it difficult. In this case, your mentor will want to know so that they can start to help you address this. Sometimes people spend too long on planning because they have perfectionist tendencies.

Perhaps they agonise too much, overthinking details. Let's be clear – there is no such thing as a perfect lesson plan, so don't waste your energy and sleep trying to write one. It helps to accept that good is good enough – you don't have the time to be outstanding all of the time! A lesson plan is your best guess as to how learning might develop. Plan the important things – where you are heading, the practicalities of how you will get there and a back-up plan if things go wrong. Accept that you won't know what is going to happen until you get into the classroom. It can also be useful to work out on a day-to-day basis what you want to achieve within the day and allocate your available time accordingly. That means that you will end up spending less time planning a given lesson if you have a lot to do that day, and more time if you have less to do.

There may be other reasons to explain why for some people lesson planning takes up too much time. A strategy that can help everyone is to set yourself deadlines or cut-off points. As a general rule of thumb, try to avoid spending longer than three hours planning any one lesson. If you are already spending three hours planning each lesson, aim to cut this down to an average of maybe one hour per lesson by the end of the ITE period. Normally, beginning teachers have more lessons to teach as they go through the training year, but the average total time spent on lesson planning might remain the same. This doesn't mean you haven't made progress; on the contrary, it means you are planning more lessons in less overall time and this is good preparation for teaching full-time when you will have more lessons to plan and when you may well find that marking increases significantly.

Another strategy is to arrange for feedback on outline plans, well in advance of lessons. This can help you to think more clearly when writing your final plans, and thinking clearly saves time. Also, thinking in terms of a series of lessons rather than isolated lessons is a more efficient way to plan. When you think about your LOs, try and think in terms of a continuum across lessons: we are doing X today so that we can do Y tomorrow. Considering lessons as part of a sequence avoids wasted time. The time it takes to write an overview for the next sequence of lessons is time well-invested, it will save you time in the long run.

Finally, you might ask someone in your department whether they have any materials to share. Teachers don't always do this enough, and there's no point reinventing the wheel when materials can easily be tweaked class to class.

5. How much detail should I include?

There is no definitive answer to this question; it depends. What I would say is that what makes the difference to learning is *quality* of detail rather than *quantity* of detail. You should find that the detail that you are able to think through when lesson planning will change over the course of your ITE period. Early lesson plans, for example, typically include detail relating to instructions and to what you, the teacher, will do in the lesson. In later plans there may not be the same need to write this detail on every plan, because the teacher has, by this stage, internalised instructions for routine activities and can do this without thinking about it. Unlike earlier plans, later ones may include more information about differentiation or how individual pupils will be challenged or supported in the lesson. This is a detail that can only be meaningfully written into plans once you have acquired knowledge of the pupils you are teaching. My own view is that too much writing is not always helpful. For example, I think it is fine to use bullet points and abbreviations or symbols rather than writing full sentences; and headings are a useful device to signal different stages in the lesson.

6. How to become more creative in my planning/ more risk-taking in my teaching?

It is good to try new things and to learn from them. And you definitely want to take full advantage of your ITE period to amass as many ideas as possible. In terms of lesson content, the sky is the limit in ML. Provided that what we ask pupils to do actively involves them in using or engaging with the language, you can pretty much teach any content in the ML classroom. CLIL (content and language integrated learning) is one way of teaching other subject content through the medium of a ML. You might want to try teaching a one-off CLIL lesson. In terms of pedagogy, you might challenge yourself to teach a whole lesson without using technology, especially PowerPoint. So much teaching is mediated through technology that having a technology-free lesson can really help to strip things back to you and the pupils in front of you. Planning a lesson like this can be liberating. Afterwards, you might want to reflect on what difference this made to your relationship with the group. Another lesson that can move you forward in your pedagogical understanding is a lesson conducted exclusively in the TL. Carefully planned, such a lesson can be a real confidence boost for pupils and valuable learning experience for the teacher. To squeeze as much learning out of this as possible, it is a good idea to build in ten minutes at the end for pupil feedback in English and discussion of what you did that helped them learn.

If you are looking for ideas to vary your teaching repertoire, you might want to arrange for a swop shop with other beginning teachers or perhaps a Teachmeet with other teachers. The ALL (Association for Language Learning) organises such events in different parts of the country, but if there is not an ALL branch near you, you might still be able to arrange this informally. Otherwise there are numerous websites offering ideas and resources specifically for ML; for example, the TES teaching resources website has a ML tab, many of the resources can be downloaded free of charge, Lightbulb Languages is free and, for a small annual subscription, TeachIt Languages (endorsed by AQA) offers high quality resources tailored to exam board specification requirements. See also suggestions in the annotated list of sources at the end of this book.

7. Pitching the lesson at the right level for the class.

Accept that there is no quick fix, this will take time. But there are things you can do which will help. The first of these is to discuss outline plans with the class teacher and write your final plans in the light of class teacher feedback. Another strategy is to ask for feedback on this when you are observed teaching; you might even ask the observer to make this the focus of the observation and lesson debrief. Perhaps you can arrange to observe a parallel class and make notes on what you notice? You may also find it useful to observe the same class in different subjects and see how other teachers are stretching the same pupils, particularly in terms of challenging them to think.

Some beginning teachers find it helpful to factor into lesson plans time for pupil feedback on particular tasks or activities. Think carefully about the questions you ask and how they might be answered. You might want to do this first with a class with whom you have a good relationship. Written feedback can also be effective, so that pupils can say what they felt was a barrier in a given task or activity or about a particular skill. Over time, with experience and reflection, you will learn to understand the difference between a worthwhile challenge and an unnecessary difficulty and this will help you a lot in your planning. In the meantime, this is something you could include as part of your own lesson evaluations. From time to time ask yourself: Was the lesson sufficiently challenging for everyone? Was the lesson too difficult in places? And how do you know?

8. The extent of prescription inherent in the template I am expected to use to write lesson plans.

I am tempted to say, don't knock it until you've tried it. Try and identify the positives within the proforma you are expected to use. If you still feel that the template is making it difficult for you to write lesson plans that are helpful to you, then I suggest you need to talk to someone about this. Have a conversation with whoever has set this expectation, your mentor or tutor. Explore together what the issue or issues seem to be. For example, is it an issue of the time involved in completing the template? Do you have to complete each section each lesson? Is it an issue of not having space to show thinking that is important to you? Would it be possible to use a hybrid that includes the best of the given template and your own ideas?

9. How to balance adapting to a school vision and finding your own style of teaching.

Balancing school and department vision with your own style of teaching can be exciting but daunting at the same time. There are a few points worth bearing in mind here. The first is that the ITE period is very much the start of a journey. You will not learn everything you need to know about teaching ML by the end of that period and learning how to teach your subject is just one part, admittedly a very important one, of learning to become a teacher and joining the teaching profession. So, you may not find your own style of teaching by the end of your ITE period, but you may have begun to form a firmer idea about the kind of teacher you want to be and the kind of school you ideally see yourself working in. As a qualified teacher, you may well find that you need to fit in with a particular school vision. In most cases this is part of what it means to be a teacher in a particular school. If the school vision matches your own vision you are lucky, this is the ideal situation. As a beginning teacher you will probably have spent time in at least two contrasting schools. Even if you didn't particularly share the vision or ethos of either school, at least that experience will have informed your views about the sort of school you are looking for. If you feel that the school vision is restricting opportunities for you to progress, as well as you might as a beginning teacher, then it would definitely be worth having a chat about this with your school mentor.

10. How to show that you are taking on board advice but at the same time feeling that you are establishing your own way of doing things.

This can be a tricky dilemma. On the one hand, the beginning teacher is grateful for the advice and support of more experienced colleagues, but on the other hand s/he does not want to become a clone. The resolution of this

Developing your planning abilities

dilemma might depend on your relationship with your mentor or the person who is advising you. It might help the mentor to see you more as a colleague and get more of an insight into your thinking if you had the opportunity to do some joint lesson planning. Joint lesson planning is an opportunity for the beginning teacher to be proactive in bringing their ideas to the table. For example, if you and your mentor teach parallel classes, then perhaps you could jointly plan the same lesson for both of you to teach to your respective classes. Ideally, you would then also observe each other teach the same lesson and jointly debrief each one.

11. Striking a balance between engaging pupils and progressing pupils in their learning.

This can be a quandary for beginning and experienced teachers; lots of people find this difficult. On the one hand, it is important for pupils to be engaged in lessons, without engagement there can be no learning. On the other hand, we need to ensure that pupils are learning, and making progress in lessons and engagement does not always equate with learning. A good example of this in ML arises through games such as SPLAT that only actively involve two pupils at a time. If you are lucky, the whole class is engaged in watching the action at the front of the classroom, but what are they actually learning? More often than not, it is only the two pupils with fly squatters in front of the board who need to process the language and who are able to learn from the activity. I am not sure you can justify planning to spend ten minutes of a 60 minute lesson (possibly the only lesson or one of only two lessons that week) on such an activity. A better idea would be to run this as a desk-based activity with pupils working in groups of three or four. That way you combine maximum engagement with optimal learning; everyone is engaged in using the language and motivated by the game. However, such a solution may not always be possible. At the end of the day, it is learning that matters. Teachers are paid to promote learning and increasingly, within the performance driven culture of English schools, to secure good exam results. When lesson planning therefore, time spent on high value learning activity needs to be prioritised and, all other things being equal, expectations of learning should increase as the lesson progresses. Another way of looking at this is to promote language enthusiasm by doing activities outside of the classroom as well; for example, the Foreign Language Spelling Bee competition (you can find out more about this competition at http://www.flsb.co.uk/). If you do decide to go down this route, then consider how you might evaluate pupils' response to extracurricular activity and use this to inform your classroom teaching.

12. Not knowing what a well-structured lesson looks like. How do I structure lessons? It doesn't always look the same when observing.

I'm sure that universities and other ITE or training providers will offer advice on how to structure lessons. And if not, or if you are still not clear on this, please ask for further help. If you have not had any ML specific input on structuring lessons, the PPP model is a good starting place. Some schools have a particular proforma that they like teachers to use to structure their lessons. This might be a useful starting point for you. If you are finding that lesson structure is not always evident when observing ML lessons, find out where there is expertise in teaching and learning elsewhere in your placement school and arrange to observe lessons in other subject areas. Think through how you might apply principles observed to the planning and teaching of ML lessons. For example, consider how you are linking up different parts of your lessons. You need this to be clear in your own head before you teach the lesson.

13. Timing of lesson / activities within the lesson.

Before you start teaching yourself, it can help to observe experienced teachers and make a timeline of what is happening in the lesson. Notice how long is spent on different activities. If you can, compare this with the lesson plan afterwards. When you are observed teaching, ask observers to note the start and finish times of activities in the lesson, compare this with what you had planned. Informal observers might also annotate your lesson plan, to show actual start and finish times, as well as anything on the plan that didn't happen or anything that did happen that wasn't on the lesson plan.

14. I feel like I'm getting nowhere with this class. What can I do?

First of all, this may not be a planning issue as such. This is a feeling that many teachers experience or will have experience of at some stage in their career; this dilemma doesn't just affect beginning teachers. Having said that, it can be extremely frustrating and demotivating if you have spent ages planning lessons and the class do not respond in the ways you had intended. My advice would be to speak to your mentor or the class teacher about this; speak to the class and elicit some opinions from the pupils, what do they want to do more/less of? If the relationship is poor, then you might use question prompts to elicit written pupil feedback. If so, you might need to pay particular attention to the comments of more reliable pupils in the class rather than taking all feedback at face value. Consider also asking someone to observe, the chances are that the situation is not actually as bad as you thought!

A look ahead . . .

The research cited at the start of this chapter tracked the same student teachers into their first two years of teaching. The researchers found that learning how to plan did not stop at the end of the ITE period. On the contrary, during their NQT year and beyond, beginning teachers reported that they were still learning a lot about planning (Mutton et al., 2011). In the next chapter, we will consider how you might expect your planning to progress beyond the ITE period.

CHAPTER

Next steps

Introduction

This chapter is about looking ahead: it concerns how lesson planning might continue to develop beyond the ITE period. We will be considering the different experiences of five recently qualified teachers (RQTs) in ML and how their planning and understanding of the point of planning have progressed. The aim here is to give beginning teachers some insight into how they might expect their own planning to develop in the early years of their careers, and the sorts of professional development experiences that can help make a difference to their planning and learning about planning.

In what follows, I have deliberately not included any references. This is so that the voices of the teachers can be represented here as naturally as possible and their views and ideas can be given centre stage. The annotated bibliography at the end of the book includes recommended further reading that relates to points that they raise.

Pen portraits of five RQTs

All five of the teachers you are about to meet completed their PGCE at Newcastle University; at the time of writing, all five were still teaching ML in different schools in the North East of England. For anyone unfamiliar with the North East it is worth highlighting the local context. Probably the most significant fact is that uptake of ML at age 14 is consistently lower than any other region of England; none of the local authorities across the North East appears in the top ten authorities with highest participation rates. For many teachers of ML working in the region, motivation is a key factor. Motivating young people, and to some extent parents and school leadership teams, to see the point in learning languages can be a particular challenge in this part of the country.

Pen portraits are presented below. Each teacher is introduced with brief background information about their teaching context and more detailed information about their 'signature dish'. Signature dish refers to an aspect of their practice that has become an integral and distinctive feature of their ML teaching; in other words, an idea that they have made their own.

Will

Will is in his third year of teaching; he teaches full-time and is currently in his second school. His current school is a larger than average 11–19 secondary school, with a large sixth form, located in a market town. French, German and Spanish are taught at the school. Will teaches Spanish (up to A-level) and French; he is also a form teacher.

Will's signature dish

Will is a teacher who thrives on new ideas. He says 'if I was only ever doing what I did I would never learn anything new'. As a result of trying out lots and lots of different ideas, Will has developed a few core activities which he tends to use in most lessons. One of his core activities is a 'treasure hunt'. This is an activity that he first adopted during his PGCE year and that he has refined over time to include different levels of challenge. He loves the discovery element of the activity and still really enjoys using it in lessons. He finds that it works particularly well at Key Stage 3.

The mechanics of the 'treasure hunt' are as follows. Pupils have a given time to find information, or 'treasure', from sheets that are stuck around the walls of the classroom. Once they find the information they are looking for, pupils write this down on a response sheet. Within the given time pupils try to find out as much 'treasure' as they can. The completed pupil response sheet doubles up as a vocabulary sheet or point of reference which pupils stick

	J'habite		**Gold**
	Je n'habite pas		*Bringing learning together*
Bronze: Find the English.	dans un village		I live in a city.
	dans une ville		
	dans une grande ville		
	à Chester-le-Street		
	en Angleterre		I live in Chester-le-Street in England
	en France		
	en Espagne		
Silver: Find the French.		in a house	
		in a semi-detached house	I live in a house in the countryside in France.
		in a flat	
		at the seaside	
		in the countryside	
		in the mountains	CHALLENGE: Freestyle your own sentence!
		in the city centre	

FIGURE 8.1 Example of a treasure hunt pupil response sheet

in their books. Figure 8.1 shows an example of a response sheet. It was used with a Year 7 mixed ability class, in a lesson called *Où habites-tu?*

Will has adapted this activity since his PGCE days. He is much more aware now of the potential for differentiation that this activity offers. During his PGCE days he would have one expectation of all pupils. Now he thinks in terms of different expected outcomes for pupils. This helps him in his planning. It means he has to think through in more detail questions such as: What do I want my end point to be? What is my highest expectation for some pupils in this class? What is the minimum end point that would represent worthwhile progress or a worthwhile achievement for other pupils? These days he has three levels of expected outcome for pupils, corresponding to bronze, silver and gold 'treasure':

- Bronze = minimum expectation of everyone in the class
- Silver = is a bit more developed and involves pupils writing TL words or phrases
- Gold = links the bronze and silver 'treasure' together, pupils write whole sentences in the TL

At the end of the activity, progress is reviewed with the whole class. Will goes through each of the items with the class and sees discussion of 'gold' items is an opportunity for all pupils to learn from listening to each other.

A further development since PGCE days is that Will now uses the 'treasure hunt' for different purposes:

- to introduce new language (as in the example above, using pictures + TL labels)
- to practise different verbs or tenses by asking pupils to find the best verb or verb form to complete a gapped text (with GCSE and A-level classes)
- to consolidate or practise particular language in preparation for homework

Thinking through how the activity is best used involves thinking through the relevance of the language introduced or practised in this way. Again it helps Will with his planning to consider questions such as: What will pupils be using this language to do? How will it help them? In the lesson above, for example, pupils went on to practise manipulating the treasure hunt structures with different vocabulary, they did a listening exercise with native French speakers talking about where they live, and by the end of the lesson they were given four minutes to write the best possible answer to the big question: *Où habites-tu?*

Catherine

Catherine is in her third year of teaching; she teaches full-time and is currently in her second school. Her current school is a larger than average 11–19 secondary school, with a large sixth form, located on the outskirts of a large conurbation. French, German and Latin are taught at the school. Catherine teaches French; she also speaks Spanish and runs a voluntary Spanish lunchtime club.

Catherine's signature dish

Catherine's thinking about her own role in the classroom has changed since PGCE days, she explains: 'I try to put more work into my planning because in the lesson I want the students to be working more than me'. She plans lessons where pupils are expected to take responsibility for their learning, and expected to think for themselves. In the classroom she has become more fluid in her approach and more responsive to pupils' learning needs as they arise. Her favourite teaching tool to help her do this is the mini-whiteboard (MWB). She has a full class set of MWBs in her classroom and really likes the way she can pull them out as and when needed in the course of lessons in order to assess progress. This suits the way she now teaches.

Because she uses MWBs frequently, her pupils are familiar with the practicalities and routines involved and this saves time. They are also familiar with the routine TL phrases that are used when the MWBs come out. This includes phrases typically used by the teacher such as: *Sortez les tableaux! Trois, deux, un – montrez! Montrez-moi les tableaux! Tu es le gagnant! Vous êtes les gagnants! Essuyez les tableaux!* ; and phrases used by pupils such as: *Est-ce que je peux avoir un feutre? Est-ce que je peux changer de feutre? Mon feutre ne marche pas!*

The boards provide instant feedback on what pupils are able to do at any given point in time and this helps the teacher to diagnose progress of the whole class. Catherine really likes to use them for grammar teaching purposes; for example, inviting pupils to conjugate verbs or write down one specific verb ending. Usually this takes the form of verbal questions, planned in the lesson, based on her knowledge of potential pitfalls and of the class; sometimes, she prepares a PowerPoint slide in advance with multiple choice questions that pupils can quickly answer on their MWB.

She finds the MWB particularly useful as a way of checking for any misconceptions before pupils write up what they have learnt in their exercise books. Where misconceptions do arise, she will challenge pupils to explain their answers; and rather than correct them herself, she encourages self or peer correction. The key point here is that pupils are having to apply themselves. The pupils might work individually or they might work in pairs. Often there is an element of competition with points for the first team to write the correct answer; and individual pupils take over Catherine's role as questioner.

Josh

Josh is in his second year of teaching; he teaches full-time and is currently still in his first school, but is moving shortly to teach in another school within the same trust. His current school is a larger than average 11–19 secondary school, with a small sixth form, located in a large industrial town. French, German, Spanish and Latin are taught at the school. Josh teaches French (up to A-level) and some Spanish.

Josh's signature dish

Josh strongly believes that an important part of his role as ML teacher is to broaden minds. He explains: 'there is an outside world out there and in that outside world languages do exist'. He likes to bring something of his own flair and personality into lessons and particularly from his background as a bilingual French and English speaker. He has numerous family members and friends living in France and has taken advantage of his contacts to produce various short video clips. The clips feature Josh's family and friends speaking to camera in French.

This is something he first started doing during his PGCE year. In those early days, he would use the clips as a motivational hook to engage pupils at the starts of lessons. Since then he has found ways to go a bit deeper; for example, by exploiting the transcript and linguistic content of clips. For this he might provide a transcript or gapped transcript for pupils to read and analyse; he can use this transcript to expand vocabulary, develop understanding of particular structures or as a framework to scaffold speaking or writing tasks.

In the early days, clips tended to centre on the topics Josh was teaching; for example, one video featured a family member showing what items he packed in his suitcase. Since then, he has produced clips for a wide range of cultural topics such as Christmas, Mardi Gras, music and youth culture. These video clips make French real for pupils; they bring the subject alive and make pupils curious about French and people who speak French. Josh capitalises on this by inviting pupils to ask questions, as Josh explains 'that's where the engagement lies'. He finds that this works with everyone, they can all engage with it and the questions pupils ask are different. For example, some pupils might ask about the people in the videos; others about the theme of the video. There is scope here for pupils to ask questions in French or in English. A possible next step would be to introduce Skype. This is something that pupils themselves have requested because they would now like to talk with the French speakers from the videos and get to know them even better.

Marilu

Marilu is in her second year of teaching; she teaches part-time and is currently in her third school. Her current school is a much smaller than average 11–16 secondary school, located in a very large industrial town; the proportion of pupils with SEN is well above the national average. French and Spanish are taught at the school. Marilu teaches both languages but mainly Spanish.

Marilu's signature dish

Marilu finds that pupils in her current teaching context respond well to routines. Routines help them feel safe and increasingly confident in her lessons. A particular routine that she has developed since PGCE days is sharing learning objectives in the TL at the starts of lessons, and exploiting the wording of these objectives for linguistic purposes.

Marilu uses a PowerPoint slide to support this part of the lesson. There is an example below in Figure 8.2. Typically the writing on the slide is all in the TL and organised into three sections, from top to bottom:

1   A big question which establishes the focus of the lesson, e.g. *¿Qué tipo de música te gusta?*
2   The main learning goal or overarching LO for the lesson which is always expressed with an infinitive form, highlighting what pupils are going to learn to do, e.g. *Hablar de la música que te gusta.*
3   Three steps or mini objectives which make up the main learning goal; these are also expressed using the infinitive e.g. *Reconocer diferentes tipos de música en español.*

The use of the infinitive form is significant. Over time, Marilu deliberately plans to extend the range of verbs that she uses at this stage in the lesson. At the start, she uses them in conjunction with '*vamos a . . .*' [we are going to]. She begins with verbs that are needed most frequently: *escuchar, hablar, escribir* and *leer* and consistently uses the same icons on her slides to refer to those verbs. Then she gradually introduces more verbs and more vocabulary, always starting with cognates and familiar language that can be recycled.

In her planning, she allows about three minutes for the sharing of LOs. She has established a set routine for this. Each section of the slide is revealed in turn, starting with the three learning steps, and a similar procedure is followed for each section:

1   Pupils discuss the three steps in pairs for 10 seconds. The steps are then read aloud in Spanish and discussed as a class in English *[¿Que significa. . .?]* Everyone is expected to participate; Marilu uses lollipop sticks with pupils' names to randomly invite pupils to translate. The steps are then linked to the four icons on the bottom of the slide, e.g. using *Vamos a . . .*
2   Pupils read aloud and focus on the overarching LO for the lesson with questions from the teacher, e.g. *¿Que significa. . .?*
3   Pupils read aloud and think about the big question – this might also be an opportunity to discuss with the class what they already know in response to this question.

It is worth pointing out that before Marilu started teaching these classes, there was no culture of TL use in the department. It took her about two months to establish the routine and reach a stage where she felt that pupils were really benefitting from this in terms of their language learning and confidence. As Marilu explains: 'if you do it from the beginning they know this is the way your lessons are going to start'.

Next steps

Viernes, dos de diciembre

¿Qué tipo de música te gusta?

LO: Hablar de la música que te gusta y no te gusta.

Reconocer diferentes tipos de música en español.
Hablar de la música que te gusta y no te gusta
Dar razones con el adjetivo correcto

FIGURE 8.2 Example of a learning objectives slide

James

James is in his first year of teaching; he teaches full-time. His current school is a smaller than average 11–19 secondary school, with a shared sixth form, located on the outskirts of a large conurbation; the proportion of pupils with SEN is above the national average. French and Spanish are taught at the school. James teaches both languages, predominantly at Key Stage 3; he is also a form teacher.

James's signature dish

A distinctive feature of James's lessons is the award of 'linguist of the lesson'. The idea is simply to recognise and celebrate individual pupils who have done well in French or Spanish lessons by making time at the end of lessons to announce and applaud the linguist of the lesson. James has an attractive, colourful poster on his classroom wall to promote this award. Figure 8.3 shows what this looks like.

James finds that the element of praise makes more of an impact on his younger classes or classes where there are issues of pupil self-image. He sees this scheme as a way of celebrating the distinctiveness of ML as a school subject, particularly the ability to speak another language. It helps to establish a classroom culture where risk-taking is actively encouraged and pupils are supportive of each others' efforts. It is also very inclusive, celebrating different ways of being a good linguist. For example, the linguist of the lesson might be a pupil who:

- was willing to try and give answers;
- was willing to read out loud or perform in the TL at the front of the class;
- was willing to experiment with the language to say or write something new;
- showed improvement in their pronunciation or spelling;
- showed initiative in using the language spontaneously or without being prompted;

FIGURE 8.3 Linguist of the lesson poster

- showed progress in memorising words, phrases or chunks of language;
- was able to make links between the TL and English;
- asked a question/s that showed they were thinking more deeply about the subject;
- in some way made an exceptional effort in class.

This is an idea that James introduced into his own practice at the start of his first year in teaching; it has subsequently been adopted more widely across the languages department in his school.

Interviews with five RQTs

Each of these teachers kindly met with me on two occasions to discuss lesson planning. What follows is a summary of some common themes that emerged in those recorded interviews. There were three main interview questions:

- How are you planning now?
- How has your planning changed since PGCE?
- What has helped you get better at planning?

How are you planning now?

For the most part lesson planning is based on a departmental scheme of work or, in some cases, a progression grid which is a medium-term plan with skeleton lesson plans that can be adapted for individual classes. The departmental scheme of work is sometimes used as a starting point for planning one skeleton lesson that is then adapted for different, parallel classes in the same year group. In some cases the scheme of work is based on a textbook; in one case, it was written entirely by the Head of Department; in others, there is a departmental approach to planning with collaboratively planned schemes of work and shared resources. For example, the departmental scheme of work might be structured around big questions for each lesson, agreed upon by the department.

In some cases, RQTs themselves have had responsibility for drawing up longer-term plans for others to use; for example, responsibility for writing a progression grid covering half a term's work for one year group. Such a grid breaks down the half term into two or three chunks of individual lessons that are thematically linked; for each lesson, the grid details LOs, a suggested lesson outline and expected progression in pupils' learning. The process involves discussing initial ideas with colleagues, drafting an outline structure for each of the lessons, sending this to the rest of the department for feedback, then writing up the completed progression grid.

This background already gives some indication of the extent to which teaching contexts can vary. Nevertheless, some common themes emerged, as follows.

Knowing more about the pupils you teach

Planning is informed by teachers' knowledge of the pupils they are teaching, to an extent that is not possible within the time constraints of the PGCE year. Knowledge of pupils is not restricted to school data. As Josh explains: 'your own knowledge of the students helps massively. Data can inform you to a certain extent about certain things but we know the students as individuals as well, what their strengths are and what their weaknesses are. When you're spending a lot of time with the students you get to know them'. Getting to know students includes learning about them as people. Marilu adds: 'sometimes you cannot engage the student because you don't know what they like. If you know their hobbies at least you can connect the lessons with that and you can relate. But it takes time, it's not going to happen overnight'.

Teachers recognise that it makes a massive difference how often you see classes; during your ITE period you see them a lot less and you don't know them as well. Knowing your pupils means that planning is informed by more realistic expectations of learners or groups of learners. This relates to expectations in terms of prior learning and in terms of what progress can be expected within a given time. Planning is also much more meaningful when you are planning for *your* classes and *your* kids, *your* responsibility. This is rather different from the PGCE year when you only have partial responsibility for classes.

Building up a bank of activities and resources

Teachers build up knowledge of what works well with particular classes or when teaching particular topics. They also accumulate their own bank or repertoire of resources and activities that they can draw upon when planning lessons. James, for example, is developing a bank of core activities that are adaptable across key stages and across topics. For instance, he has a generic template that he uses to design Battleships boards. Many young people are familiar with the format of Battleships; the game can be used in ML in order to practise forming and saying sentences. James has used Battleships with topics as diverse as jobs, booking a hotel room, describing people and hobby preferences. He finds that the game is not only engaging for pupils, it also helps promote progress in speaking. This fits in with his philosophy that 'engagement + progress = motivation'; when pupils can see they are progressing, they are motivated. Downloadable Battleships templates are available online (for example, from www.teachitlanguages.co.uk).

Josh uses core resources at the start of the year, to gauge or diagnose the strengths and weaknesses of new classes. After that he is constantly challenging himself to try different things to meet the learning needs of the pupils he is teaching. He has already accumulated a suitcase full of resources and his repertoire is getting bigger and bigger. His bank of resources includes different techniques, approaches and methods to achieve similar goals. As a result, his planning has become more diverse.

Approaching lesson planning in individual ways

Planning lessons is an individual thing, people plan in different ways. What everyone has in common is that they have developed their own individual ways of going about lesson planning and they are able to articulate those. Josh, for example, has stripped back his lesson planning to three key points which he thinks through at the planning stage:

- knowing where you're heading
- aware of what could go wrong
- prioritising lesson time and what to spend quality time on in the lesson

In Box 5.1 Will explains his approach to lesson planning.

Box 8.1 Will explains how he plans his ML lessons

I've got certain routines that I always follow, that go with school routines. At the start of the lesson my expectation would be that they all stand behind their chairs, pencil cases out, register in the TL, before we sit down. I explain the objectives and then we'd start some kind of starter to either recap what we've done before or a thinking starter. Normally we then go straight onto something new, presenting language in some way. There's always new language, then doing something with that language, maybe speaking practice. I'd normally use the first 10–20 minutes for a lot of mini-whiteboard work, a lot of pairwork. Then there'd be maybe another core kind of activity which is normally reading or listening; then after than would be production of writing or speaking. Sometimes in the middle it might vary, I might present the language and do some speaking straight away and develop that with a bit of listening – what could we add on now?

It's about chunking the learning, I suppose. I don't like to think of it in terms of progression in 20 minutes. I like to think what do I want them to learn at this point? How am I going to get onto this bit?

At KS4 it maybe has to vary because sometimes if we're doing translation work that might be a full hour, just pure translation work. Or you can end up doing a reading that might take a full hour to do. Towards KS4 the presentation aspect might reduce or the way something is presented may be different. I think at KS4 the presentation moves much more into something that is more challenging in how you plan it. It can't just be putting pictures on the board and saying what they mean. Those skills should be developed further down the school.

At KS5 the way I approach my lessons is to consider probably two skills I want to work on in the lesson. Always framed with a big question. Always with some kind of production at the end and I really consider at KS5 in particular that translation from English is production.

What is noticeable about this is that Will has a very clear idea of what a lesson will look like and how it will differ at different key stages. He has a different planning formula depending on what key stage he is planning for. Implicit in this is a progression in pupils' learning. For example, a feature of Key Stage 3 planning is to break lessons down into chunks of learning; whereas at Key Stage 4 lessons might focus on developing just one skill area.

Developing a longer-term view of planning

When lesson planning, teachers are consciously thinking about the longer-term view. Planning is informed and guided by end goals and the overarching point in what they are teaching. This might mean knowing how your LO are linked to a longer-term teaching plan such as a scheme of work. So you know where you are heading, you know where you can spend more time in the short term and where you can't and how you can move things about. Knowing what goes before and what comes after makes a big difference to the lesson planning of RQTs; it means they are no longer planning isolated lessons and they are no longer planning from scratch.

An important part of the planning process for Catherine is to look at the half term ahead and get the larger view first, this reminds her of where she is heading. Then she likes to plan for the week ahead, starting with the bigger picture for the week and then identifying one aim per lesson, linked to progress. In Box 8.2 Catherine explains how she plans her lessons for the week ahead.

Box 8.2 Catherine plans her lessons for the week ahead

In a week I'd normally like to get through a double page spread in the textbook. Personally I like to use the textbook for some things but I don't like to just say exercise 3, exercise 4 etc. If there's a good text in the book I'll use it. So I'll start with the double page spread and then I like to go out of the book and start to break it down.

I like to look at many different things, e.g. if I've got them last lesson on Friday they're going to less receptive to new input than first lesson on a Wednesday. So then I think doing a new piece of writing is probably best on the Wednesday. If we're going to do more speaking practice or tasks, Friday might be better. I also like to get a balance of skills in. I don't want a week where all we do is writing or a week where all we do is speaking. Then I'll think about how many lessons we've got and how many homeworks and then try to plan that way.

And then, it sort of happens automatically. I don't think that I think about every step – every step of what needs to happen in that lesson – it just comes. I think I look at the double page spread and think I want to exploit that listening so that's going to take lesson one and I might make a quick note of that. And then second lesson I'll think let's exploit the reading, then I'll go back to my first lesson, the listening, and break it down. There's other skills coming in as well (such as translation, reading aloud) but it's all coming from that one piece. Then I always like to think when I'm planning how can I differentiate? What can I have in place to extend students who finish early?

She is using the textbook as a starting point for more detailed planning. She uses the textbook selectively as a resource to provide a balance of skills over a series of lessons. For each lesson she will exploit one key activity or skill area.

The longer-term view also means knowing how what you are teaching fits in with the bigger picture of public examinations and what will be important then. James explains how this bigger picture informs his planning: 'Lesson planning is always linked to a bigger picture I've got in my head about where students are going. For example, if we're doing jobs in French (les métiers) this is also directly linked to the grammar point of gender and how some words change, and gender will be important for GCSE etc. etc. and I will tell pupils about why it's important when I teach it'.

Implicit lesson planning

When they go into lessons, teachers carry a lot of implicit lesson planning in their heads; written plans do not cover everything that the teacher has thought through to make the lesson successful. In fact, written plans tend to be quite short and in most cases this is a significant change since PGCE days. A further significant change is that, as RQTs, they feel more comfortable in the classroom and better able to make decisions in the lesson itself. They have moved away from relying on the written plan, or script, as an aid or crutch. They are able to think on their feet and adapt lessons in response to learners' needs or in response to things that come up in the lesson, and this is implicitly built into lesson planning. It seems responsiveness becomes progressively easier with experience, commensurate with the ability to pre-empt how you might need to respond. In short, important decision making for learning happens both before and during the lesson, and not every aspect of pre-lesson planning for learning is written down.

How has planning changed since PGCE?

When you have more classes to teach and more is expected of you in terms of other professional responsibilities such as marking, data collection and reporting to parents, planning needs to take less time than it did during the PGCE year. 'You have to learn to plan efficiently' is how James puts it. On the whole, lesson planning is easier and takes less time. People are able to make more efficient use of the limited time available to them for planning.

It seems that planning also becomes more effective in the sense that it leads to better learning than was the case during the PGCE year. This is how Will sums up how the quality of his planning has progressed: 'sometimes a lesson can take me far longer than I feel it should take me but I'm still planning it much more effectively than on the PGCE. On PGCE you can spend hours planning one lesson. I could still, depending on what I'm doing, spend hours planning one lesson but it would be a thousand times better than the same amount of time I spent on lessons as a PGCE student'.

So, planning has become both more efficient and effective. But what about the thinking behind the planning? How has that progressed since the ITE period? The main ways in which the thinking of these teachers seems to have progressed include the following:

- Thinking more critically about the purpose of activities and how they fit into the lesson;
- Prioritising activities or experiences that make most difference to learning;
- Anticipation of subject-related difficulties;
- Enhanced understanding of ML pedagogy;
- Taking account of the needs of the pupils you teach and of your teaching context;
- Anticipation of how learning might develop in the classroom;
- Reflecting more critically.

Thinking more critically about the purpose of activities and how they fit into the lesson

Teachers are consciously thinking through the potential and the purpose of activities. Potential means the inherent potential in a given activity for promoting language learning; purpose relates to the specific learning purpose for which you want to use that activity in a given ML lesson. Rather than thinking in terms of an isolated activity to fill time, teachers are considering how this activity supports the overall aims of the lesson or current scheme of work for that class. We have already seen how Will and Josh have exploited the learning potential of activities that are core to their practice. James is also more aware now of the learning potential of specific activities and Battleships is one of his favourites. Box 8.3 outlines the ways in which he now exploits the game of Battleships as a learning opportunity.

Box 8.3 Exploiting the game of Battleships

For James, the biggest purpose of Battleships is speaking practice in the TL. The game element and the fact that pupils play this in pairs helps to loosen inhibitions and this can be an important consideration for some of the classes he teaches. He finds that Battleships works especially well with Year 9 classes, at an age when pupils can feel particularly self-conscious about speaking in front of their peers. The game disguises the fact that pupils are doing a speaking task and if pupils are not used to speaking in the TL, this can be a good way in.

He has used the game in a variety of different linguistic contexts, such as:

- Linking the content to GCSE role-play, both in terms of using different role-play situations and using the sorts of symbols that are used in the GCSE exam (e.g. reserving an hotel room);
- Drilling particular structures and vocabulary needed for a topic;
- Practising particular points of grammar, such as verb paradigms;
- Practising translation from English into the TL.

He also exploits the whole game as an opportunity to use more TL :

- Incorporating into the game TL phrases for pupils to use (e.g. ¡*Tocado*! ¡*Agua*! ¡*Hundido*!) also rubrics and instructions can be written onto the board in the TL (e.g. *Para jugar, coloca los barcos en la tabla.*).

And he is aware of ways of adapting the game to different levels of difficulty, commensurate with his expectations of different classes, for example:

- Varying the extent of TL instructions (Having all instructions in the TL, including words for different types of boat and words to say 'hit' or 'missed' might be appropriate for higher end KS3 pupils, definitely KS4 whereas at a simpler level, less TL would be prevalent on the Battleships board)
- Conjugating verbs would be more difficult than using pre-learnt, prefabricated phrases

Finally, the pairwork element of the game serves a cross curricular purpose in promoting collaborative learning. James links this with his expectations of pupils and the classroom culture he wants to establish.

- The rule is everyone has to speak
- It's OK to make mistakes, that's part of language learning
- And we're all in this together, we're all going to do this

James is clearly aware of how the board itself can be exploited in different ways to support different linguistic objectives. This awareness has come from his experience of using the game with different classes and in different ways. TL use is also factored into his thinking; he is not only thinking in terms of practising the content language of the game, he is also exploiting the opportunities for 'real' or spontaneous TL communication around the game itself. Some of the potential for spontaneity is specific to the game of Battleships (e.g. the words for 'hit', 'missed' or 'sunk'); other possibilities extend beyond this game to other paired activities and games (e.g. the language used to negotiate turn taking, or that used to express your feelings, especially if you have won or lost the game). He is also aware of the potential for differentiation and for varying what language he wants pupils to be practising through the game. Finally, he also knows and understands better how he wants the game to be set up in order to maximise the learning of the pupils he is teaching. And he has learnt how to exploit this key activity to help establish a distinctive ML culture in his classroom.

There is more linking up of different parts of the lesson and this makes planning feel more fluid. As James explains: 'even though I have my bank of resources I'm not just going to pick any one. I'm going to pick one that is relevant to the lesson in question and it has to be in a place in the lesson which is suitable, relevant, appropriate and is linking in to what we're doing and always building on prior knowledge. Not just prior knowledge from lessons ago but prior knowledge from maybe 10 minutes ago in the lesson'.

Going back to the example of Battleships, we can see how thinking has become more purposeful and more fluid since PGCE days. During the PGCE, beginning teachers may well have used Battleships as an isolated, fun activity to engage pupils perhaps at the end of a lesson or as a treat. These days, Battleships is seen as serving a learning purpose that is integral to the lesson it is used in. The lesson might be structured something like this:

Next steps

1   Drill key language that will be practised in the game
2   Listening exercise based on key language
3   Model Battleships with pupil/s
4   Battleships in pairs
5   Written plenary activity based on key language of lesson

Prioritising activities or experiences make most difference to learning

Teachers are not just thinking about what works, they are also giving throught to which activities or experiences make the most difference to learning. Teachers understand that some activities promote better learning than others or have a higher learning value. Again, this is rather different from their memories of the PGCE. Will recalls: 'looking back on some of the lessons from PGCE it was like I knew what I wanted to do but it was more a case of let's do lots of activities to get through the hour and what will happen if I run out of things to do? Whereas now I go the other way. In fact, I want more time most of the time'. When planning lessons, Will and his colleagues are more conscious now of prioritising what will most help the process of ML learning, both in the short term and in the longer term.

Understanding about learning value has implications for how teachers plan to prioritise learning time in lessons. Josh explains how his thinking about timing has progressed: 'you learn where and when to spend time in lessons. As a trainee you'd spend time on things and at the end of the lesson think it wasn't worth that time. I should have spent less time on that so that I could spend more time on that. So, the allocation of time is a bit imbalanced as a trainee- now you know what's going to be difficult and what's going to need time'.

Another implication of this focus on learning is that planning tends to identify one main aim or learning goal and lesson time is prioritised to ensure that pupils achieve that goal in the time available. This is rather different from PGCE days when, for example, Catherine used to think that she needed to have some listening, speaking, reading and writing in every lesson. These days she might plan a whole lesson around a listening exercise. This might involve listening to the same piece three or four times with different tasks and then a reading practice activity or translation based on the transcript.

Marilu reflects on how her lesson planning has changed since PGCE days: 'what I used to do for one lesson was to have lots of ideas and then I was a mess! I thought I needed lots of activities and the students are going to learn in this way. I think more carefully now about what I want to achieve by the end of the lesson, one specific thing. What do I want them to learn? What do I want them to take from my one hour lesson? Is it listening? Speaking? Grammar? Vocabulary? After that my second question is how can I structure the lesson? What can I do first?'

Anticipation of subject-related difficulties

With experience, teachers are better able to anticipate subject-specific misconceptions and difficulties and can refine their planning to try and pre-empt those. It is easier now for teachers to put themselves in the position of their learners. In principle, this helps teachers to see how they can break down the learning, and make it more accessible to more pupils. The more often you teach that topic or particular grammar point, the more opportunity you have to try a different approach and further refine your own understanding of some of the concepts involved. Josh explains how particular difficulties arise when teaching elements of French grammar which don't exist in English:

> They struggle with understanding reflexive verbs. The idea of reflexive verbs is hard to understand because of the nature of reflexive verbs. We (French teachers) know what they are so it's a matter of finding different ways to teach it. For example, using props like false teeth, wigs etc. Another example is gender. They struggle with feminine and masculine. They struggle with the concept that it's to do with words it's not to do with people. It's not female and male, it's feminine and masculine – but they see that as girl and boy.

Enhanced understanding of ML pedagogy

Will gives a different example to show how his understanding of subject pedagogy has changed and the difference this makes to his lesson planning. He explains: 'as a PGCE student if I was presenting places in town, I would first present maybe nine places and then maybe build up with 'il y a . . . or il n'y a pas de . . .'. First the words and then add on the structures. But now I would integrate it all from the beginning so that they're learning the structures right away and they can do something with the words they are learning'. He has come to realise the value of learning prefabricated chunks of language, or learning words in context, as opposed to learning individual words. As Will puts it: 'it's knowing to plan for what they're going to get a lot of learning out of'.

Marilu provides an example of how these different strands can come together. She likes to begin all of her lessons with a formal standing start to the lesson and some speaking practice. This is what works for her in her current teaching context, as she explains in Box 8.4.

Box 8.4 Marilu's formula for starts of lessons

I always start my lessons with speaking. The reason is that I like to do the hardest part at the beginning of the lesson always. For me the hardest part is the listening and speaking, so I try to speak in the TL all the time, especially at the starts of lessons. This is the routine I have built up.

When pupils first arrive at the lesson they stand up and I formally open my lesson with

!Buenos dias¡ !Buenas tardes¡

They know then that they are in my lesson, my house. Then after that they greet each other, they have 10 seconds to say hello to each other. Then I ask how are you? If you are fine, then why are you fine? Or if not, then why don't you feel well? Pupil use the language they have learnt from different topics to expand on their reasons. Maybe it's the weather they can talk about the weather; maybe it's something about the family, they can speak about their family; maybe it's because it's Friday or because they are going to do something at the weekend etc.

When they finally sit down, I might say sentences in the TL from the last lesson- to see how they will cope. They listen and write them down at the back of their books- so they're listening, still listening to Spanish. Then I call out names at random, using lollipop sticks, and pupils say the sentences back to me in English. Then after this, I present the LO for the day in Spanish and I always try to include new words in this, especially verbs.

*At the beginning they couldn't even say 'Hello! How are you?' They were not used to the target language, they'd just laugh. But now when they talk in Spanish it's become normal for them, it's a routine, and it's fun. I do it little by little, the first thing I teach a new class to say is **!Hola¡** and it takes about two months to establish the routine I've described.*

We can see here that Marilu is taking a longer-term perspective. Over time she has gradually and systematically created a routine where speaking and listening become a habit. She builds up small steps of progression, so that over time pupils are able to initiate and respond to greetings, ask and answer questions about how they are feeling and use a range of familiar language to give reasons for how they are feeling. Increasingly, within the framework of this routine, there is scope for pupils to play with the language and take risks with the language, as they use what language they do know to say things that they want to say.

Taking account of the needs of the pupils you teach and of your teaching context

Knowledge of their pupils helps teachers to anticipate their particular needs. This seems to be a regular feature of the planning of these RQTs. This might mean anticipating where their pupils are going to take longer or where they're going to need extra help; it might also mean knowing what they respond well to, what helps them to focus and engage well in their language learning. Catherine gives an example of what this might mean in practice: 'you know the class so you know what works e.g. my Year 9 set 4 they like a lot of structure, a lot of discipline and they like to do an exercise, go through an exercise and very much dissect a text. Whereas my Year 9 set 7 are a much smaller class, very different. They like to have the text in their hand maybe translate it verbally, then translate it writing it down, then pick out bits – so it's a different style. So I think once you know your class you know what works. That can take the first half term to get to know your class, before you know what works'.

Some factors affecting learning, or attitudes to learning, are inherent in a particular teaching context. In some cases, when disaffection is combined with low levels of English literacy and low aspirations, this presents serious barriers to ML learning. In Box 8.5 Josh explains a bit more about the context where he is teaching and how this influences the thinking behind his lessons.

Box 8.5 Josh explains about his teaching context

I've never taught outside the NE but in the NE there's a certain culture. So in the school I've taught in there was a kind of initial blockade in terms of accepting and understanding why it's important to learn a modern language. Once that blockade is down it's a lot easier to get through and get a response from pupils.

Next steps

> *Another difficulty in the NE is the actual grasp of the English language. A lot of students find English quite hard, let alone French. The control of the English language is still an issue for certain students. It's also a difficulty for them to understand why they're doing French or Spanish when they feel their grasp of English isn't strong enough yet. Or some parents come in and say things like 'Why is my son having to do French when his English grade is that low?' What I try to get them to understand is that they (French and English) help each other. French helps English as much as English helps French. It's collaborative and both languages benefit from each other.*
>
> *I know the students. I know they use the present, the past and the future tenses in English without thinking about it. But they don't understand how it works. They don't understand why certain things are there and why certain things are mistakes.*
>
> *Seeing the links between French and English, and how languages evolve and change, that's an element of languages I try and bring into my teaching. I say to students 'look you're saying French is not useful to you but look you're starting to understand more about your own language, you're starting to understand how it works, how we express things'.*

Rather like Marilu earlier, Josh has adapted his teaching approach to take into account the particular teaching context that he finds himself in. He is thinking more broadly about his pupils and barriers to their ML learning and making links to other aspects of their school curriculum. As a RQT he has more opportunity to address deeper issues and to factor those into his lesson planning. The approach he has taken is helping him to win over pupils and parents to the point of learning languages; he is also educating them in the widest sense of the word.

Anticipation of how learning might develop in the classroom

At the pre-lesson planning stage, these teachers are able to anticipate more how things might go in the classroom, how learning might develop. An important part of this might be thinking through how you want particular conversations to go and pre-empting any possible pitfalls. As Catherine explains: 'If you're looking for a reading text, I don't know how but your mind sort of thinks . . . you'll anticipate what they'll pick up on, what questions to ask and you can anticipate or plan how the conversation will go. You allow the students to lead it. In fact, you're leading it but they think that they're leading it. Whereas when you're training all you think is that we're going to do this reading, not how will that conversation go'.

Reflecting more critically

Asking 'why am I doing this?' becomes much more important for RQTs and especially when ML curriculum time is limited. They routinely reflect critically on questions such as: Why this activity? Is it actually relevant to the main learning goal or what I want pupils to achieve in this lesson? In Box 8.6 Josh gives an example of how critical reflection has impacted on his planning and his practice.

Box 8.6   An example of critical reflection

Sometimes on PGCE there's so much going on when you're training, you've got a lot of boxes to tick and sometimes without necessarily thinking why am I doing this? I'm at a stage now where if I don't think it's getting them anywhere or it's not useful to them – I am going to question that, I am going to say 'Why am I doing this? What's the reason behind it? I don't understand it.'

At the end of the day, I'm the one responsible for the class. So it's up to me to do something about it. So I thought about the point of sharing LOs at the starts of lessons. I came to the conclusion that LOs are extremely important, it's what we want them to achieve. They need to know where they are going, what the end point is and why. But if they're just reading them they're not going to know that.

So, it's finding a way to make sure they listen and hear it and engage with the objectives. Because if **they** don't get it what's the point? I know the objectives, I know where I want the lesson to go, I don't need to tell myself that!

For example, if the LO is 'to recognise the future tense', these are some of the ways I might engage the students in thinking about the LOs

- get one of the more confident pupils out to the front to read out the LO and then to mime something specific to that LO to engage the interest of the rest of the class
- right away after that ask questions about the LO, such as:

- what do we know about the future tense in English?
- how would you use the future tense in English? Give me a sentence in the future tense in English.
- tomorrow is a future time phrase. What other time phrase do we use in English with the future tense? What's tomorrow in French?
- why do we have the future tense? What do we use it for?

Critical reflection has helped Josh gain a deeper understanding of the purpose behind what he is teaching and helped him think creatively and positively about possible outcomes.

To sum up, we have seen that planning is no longer about cramming lessons with activities simply to fill the time or to keep pupils occupied: there is more thinking about and greater anticipation of how to exploit learning potential in the lesson. The thinking behind lessons draws on teachers' developing understanding of ML pedagogy, knowledge of their particular teaching context and their evolving views about the sort of ML teacher they want to be.

What these RQTs think now about planning and lesson plans

The point of planning makes a lot more sense now to RQTS. Lesson planning is not about isolated lessons, it's part of something much bigger. Or, as Will puts it, 'Good planning allows for good learning – I'm not sure I considered that as a PGCE student'.

These teachers have an instinctive sense of how important planning is and can be for teaching and learning. James explains how planning helps him as teacher: 'a tightly planned lesson with a clear structure generally for me is a more successful lesson, more successful in terms of behaviour management because the pupils have something to focus on and generally pupils are learning more'. He also describes it as a creative process: 'you can visualise all that's going to really engage them and it may be tricky but you plan how they will cope – in a good way'.

Part of making sense of planning is an awareness of its limitations. In ML, for example, there are limitations to the usefulness of scripting what you are going to say in the TL. Scripting is a helpful planning device at the start when establishing routines and relationships with new groups in order to ensure that the same phrases and structures are used consistently in predictable classroom situations. However, once those phrases have become embedded in practice, scripting can be more of a hindrance than a help to learning. James, for example, sees it as indicative of his development as a teacher that he is now less dependent on scripting. He is also developing the confidence to build unscripted TL conversations into his teaching. For example, with a small Year 10 class he recently talked to them in Spanish about his weekend. The conversation was unscripted and unplanned. James explains what happened: 'they were following the gist and the general topic of what I was saying. And then they started to chip in and ask me questions in Spanish. The questions weren't formed brilliantly, there were mistakes but I understood what the questions were and they understood the answers'. Ultimately, in order to be fully responsive in the classroom, the ML teacher needs to be 'in the moment' rather than reciting or remembering a script. It takes time to reach that stage as ML teacher where you are secure in knowing your own unscripted TL use is helping learning and making a difference to pupil progress over time.

Teachers are developing the classroom awareness needed to know when something is not working as well as it should be and the professional judgement to know when this warrants stopping the planned lesson in order to remedy a particular point and when not. Will, for example, explains: 'I think I've definitely developed responsiveness because you have to be able to learn to go off the lesson plan. You've got to be able to cope with and respond to what's in front of you. There's no point in powering through a lesson plan for the sake of powering through it'. This is one of the lessons that RQTs have learnt the most about planning.

This is how Josh reflects on his experience of learning to plan:

> I think I know what I want now and I think I know what I want them to achieve. I know that, so I'm really confident about what I want and what it will look like in my own head. Obviously it's still a work in progress. Understanding of how MLs are learnt will continue to develop. Everyone is different, everyone has a different relationship with languages, and a different relationship with language learning. But I'm secure in knowing what I want my classes to look like, what my expectations are and what I expect from them.
>
> I know that I'm learning to plan every single time I plan. I don't think that'll ever go away - the learning stage. Sometimes I feel it's interwoven it's not just a question of learning to plan because we probably know how to plan, we know the structure, we know the bits that need to be incorporated. But it's always a work

in progress, there's never a finished version of it and that's why I enjoy it. I enjoy it in the sense that we can always do something in a different way and that's what I mean by we learn all the time, we keep learning. There's always a different way of doing it, a different way to address a certain point or bit of information.

In the short term, Josh has a clear vision of where he is heading and why. Longer term, he knows that he has already progressed considerably in the few years he has been teaching; but he also accepts that understanding how ML are learnt and how best to plan for ML learning is going to be an ongoing aspect of his professional learning.

What hasn't changed since PGCE

It is also worth noting that some aspects of planning have not changed since PGCE. Some degree of planning still goes into every lesson that these teachers teach and they still like to write down what they are planning to do that lesson. It helps to keep them focused and acts as a reminder of particular details.

In addition to this, there are still some occasions when lessons are thought through in detail and considerably more time is devoted to planning those. Those occasions might include:

- High stakes lesson observations, such as those linked to performance management where the lesson outcomes matter not only for pupils but also for teachers;
- Changes to the subject curriculum which require careful thinking through so as to embed them in practice;
- When things go wrong and extra planning and reteaching is needed to unpick misconceptions or to ensure that pupils correctly grasp particular learning points.

In terms of actually putting a plan together, or structuring a lesson, teachers are still essentially doing what they first learnt to do in their PGCE days, namely starting at the end and working backwards. In a sense then, the essence of lesson planning hasn't changed. There is, however, one significant difference. When they plan lessons as RQTs, they are doing so with a greater and more explicit understanding of why they are doing what they are doing. This applies both to what they are planning to do in the classroom and to the planning process itself.

What has helped you to get better at planning?

The biggest single factor that has made a difference to planning is experience of teaching. To a certain extent planning gets easier the more often you do it and planning for ML learning improves with the experience of trial and error. Or as Catherine puts it: 'teaching informs planning and vice-versa; planning can only improve if you've taught it'.

This is how James sums up how experience has helped his planning: 'just being a teacher day to day is probably the single most helpful thing that will help your planning and that's not really about anyone else's influence it's just understanding the reality of the job. And that you have to plan efficiently or you won't be able to do the job successfully'.

Teachers learn from lessons that don't go to plan or lessons that were not planned as well as they could have been. Perhaps the choice of activity was not appropriate or perhaps the activity was not entirely suitable at that moment. This is how Catherine highlights that you learn from bad lessons as well as good:

'Unless you make a mistake you don't see how to make it better. For instance, I firmly believe that you need to know exactly what the aim of the lesson is. But I think I only knew that from seeing lessons where the kids were almost just going through the motions because they had to. Now it's more focussed – these 55 minutes are going to be useful this is what we are going to do'.

Experience means you are not starting from scratch. Those who have taught longer are now reaching a point where they have taught most topics and have built up a bank of resources and ideas for teaching those. With experience you know where things can go wrong and what you can spend more time on. You develop scenarios (what if...?) that you can draw on to help you think on your feet in the classroom. You develop a sense of perspective that helps inform your planning and expectations in the shorter term. And you have more knowledge of the pupils you are teaching, as learners and specifically as language learners.

And yet, crucial though experience is, on its own it does not account for all the progress that people have made in their planning and particularly the thinking behind their planning. The next subsection considers some specific opportunities and activities that have made a difference.

Professional dialogue

Talking about planning with your colleagues can be hugely beneficial, both to yourself and to them. These might be quite short, informal chats. Perhaps you just want to get or share some new ideas. We all need new ideas every now and again, because otherwise we get bored and particularly in ML where you need lots of ideas for revisiting and recycling key points. Or perhaps you have a mental block and need a bit of help from a colleague. This is a point that Will can relate to:

> I think when you can't see a way to do it, like knowing the end point but not knowing how to get there. When you talk about it you can kind of hear yourself, OK that's not going to work. Sometimes planning can be very insular, sitting at your computer click, click, click.

Talking to subject colleagues beyond your department is possible through various online communities. For example, James and Catherine use the UK-based Facebook group 'Secondary MFL Matters' and recommend it as a professional forum in cyber-space for sharing ideas, reading about other people's experiences and asking others for suggestions. Sharing ideas like this can cut down the time needed for planning.

Further, more formal opportunities for professional dialogue arise in relation to collaborative planning, team teaching and mentoring.

Collaborative planning and team teaching

Joint or collaborative planning continues to make a difference to teachers' professional learning beyond the ITE period. Josh describes his experience of planning as part of a small group of ML colleagues:

> The whole process would be planning together, teaching together and then evaluating together. We planned the lessons about health. We invented these characters. Each character was linked to a different tense. And then we created those lessons, we bounced ideas off each other.

> Team planning or planning as a group is one of the most helpful ways for me to plan. It helps me because you can see the ideas before the lesson is created and you can talk about it. Just by talking about it and going through it bit by bit that does help. It's something I would do every time if it was possible. When you're typing it you're writing it and you going through different options in your head but actually saying it to someone else really does help.

For me, this highlights planning as a creative process and the creative potential that is unleashed when teachers plan together; and joint planning as a RQT is perhaps more truly collaborative than typical experiences of joint planning with a mentor during the PGCE year.

Mentoring

As a NQT in the UK you can expect to be mentored. The mentor may not always be a subject specialist. Nevertheless mentoring continues, in principle at least, to provide opportunities for formative professional dialogue about planning. James's experience of NQT mentoring has been very positive. In particular, he has found that external input in the form of feedback from observers helps him to think about what he is planning to do in lessons; for example, an observer might say 'maybe you could try doing this ... because I know it has worked for me'. Marilu has made progress thanks to a mentor who has helped her to identify and plan for subject-specific development targets and to make those the focus of a plan, do, review cycle.

Subject-specific Continuing Professional Development (CPD)

Subject-specific CPD has been particularly helpful. ALL, the professional association for ML teachers in the UK, provides regular training and professional development opportunities. James, for example, attends a TL support group for ML teachers, organised by ALL North East. Participation in this supportive group of like-minded colleagues has helped deepen his understanding of the central role of speaking in language learning, given him different teaching strategies to try in the classroom and inspired him to plan for more sustained pupil TL use in his second year of teaching.

Other experiences that these RQTs found helpful

- Marking for misconceptions is useful and helps tailor lesson plans to the needs of pupils you are teaching.
- Teaching the same lesson again to a parallel group or groups helps you see how you can refine the lesson structure and strip it back to essential elements.
- Observation of others, either in your own department or in another school, increases awareness of what is possible and this informs your own planning.
- The experience of learning another language yourself as a teacher helps to put you in the position of the learner and to pre-empt likely difficulties or misconceptions.
- Keeping a record of what you have taught and what you have covered in lessons helps you to plan more efficiently; it saves time next time you teach that same topic.

And finally . . .

Teachers were asked to suggest one final piece of planning advice for beginning teachers. This is what they said:

Catherine	'Do joint planning with your mentor'.
James	'Don't be afraid to try new things and to learn from that'.
Josh	'Talk about lessons you are planning as much as you can'.
Marilu	'Plan for one target at a time, you cannot learn everything at once'.
Will	'Learn to exploit what you've got'.

Summing up Chapter 8

It is difficult to separate out what has helped these teachers get better at planning from experiences that have supported their practice in a broader sense. What is clear is that learning to plan, like planning itself, is an individual process. To an extent, how you learn to plan depends on the school context you find yourself in, how planning is conceived within that context and the value placed there on professional learning and development. However, it does seem that opportunities to talk about and get feedback on planning are hugely important for continued learning beyond the ITE period.

References for Part IV

Black, L., Gordon, A.L., Hughes, C., MacArthur, R. and Sandy, S. (2017) *Effective mentoring of trainee teachers (e-Book)*. Association for Language Learning. Available to purchase from: https://www.all-languages.org.uk/product/effective-mentoring-trainee-teachers-e-book/

Burn, K. (1997) Learning to teach: the value of collaborative teaching. In D. McIntyre (ed.), *Teacher education research in a new context: The Oxford internship scheme*, pp145–161. Paul Chapman: London.

Cambridge International Teaching and Learning Team (n.d.) *Getting started with reflective practice*. Available at: https://www.cambridge-community.org.uk/professional-development/gswrp/index.html (accessed February 2019).

Capel, S., Leask, M. and Younie, S. (eds.) (2016) *Learning to teach in the secondary school*. Seventh Edition. Routledge: London.

Department for Education (2011) *Teachers' standards*. Available at: https://www.gov.uk/government/publications/teachers-standards (accessed July 2018).

Department for Education and Skills (2001) *Teaching and learning in the foundation subjects*, DfES: London.

Gibbs, G. (1988) *Learning by doing: a guide to teaching and learning methods*. Further Education Unit, Oxford Polytechnic: Oxford. Please note, Gibb's reflective cycle is widely available on the internet, for example from https://www.cambridge-community.org.uk/professional-development/gswrp/index.htm.

Hardman, F.C., Bramald, R., Leat, D. and McManus, E. (1994) The importance of bad lessons. *Teacher Education Reform: current research*, pp147–156. Paul Chapman: London.

James, C.R., Dunning, G., Connolly, M. and Elliott, T. (2007) Collaborative practice: a model of successful working in schools. *Journal of Educational Administration*, 45(5), pp541–555.

Lightbulb Languages website, https://www.lightbulblanguages.co.uk/ (accessed February 2019)

Lofthouse, R. (2018a) Improving mentoring practices through collaborative conversations. *CollectivED*, Special Issue, June 2018, pp14–15. Carnegie School of Education, Leeds Beckett University. Available at: http://www.leedsbeckett.ac.uk/-/media/files/research/bursaries-2015/ncs-collectived-special-edition.pdf?la=en (accessed October 2018).

— (2018b) Mentoring as part of career long professional development and learning. *CollectivED*, (5), pp28–36. Carnegie School of Education, Leeds Beckett University. Available at: http://www.leedsbeckett.ac.uk/-/media/files/research/collectived-sept-2018-issue-5-final.pdf?la=en (accessed October 2018).

Lofthouse, R. and Birmingham, P. (2010) The camera in the classroom: video-recording as a tool for professional development of student teachers. *TEAN Journal*, 1(2). Available at: https://ojs.cumbria.ac.uk/index.php/TEAN/article/view/59 (accessed July 2018).

Mutton, T., Hagger, H. and Burn, K. (2011) Learning to plan, planning to learn: the developing expertise of beginning teachers. *Teachers and Teaching*, 17(4), pp399–416.

PDC in MFL (2012) *Research for Language Teaching*. Available at: http://pdcinmfl.com (accessed November 2018).

TeachIt Languages website, https://www.teachitlanguages.co.uk/ (accessed February 2019)

Final reflections

I set out to make planning more visible to beginning teachers, in order to help them plan ML lessons that will make a difference to the lives of pupils they are teaching. Various exemplary materials and commentaries in this book were intended to do just that by illustrating what planning for learning might look like and the decisions upon which that planning was based. I do want to emphasise, however, that the plans presented here should not be misconstrued simply as recipes, which are telling beginning teachers what to do and say in the classroom. A lesson plan is never going to be an exact prediction or foolproof recipe, regardless of how detailed it is. At best, a lesson plan is a guide to help the teacher.

Classrooms and teaching contexts differ in a seemingly infinite number of ways and it has been a challenge to represent a variety of them in the book. Beginning teachers are not only new to the school and the classes they teach, they are also new to teaching. It takes time to be able to take account of contextual factors when planning lessons, particularly knowledge of the pupils you are teaching. Collaborative planning with a mentor can help start to plug that knowledge gap early on. However, it still takes time to work out what works for whom, under what conditions and why. This is a challenge for any teacher who moves to a new teaching context, beginning or experienced. In ML, there are particular contextual factors that make a significant difference to planning for learning. For example, planning for classes who have had virtually no exposure to the TL is very different from fitting into a department with a long-established culture of TL use.

Added to which, progression in learning does not necessarily proceed in a predictable, linear fashion; learning a language is not a simple matter of learning more and more words or becoming increasingly accurate. For example, in the final chapter, 'Linguist of the Lesson' reminds us that there are many different ways to be good at languages. Progress in ML is slower and more diverse in nature than current orthodoxy might have us believe, particularly the notion of predetermined level descriptors and the notion that progress can always be evidenced within the course of a single lesson. This is why, for me, it is more meaningful to plan in terms of long-term learning goals and longer-term progression in learning, rather than thinking that progress in learning can and needs to be measured in every lesson.

The attention to detail on lesson plans and mini-plans in this book, particularly in the first three chapters, may seem excessive. However, attention to such detail in the early stages of learning to teach will reap benefits later on and it is very important to keep this bigger picture in mind. This applies, for example, to the fundamental skills of drilling and TL modification. With practice, both of these will soon get easier. You will be able to use appropriate techniques more fluently in the classroom and you will be able to do so without the same need for detailed scripting. More importantly, with experience comes the ability to use those skills more intuitively in the classroom, as and when the need arises. It is my view that, over time, conscious reflection (e.g. through lesson evaluation) can help teachers develop this more intuitive feel. That said, in the early stages of learning to teach, drilling sequences and your own TL output need to be planned and this takes time. Longer term, however, the benefits are that you can be more responsive to pupils' needs as they arise in the classroom.

It strikes me now that learning *about* planning is not the same as learning *to* plan. It is nevertheless helpful. Learning about planning helps make planning visible and an awareness of what is needed or involved might be a first step towards achieving it. Learning about planning means you can be proactive in creating sequences of lessons, individual lessons and learning experiences which are informed by your understanding of successful language teaching and learning and which accord with the values and beliefs that underpin your practice as a languages teacher.

Ultimately, for me, planning for learning is a creative process. But there is a possible tension here if teachers are not given the freedom to take control of that process. It is a matter of concern that if teachers are asked to deliver lessons that they have had no part in planning, then teaching itself becomes automated and understanding of the creative potential of planning and how it might impact on teaching and learning is lost.

But no school or department is without its challenges. It is understanding those challenges and being proactive in addressing what is within our influence or control that makes us better teachers and educators. In the final chapter, teachers stressed the value of trying out new ideas and learning from that; I would like to strongly endorse this willingness to experiment. This is not a matter of experimenting for the sake of it. Rather, it is the idea of being proactive in making informed changes to your practice with a view to improving it and deepening your understanding. Purposefully and systematically planning for and reviewing the impact of such changes to practice will enable you to learn more from the 'experiment'. For me, this is intelligent planning and there are some good examples of this in the book. The '*Déjeuner du Matin*' lesson was planned as an experiment to deepen understanding of the learning value in studying a French poem; the Independent Reading Skills lesson was planned to see what impact a more pupil-centred approach would have on pupil behaviour. These examples show the potential of lesson planning for creative thinking and problem solving in order to promote better learning. Ultimately, this is the sort of planning that will make the biggest difference to the learning of beginning teachers and, longer term, to the lives of the pupils they are teaching.

Happy planning!

Annotated list of further reading and sources

Here are some suggested reading and sources of advice to further support and deepen understanding of lesson planning for beginning teachers. This includes works that have already been referenced in the book, together with other texts and sources.

Atkinson, T. (2000) Learning to teach: intuitive skills and reasoned objectivity. In T. Atkinson and G. Claxton (eds.) *The intuitive practitioner: on the value of not always knowing what one is doing.* Chapter 4, pp69–83. Open University Press, Magraw-Hill Education: Maidenhead, Berkshire.

■ Beginning teachers sometimes struggle to conceptualise the relationship between deliberate, reasoned planning decisions, formalised in a lesson plan, and more intuitive decisions that are made in the classroom. Atkinson unpacks the relationship between planning and intuition (reflection in action) in an accessible and highly relevant way for beginning teachers and/or their tutors and mentors, and considers implications for teacher education.

Christie, C. (2016) Speaking spontaneously in the modern foreign languages classroom: tools for supporting successful target language conversation. *The Language Learning Journal*, 44(1), pp74–89.

■ This article is based on Colin Christie's PhD research into spontaneous speaking. It is a very helpful read, both in terms of explaining theoretical perspectives and offering practical guidance. Transcripts of classroom exchanges are used to illustrate key points and provide insight into what is possible.

Clark, C.M. and Yinger, R.J. (1987) Teacher planning. In J. Calderhead (ed.) *Exploring teachers' thinking.* Chapter 3, pp84–103. Continuum (formerly Cassell Academic): London.

■ I can recommend this chapter for anyone interested in deepening their understanding of planning as decision making, and of teachers as reflective professionals and thinkers. It reviews what is known about the planning of experienced teachers, and discusses important themes that have been introduced in this book, for example, the cyclical nature of planning and the relationship between pre-active and interactive stages of teaching. The authors argue that success depends on the teacher's ability to manage complexity and solve practical problems.

Council of Europe (2001) *Common European Framework of Reference for Languages: Learning, teaching, assessment.* Cambridge University Press: Cambridge. Also available at https://www.coe.int/en/web/common-european-framework-reference-languages/ (accessed November 2018).

■ As a language learner you may well be familiar with the Common Reference Levels (A1-C2) that form the basis of this reference book. The book presents a framework that was more than 30 years in the making, the result of collaboration between language experts from across Europe and beyond. It describes and analyses different competences that contribute towards language proficiency and different levels of proficiency in each. If you are interested in the bigger picture of what is involved in learning to communicate in another language, then this is the book for you.

Coyle, D. (2005) *CLIL: Planning tools for teachers.* University of Nottingham, School of Education.

Available at: https://www.unifg.it/sites/default/files/allegatiparagrafo/20-01-2014/coyle_clil_planningtool_kit.pdf (accessed November 2018).

■ This is a useful booklet for anyone interested in planning specifically for CLIL. The author, Do Coyle, is a leading authority on CLIL; she talks the reader through what is involved in planning for CLIL and covers modules of work and individual lessons.

Dörnyei, Z. (2001) *Motivational strategies in the language classroom.* Cambridge University Press: Cambridge.

■ This is a very popular book dealing with a notoriously difficult construct – motivation. The author engages with this topic in clear and very readable terms. The book combines theoretical perspectives with lots of practical advice. It includes a checklist of 35 motivational strategies that teachers can use with language learners and which can inform lesson planning.

Driscoll, P. and Macaro, E. and Swarbrick, A. (eds.) (2014) *Debates in modern languages education*. Routledge: London.

- This book covers a range of issues of particular relevance to teaching ML in the UK. The chapters are all written by experienced experts in that particular field. Many of these are of direct relevance to pedagogy and planning. For example, I can recommend the chapters on formative assessment (written by Jane Jones) and grammar (Ernesto Macaro). And I also recommend the chapter by Mary Ryan, who argues a strong case for creativity in the ML classroom.

Hawkes, R. *Rachel Hawkes language learning website*, www.rachelhawkes.com (accessed November 2018)

- Rachel is Director of International Education and Research for Comberton Academy Trust; she is also a language teacher and former president of ALL. Her website contains ideas and strategies for promoting, teaching and learning languages, as well as many presentations that she has given to teachers, and is well worth a visit.

- Rachel is also a leading authority on the promotion of spontaneous L2 teacher-learner interaction. In 2012 she completed her PhD, entitled 'Learning to talk and talking to learn: how spontaneous teacher-learner interaction in the secondary foreign languages classroom provides greater opportunities for L2 learning'. You can download the full PhD thesis from her website. It is highly articulate and readable. I would particularly recommend Chapter 4 (review of L2 talk in the secondary classroom context in England), Chapter 6 (discussion of the actual teaching strategies used to generate L2 spontaneity) and the Conclusion. Rachel's work highlights the central role of the teacher, including important planning implications for promoting teacher-learner L2 interaction.

Jones, B. *The Barry Jones Archive*. Available at: https://www.all-languages.org.uk/student/barry-jones-archive/ (accessed November 2018).

- Barry Jones was a highly respected, influential and inspirational teacher educator, well known throughout the UK. Before he died in 2015 he selected some of his publications which he felt would be most useful for future student teachers and bequeathed them to ALL. These cover many themes covered in this book, notably grammar, creativity, cultural awareness and target language use, and more. As Barry writes: 'the readings are full of tried and tested teaching ideas. They may work with some classes, but not with others. The thing is to try them and then ask yourself why they did or didn't work'.

Lightbown, P. and Spada, N. (2013) *How languages are learned*. Oxford University Press: Oxford.

- This is an award-winning book and, in my opinion, deservedly so. It is a reference book for anyone who is interested in second language acquisition and learning. The book provides a comprehensive introduction to relevant theory and research, and relates this to teaching and learning in the languages classroom. It is clearly written and highly readable.

Lin, M. and Mackay, C. (2004) *Thinking through modern foreign languages*. Chris Kington Publishing: Cambridge.

- This book introduces and discusses a particular approach to teaching and learning in ML, designed to promote metacognitive awareness. It contains 20 exemplars of different Thinking Skills lessons in French, German, Spanish and English. Those take the form of accounts of lessons written by the teachers who taught them, together with photocopiable resources. There is detailed consideration of lesson preparation and classroom procedures.

Littlewood, W. (1981) *Communicative language teaching*. Cambridge University Press: Cambridge.

- The fact that this book was in its 30th printing in 2010 gives some indication of its popularity. It was Littlewood who introduced the distinction between pre-communicative and communicative activities. In this book he unpacks in a very clear and accessible way the thinking behind this distinction and implications for practice. The book includes lots of examples of activities to illustrate key points.

Macaro, E. (2003) *Teaching and learning a second language: a guide to recent research and its applications*. Continuum: London.

- This is an extremely useful book for beginning teachers of ML to read. It was written for teachers and, in my view, it brings together in one book everything that a beginning teacher needs to know in terms of relevant research into teaching and learning languages. It is written in a methodical, readable style and key concepts are clearly explained. I would particularly recommend the chapter 'Theories, Grammar and Methods' for its implications for planning (Chapter 3).

Maley, A. and Peachey, N. (eds.) (2015), *Creativity in the English language classroom*. The British Council. Free to download at: http://englishagenda.britishcouncil.org/continuing-professional-development/cpd-teacher-trainers/creativity-english-language-classroom (accessed November 2018).

- This is an edited collection of short papers written by experienced English language teaching (ELT) researchers, practitioners and professionals. Papers explore practical classroom activities that demonstrate what creativity is really about and include classroom procedures that teachers can incorporate into their planning, in order to promote creativity in their classrooms. Many of the examples can be transferred to the context of teaching ML in secondary schools in England.

Mutton, T. and Hagger, H. and Burn, K. (2011) Learning to plan, planning to learn: the developing expertise of beginning teachers. *Teachers and Teaching*, 17(4), pp399–416.

- This paper is likely to be of interest to beginning teachers and their mentors. The topic of learning to plan and implications for teacher education is one that little has been written about. A key focus of the paper is how beginning teachers progress in their planning, within and beyond the ITE period. Many of the points made in Chapter 8 of this book are included in this paper (e.g. less reliance on scripting, becoming more responsive in the classroom, the value of collaborative planning).

Richards, J.C. and Rodgers, T.S. (2014) *Approaches and methods in language teaching*. Third edition. Cambridge University Press: Cambridge.

- This is a very comprehensive reference book, covering approaches and methods used in language teaching around the world, and the theories of language learning on which they are based; it also provides a historical perspective, covering the start of the twentieth century right up to current day. For example, in addition to CLT, there are chapters on CLIL and on task based learning. Highly readable, informed and informative.

Williams, M. and Burden, R. and Lanvers, U. (2002) 'French is the Language of Love and Stuff': student perceptions of issues related to motivation in learning a foreign language. *British Educational Research Journal*, 28(4), pp503–528. DOI:10.1080/0141192022000005805

- ■ This article reports on an investigation into the motivation of secondary school students in the South-West of England to learn foreign languages. This is recommended reading for those who are curious to know more about motivational theory as it relates to language learning. A range of literature and research is reviewed in a clear and accessible way; key concepts and issues are explained well.

Wringe, C. (1989) *Effective teaching of modern languages*. Re-published as an e-book by Routledge (2013).

- ■ The secondary school context in England has changed somewhat since this book was written. Nevertheless, the author is an experienced University PGCE tutor and the book contains a lot of useful advice that transcends time. I think it makes a lot of good sense and I would particularly recommend Chapter 2 (Planning).

http://all-literature.wikidot.com/ (accessed November 2018)

- ■ This is the site of the ALL literature project, created by ALL in 2014. The site has been regularly updated since then. The Wiki hosts contributions written by and for languages teachers and includes links to various authentic sources and ideas for exploiting them.

CollectivEd Working Papers series. Available at: http://www.leedsbeckett.ac.uk/riches/our-research/working-paper-series/collectived/ (accessed November 2018)

- ■ CollectivEd: The Hub for Mentoring and Coaching is a Research and Practice Centre based in the Carnegie School of Education at Leeds Beckett University. The centre publishes four issues of working papers per year; they are all related to the theme of collaborative practice. We have seen examples in this book, notably in Chapter 8, of the value of collaborative planning and of professional dialogue for learning to plan. Not all of the papers may be relevant or useful to beginning teachers and / or their mentors; but some of them will be; see for example, the two papers referenced at the end of Part III. I think it might be useful for beginning teachers and their mentors to know about this resource, particularly if you are in a school context where little value seems to be placed on collaborative practice. Just because it isn't happening in your school yet, doesn't mean that it can't happen.

Secondary MFL Matters Facebook page. Joining instructions: https://www.facebook.com/groups/secondarymflmatters/?ref=group_header (accessed November 2018)

- ■ An open forum for secondary MFL teachers. Currently the group has about 9000 members. A forum to share ideas that are or are not working for you. Really helpful if you are seeking out opportunities to plan lessons differently or more successfully.

https://www.lightbulblanguages.co.uk/ (accessed November 2018)

- ■ A site packed with thousands of language resources written by language teachers for language teachers. The site is regularly updated.

https://www.makaton.org/ (accessed November 2018)

- ■ This is the site of Makaton – a language programme that uses signing and symbols to support spoken speech and help people to communicate. Makaton can be a useful source of ideas for actions, gestures and mimes you can use to support spoken language in the ML classroom. If you are struggling to visualise what the use of these might look in practice, you might also want to watch Makaton signs on YouTube.

www.pdcinmfl.com (accessed November 2018)

- ■ The work of the PDC in MFL is referred to in the Introduction to this book. The web-site includes videos of classroom footage to demonstrate particular pedagogical points. Depending on your teaching context, it might be helpful for beginning teachers to see what those points look and sound like in practice (e.g. brainstorming ideas with a class, setting up a game of 20 Questions).

https://jamesstubbs.wordpress.com/index/ (accessed November 2018)

- ■ James Stubbs is a teacher, blogger, conference speaker, teacher trainer and magician! He is particularly interested in teaching through the medium of the TL and incorporating visual, auditory and kinaesthetic learning styles into everything that goes on in the classroom. He is also highly articulate and generous in sharing his ideas and his thinking. For example, his posts relating to sequences of grammar teaching are really instructive, in showing how he plans backwards.

Index

accuracy, activities for 127, 140–141
actions 15, 19, 29, 34, 41–44, 78, 83
adapting authentic materials 145
administration of tasks 45; *see also* practicalities of running activities
affective support in language learning 92–93
aims and objectives 101, 105, 154, 155, 161; *see also* learning intentions/objectives
A-level specifications 116, 122, 142
Alison, J. 98, 99
ALL (Association for Language Learning) 145, 179
ALL Literature Project 145
answers, checking 45, 71
artefacts/objects 15, 19
assessment 73–79, 102–103, 131, 155–156, 161, 163
assessment criteria 163
assistants, language 88, 126, 147
attention spans, poor 74
attitudes to language learning 193; *see also* motivations to learn
authentic material 119, 145–147, 184–185
autonomous learning 151

backup plans 25, 98
bad lessons, learning from 196
balance, aiming for 98, 115–152, 153, 155, 163, 192
Battleships 188, 190–191
Baumfield, Vivienne 100
before and after activities 79
behaviour, planning for 25, 59, 69, 95–99, 149, 195
behaviourist approaches to learning 4
Big Questions 118, 122
bluffing game 53–56
board, demonstrations/examples on 54, 77, 93, 129, 150
bottom set classes 89–95, 98, 117
brainstorming 140
broad aims 140
Burch, James 13
Burden, R. L. 147, 151, 152
Burn, Katherine 6, 172

Cambridge International Teaching and Learning Team 174
challenge, increasing the 29, 33–34, 85, 88
challenge and support 84–86, 92–95, 105, 119, 161
chanting 16
checking answers 45, 71

choice, offering 24, 140
chunks of language 4, 15, 83, 123, 126; *see also* prefabricated chunks
chunks of learning 189
circumlocution 19–20
class management 69; *see also* behaviour, planning for; routines, classroom
classroom instructions in target language 18–22, 83
classroom layout 150
classroom routines 185–186, 189, 193
cloze tests 16
coaching 176; *see also* mentors
cognates 20, 52
cognitive approaches to learning 3, 4
cognitive maturity 3
cognitive support for language learning 92, 127
coherence in plans 173
collaboration with other departments 141, 145
collaborative planning 172–173, 197
collaborative teaching 172, 197
Common European Framework of Reference for Languages 2
communication and the teacher's use of TL 18–22
communication as goal of ML teaching and learning 2–4, 15, 61, 92, 155
communication devices 18–22
communicative language teaching (CLT) 2, 3, 4, 123, 127
competitive elements 34; *see also* game elements
comprehensible input 44
comprehension: checking and rechecking 17; checking techniques 16; drilling 13, 15; and explicit grammar teaching 123; greater than production ability 44; before production 28; repeat if true 33–34; tools for checking 78; using non-verbal devices for 19
confidence, learner 2, 24, 28, 33, 41, 92, 93, 127, 136
confidence, teacher 48, 173
content, language 15, 24, 44–45, 177
Content and Language Integrated Learning (CLIL) 117, 121, 122
content-free, Modern Languages as 1
context: and drilling 15; of the familiar 69, 153, 154; grammatical 32; transfer of language across 56–61
contextualising phrases 31
contingency planning 25, 98
continual practice, need for 5
Continuing Professional Development (CPD) 197
continuous assessment 78, 103

205

Index

continuous improvement 64
co-operative learning strategies 30; *see also* group activities; pair work
corrective feedback/error correction 78, 127–136
Council of Europe 2
creativity 1, 53, 55, 124, 136–141, 178–179, 200–201
critical reflection 174–175, 190, 194
cross-curricular considerations 141
cross-departmental work 141, 145
cultural differences 46
culture, classroom 191
culture, learning about 116–122, 142
cumulative nature of language progression 116, 135, 160–161
cycle of planning, teaching and evaluation 102–103, 163, 176
cycle of PPP 4–5

data, pupil, making use of 84, 188
Dearing, Ron 3
declarative knowledge 1–2
deductive grammar teaching 129–133
departmental-level planning 165, 173
departures from the plan 149, 174, 195
dependence on the written plan 177
detail in plans, level of 83, 178, 196
diagnostic assessment 78, 85, 155
dictation activities, as a contingency plan 98
differentiation 84–86, 150, 160–161, 163, 183, 191
disabilities, pupils with 84
discipline plans 98, 100
discussion phrases 61
distinctiveness of ML as a school subject 1–2
draft plans 171; *see also* outline planning
drama department, working with 145
drilling 13–18, 27, 37, 41, 89, 161

efficiency of planning 177–178, 190
emotional aspects of ML learning 92
enabling environments 150
end of unit tasks 160–163, 173
engagement versus progression 180
English use 57, 78, 142
error correction 39, 127–136, 141
evaluation 63–64, 103–104, 163–165, 174–175
examination syllabuses 44, 123
expectations 19, 92, 161, 183
experience, learning from 6, 196
experiential approaches to learning 4
explicit grammar teaching 4, 123, 129–130, 136, 155
exposure to target language 3, 4, 20, 34, 44; repeated exposure 13, 18
extended lesson reviews 174–175
extension activities 57, 119

fairy stories 145
Fawkes, Steven 139
feedback from pupils, eliciting 45, 85, 150, 178, 179, 184
feedback on planning 171–172
fluency exercises 55, 127
focus, keeping pupils' 81
follow-up to lessons 69

Foreign Language Spelling Bee 180
form, focus on 3, 123, 127, 129
Framework of Core Content 153

game elements 27, 190–191
GCSE exam specifications 116, 191
gesture 19, 41
gist, understanding 44, 85, 142, 144, 195
good enough plans 178
government language policies 2, 3
grammar teaching 3, 122–136; authentic material 145; case usage 32; deductive grammar teaching 129–133; degree of insistence on grammatical correctness 40; explicit grammar teaching 4, 123, 129–130, 136, 155; implicit acquisition 4, 123, 130; inductive grammar teaching 129–133; and literature 142; long-term planning 155, 163; not trying to teach too much 177; noughts and crosses 39; in the PPP model 4; prefabricated chunks 15; teacher's use of TL 19
greetings/salutations, practising 59
group activities: classroom layout 150; listen and respond activities 41; listening in (to groups/pairs) 78; mouthing 31; organising groups 43, 69, 150; for peer learning 143; *see also* pair work
guessing games 20, 48–52
guided reading 71, 91

Hadfield, C. 140, 141
Hadfield, J. 140, 141
Hagger, Hazel 6
half-classes, teaching 143–144
Halliwell, S. 98, 99
Harris, Vee 2, 3, 4, 19, 133, 134, 147
Hawkins, E. 1
Hewer, Bev 157
homework 58, 69, 88, 91, 131, 177
human dominoes 125

ice-breakers 55
imitation 44
implicit acquisition 4, 123, 130
implicit lesson planning 190
in-classroom decisions 18, 25, 44, 78, 102
incremental approaches 17
independent learning 116, 142, 147–152
individual pupils, detailed knowledge of 84, 188, 193, 196
inductive grammar teaching 129–133
instructions, in TL 18–22, 83
interactions through the target language 3
interactive planning 102; *see also* collaborative planning
interactive teaching 6
intercultural understanding 116–122
internet resources 145
intonation 20, 141
introducing yourself to a class 54–55

joint planning 172–173, 180, 197
jokes 138
Jones, B. 117
joy of language learning 136–137

King, Lid 3
knowledge of individual pupils, detailed 84, 188, 193, 196

Krashen, S.D. 44
KS2 lessons 120–121

L2 *see* target language
Lamb, Terry 151
language assistants 88, 126, 147
Languages Review 3
learner autonomy 151
learner-centred approaches 147–152
learning conversations 171, 176, 197
learning intentions/objectives 72–73, 89, 105–106, 155, 194
learning needs, individual 84, 193–194
learning outcomes (students') 70, 105, 115–116, 161, 173, 192
learning outcomes (teacher's) 40
learning styles 155
learning to plan 5–6, 171–181
lesson objectives 72–73, 89
lesson observations 171, 172, 179, 196, 198
lesson organisation 69
lesson planning, process 102–111; getting better at 196–198; implicit 190; limitations 195; related dilemmas 176–181
lesson plans, written 1, 19, 106–109, 177, 196
lesson structure 70–72, 180
'letting go' activities 61
limitations of planning 195
'linguist of the lesson' 186–187
linguistic frameworks 139, 140, 141
linguistic progression across a sequence of lessons 157, 193
linguistic progression within a lesson 75, 77, 78, 91, 119, 126
listen and respond activities 41–44
listening comprehension 44–47, 88, 147
listening in (to groups/pairs) 78
literacy in L1 91, 193, 194
literature 141–147
Littlewood, W. 2, 95, 127
Lofthouse, Rachel 176
lollipop sticks 85, 185, 193
long-term planning 57, 69, 72, 106, 119, 124, 133, 153–165, 173, 189
lost property office sketch 138–139
low literacy (in L1) 91, 193, 194
lower achievers 161; *see also* bottom set classes

Macaro, E. 3, 18, 123, 127
marking for misconceptions 198
matching exercises 38, 96, 130, 131
meaning: chunks of 15; clues to 20; communication of 3; focus on 29–30; literature 142; negotiation of 127
meaningful learning 145
mediation/mediated learning experiences 150
medium-term plans 69, 72, 160
memorisation 13, 41, 142
memory games 27, 29–30
mentors 17, 142, 171–172, 173, 174, 175, 181, 197
messiness of classroom learning 4
messy, planning is 25, 102
meta-awareness of language 3, 127
metacognition 147, 150, 151
Meyer, B. 150
milling exercises 53–54
mimes and actions 15, 19, 29, 34, 41–44, 78, 83
mini whiteboards 78, 184

mini-class survey 56–61
mispronunciation, strategies for dealing with 17
Mitchell, Rosamund 2, 3, 4, 15, 123
mixed ability teaching 76, 82, 84, 125, 150
modelling: factoring in time for 89; guessing games 52; and independent learning 150; versus lengthy explanations 57; mini-class survey 57; paraphrasing 48; spot the fib 54; teacher's use of TL 18–22
Modern Languages as a school subject 1–2
modification of authentic texts 145
modified output 18–22, 25, 52, 83, 145
momentum, building 83
monitoring and checking 75, 78
monotony, avoidance of 17, 18
motivations to learn 3, 92, 122, 123, 136, 151
mouthing 31–32, 37
moving around the classroom 41
Mutton, Trevor 1, 6, 84, 171, 172, 173
Myles, F. 2, 3, 15, 123

national curriculum 2, 116, 142, 145
National Curriculum Modern Foreign Languages Working Party 2
native speakers: differentiation for native speaker pupils 84; language assistants 88, 126, 147; using to verify pronunciation 15
Network for Thinking Skills 151–152
new information, seven pieces of 15
Newmann, F.M. 145
non-linearity of planning 25, 154
non-verbal devices used by teacher 19, 25
noughts and crosses 38–39

observation of other teachers 17, 20, 198
observation sheets 21
observations 171, 172, 179, 196, 198
Odd One Out 80, 137–138, 139
one lesson a week 88, 93
one-off lessons 120–121, 136, 140, 143, 178
on-the-spot decision making 18, 25, 44, 78, 102
open-endedness in tasks 85, 161
other people's lesson plans, using 176–177
'otherness' 117
outline planning 109, 171
output modification 18–22, 25, 52, 83, 145
over-modification of TL 19

pace 52, 81, 88, 89, 92, 93
Pachler, N. 18, 19, 122, 129
pair work: Battleships 191; and behavioural expectations 97; guessing games 51; listening in (to groups/pairs) 78; mini surveys 59; mouthing 31–32; as part of challenge and support 92, 93; planning for 37–38; setting up 38; short bursts of 121; spot the fib 53; time limits on 81; true/false activities 61
paraphrasing 19–20, 48
participation, maximising 27, 29, 43, 84
partner schools 141
patterns, spotting/exploiting 4, 15, 48, 95, 123–124, 129, 140
pedagogic purpose, in PPP model 24
pedagogical content knowledge 1, 6
perfectionism 177–178

Index

Phipps, Wendy 59
phonics 81, 141
photographs 15
pictures 15, 19, 26–29, 33–34, 39
ping-pong (syllabic breakdown) 16
pitching at the right level 44, 48, 171, 172, 179
plan, do, review 6
planning checklists, drilling sequences 17; end of unit tasks 161; lesson planning 101; sequences of lessons 163, 164; TL output 22
planning proforma, outline planning 109, 110; lesson planning 107, 108; longer term planning 158; *see also* templates for lesson plans
planning for repetition practice 13–18
playing with language 137, 193
plenaries/debriefs 130, 147, 149, 150–151
poetry 139, 141, 143–144, 145
PPP (presentation, practice, production): as a continuum 23–24; definitions 4; drilling 13
practicalities of running activities 25, 69, 83
practice, importance of 5, 24
praise 18–19, 44, 92, 186–187
pre-active teaching phase 6
pre-communicative activities 27, 95
pre-completion of learners' tasks by the teacher 45
prefabricated chunks 15, 123, 191, 192
pre-lesson organisation 83, 194; *see also* resource preparation
pre-lesson planning 6
preparing pupils for an activity 24
principles of language teaching 3
prior learning, building on 69, 71, 81, 153, 160
prioritisation of time in lessons 55, 70, 88–95, 180, 192
procedural knowledge 2
production, mouthing 31–32
production for comprehension 28; *see also* speaking skills
Professional Development Consortium in Modern Foreign Languages (PDC in MFL) 3
professional dialogue 197
professional learning 171–181
Programme of Study for Modern Languages 136, 163
progress, pupils,' monitoring and checking 17
progression, pupils' 70, 77, 89, 105, 116, 153; *see also* linguistic progression within a lesson
prompt questions 31
pronunciation: acquisition of correct 15; drilling 13, 15–16; and literature 141; mouthing 31–32; planning a focus on 80–86, 120–121; and the value of repetition 17

questioning strategies 79, 85, 161

random questioning strategies 85
reading aloud 141–142
reading exercises 51
receptive language 44
referring to plans during lessons 106, 177
reflection 6, 147, 163, 174–175, 176, 194
rehearsing 19, 25, 34
reluctant learners 148
repeat if true 33–34, 78, 92
repetition: drilling 13; importance of 13, 27, 33; planning for repeated exposure 44–53; of the planning process 63; reusing and recycling familiar language 56–61

requests, in TL 18
resource preparation 25, 83, 97, 179, 188
re-teaching same lessons 198
reusing and recycling familiar language 56–61, 138–139, 154–155, 160–161
revision of previously taught language 24, 27, 52, 69, 81, 91, 149
rich input 3, 20, 34, 48, 85
Rivers, Wilga 1
Robinson, Sir Ken 141
Rogers, Bill 98–99, 100
role-play 191
routines, classroom 185–186, 189, 193
RQTs (recently qualified teachers) 182–198

scaffolding 54, 83, 85, 89–95, 121, 144, 176
schemes of work 44, 126, 142, 177, 187, 189
school vision 179
scripts 19, 24, 25, 48, 83, 195
seating plans 150
second language acquisition (SLA) 2
self-correction, encouraging 127
self-directed learning 151
SEN (Special Educational Needs), pupils with 84, 96
sentences, expecting full sentences 32, 38, 80, 83
sequences of lessons 84–85, 109, 153–165, 173, 178; *see also* long-term planning; medium-term plans
seven new pieces of information, rule of thumb 15
Simon Says 41–42
sit down on key/most difficult word 16
skills development 3, 163
skipping parts of the plan 102, 105, 149; *see also* departures from the plan; pausing activities
slowing down speech 19–20
small steps, breaking lessons down into 71, 93
songs 142
sound-spelling links 81, 120, 121, 141
speaking skills 2, 88
spontaneous learner talk, promoting 61, 92, 191
spot the fib 53–56
staircases of progression 157
'stirrers' and 'settlers' activities 98, 99
stopping activities, planning 37, 60, 89, 97
stories 132–133
strategies for comprehension 19–20
strategies for learning 147
strategies for listening 45
strategy instruction 3, 147, 151
structure of lessons 70–72, 180
subject pedagogy 1, 192–193
substitution dialogues 93–95
success criteria 97, 140, 163
successful language learning, clarification of 2–4
support and challenge *see* challenge and support
surveys, class 56–61
swop shops 179
SWOT (strengths, weaknesses, opportunities and strengths) analysis 163–165
syllables, breaking down into 15, 16

talking frames 121
tangents, pre-empting possible 144

target language: authentic material 119, 145–147, 184–185; classroom instructions in target language 18–22; consistent use of by teacher 19; and differentiation 85; output modification 18–22, 25, 52, 83, 145; principles of language teaching 3; scripts 19, 25, 48, 83; to show comprehension 78; teacher use of 18–22, 25, 84, 92, 185, 193; use by pupils to each other 58–59
teacher talk versus student talk 22
Teachers' Standards 153, 174
teaching expertise, development of 6
'teaching the new within the context of the familiar' 69, 153, 154; *see also* prior learning, building on
team teaching 197
technology-free lessons 178
templates for lesson plans 106–109, 160, 179
Terrell, T.D. 44
testing 161
testing out tasks 45
text adaptations 145
textbooks 154, 189
theory, importance of 6
thinking skills 151
thinking time 31, 53, 54, 93, 121, 151
time taken on planning 177–178
timed, pair, share 30
timing of lessons: and behavioural expectations 97; benefits of joint planning 173; including time for write-up 58, 81, 83; planning 72, 86–95; prioritisation of time in lessons 55, 70, 88–95, 180, 192; shortening sections 149; time limits 81, 140; underestimating 154
top set/high ability classes 86–89

topics 5, 134, 135
translation 20, 78, 142
treasure hunts 182–183
true/false activities 61, 92
20 questions 51

unconscious approaches to language acquisition 4, 44
units of work 154–160

variety of activities and techniques, benefits of having 84–85, 152
video recorded lessons 174
visual aids 15, 29; *see also* pictures
visualising a lesson 24
vocabulary teaching 3, 15, 41, 46
voice coaching 145
volunteers, seeking 19, 54, 56, 79; alternatives to 79, 85, 193

Ward, Wendy 61
warm-up exercises 24
well-structured lessons 180
Westgate, David 5
Williams, M. 147, 151, 152
wordplay 137
words versus sentences, as answers to questions 40
writing carefully, principle of 54
written activities, scaffolded by earlier speaking exercises 54
written stimulus, working from a 39
written work, building in time for 58, 81, 83

yes/no game 51